Yoga inVision 1

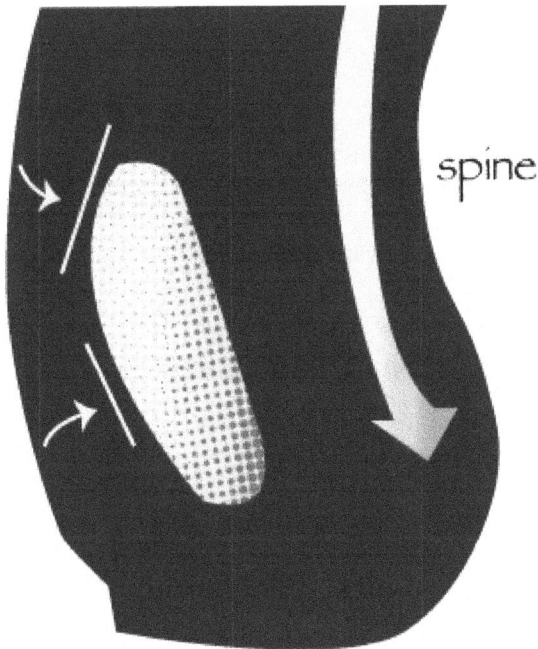

I0141811

spine

Michael Beloved

Shiva Art: Sir Paul Castagna
Illustrations: Author
Correspondence:
Michael Beloved
19311 SW 30th Street
Miramar FL 33029
USA
Email: axisnexus@gmail.com
            michaelbelovedbooks@gmail.com

Paperback ISBN: 9781942887072

LCCN: 2017902016

Table of Contents

INTRODUCTION

These Yoga Journals, comprise yoga techniques and other related practices and realizations, which I instituted in my life. The purpose of sharing this, is to encourage and give aspirants details of the practice. So long as I am allowed to use this material body, anyone can contact me. I will discuss anything mentioned in this Yoga inVision series. Supernatural contact is possible if one has the perception.

Over the years, advising many persons on the practice of yoga, I instructed students to keep a journal of psychic experiences. Many were unable to. This instruction was received by me and was followed by me astutely while practicing. I cannot overstress its value. In teaching one must sometimes give an instruction which one, as the teacher, will not practice but this instruction I practiced and continue to follow to date.

Admittedly, yoga is a lonely path. It involves working with your psyche. Still it may be regarded as the only path which will reveal the self. Good luck with it!

I spared the reader the repeated use of Swami, Sri, Srila, Lord and such titles which are routine in the Vedic literature for address divinities and supernatural yogis. The absence of these addresses do not suggest a lack of respect. Please maintain that.

Part 1

On this date, I was instructed by an astral yogi to pull the taste sense into the lung. This yogi was in the astral world. I do not know if he has a material body. Most of these entries will concern astral yogis, who may or may not use material forms. Usually I make contact with these yogis early in the morning, after midnight but before 5 am.

They check my practice and give advice. This yogi commented on my astral lung not the physical one. Since the two bodies, the physical and astral, are intermeshed, exercising an action in the astral one may involve physical participation. The taste sense is both physical and psychic, existing in both bodies simultaneously.

The yogi spoke of the earth and water taste. This refers to taste of solid and liquid foods. He recommended this:

Do pranayama breath-infusion, either standing with hands on hip or sitting in lotus posture. This should be a tight lotus. In a lose lotus or easy pose, it may be done but that will not give the full result. In all cases in asana and pranayama practice, there are final postures. If the yogi is unable to do these, he need not worry. He may substitute an easier posture but he should know that his result with be partial which is evidence of his sincerity in effort. Through that he will progress further and eventually in this life, in the hereafter, or in the next life, he may assume the final posture with the full result. One should not be discouraged if for one reason or the other, one cannot do a final form.

Yoga requires working with yourself to bring the self to the perfect stage. One must be patient with the self. One must not expect the yoga teacher to adjust everything to suit one's condition. One may surely adjust an instruction provided that one intends to advance to the perfect stage in the near future by constant endeavor to move from a primitive practice to a more advanced one.

After assuming the lotus or easy pose or after standing with hands on the hips, one should do the rapid breathing to surcharge the subtle body. After a time, the energy will accumulate in the subtle and gross forms simultaneously. One should then inhale and pull the abdomen under the chest cage. Pull it as if you are pulling up the entire lower trunk of the body. This includes the pubic and anal areas.

With willpower, mystically draw the energy upward into the two bottom chakras, then that combined power should be pulled into the 3rd chakra, which is behind the navel. Then pull that into the 4th chakra. Yogis who are not proficient should visualize this. By continued effort, they will develop the ability.

When pulling the two bottom chakras into the 3rd one, there should be a burning sensation. When the 3rd chakra is pulled into the 4th one there should be a feeling as if air is being absorbed or as if air is being compressed into nothingness. The burning sensation vanishes into the 3rd chakra, because this chakras absorbs the heated energy that reaches it from bellow. This heated energy is a combination of air, subtle air, sexual hormone energy and muscular force. For females, there is a fat-tissue energy which will be combined into this force. Please study these diagrams:

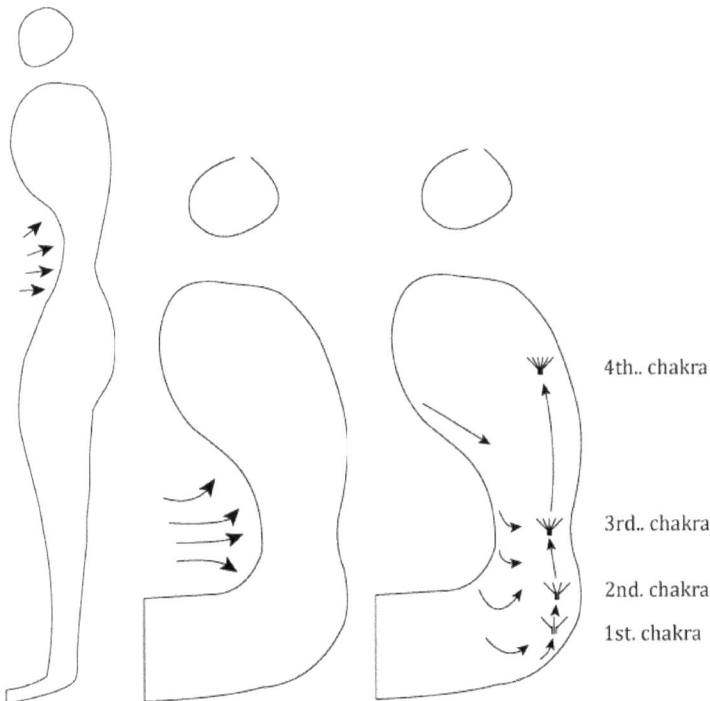

4th.. chakra

3rd.. chakra

2nd. chakra

1st. chakra

The yogi also gave this procedure for the reverse flow of energy:

Do rapid breathing either standing or in the lotus posture. After surcharging the system, push the air down the spinal chakras. This is the opposite of the first method where the infused air combined with hormonal energies rises through the spinal chakras. You begin at the 4th chakra with air. It is compressed. You push it down to the 3rd chakra where it is converted into heat energy. Then you push that to the 2nd chakra, where it is converted into a higher energy. Then you push it to the base chakra where it is converted into compressed solid energy. You then direct the radiation from the compressed solid force around the bottom of the body as in the diagram below. From around the bottom, where the energy makes a U-turn, you direct it to the causal body, the cove in the central chest.

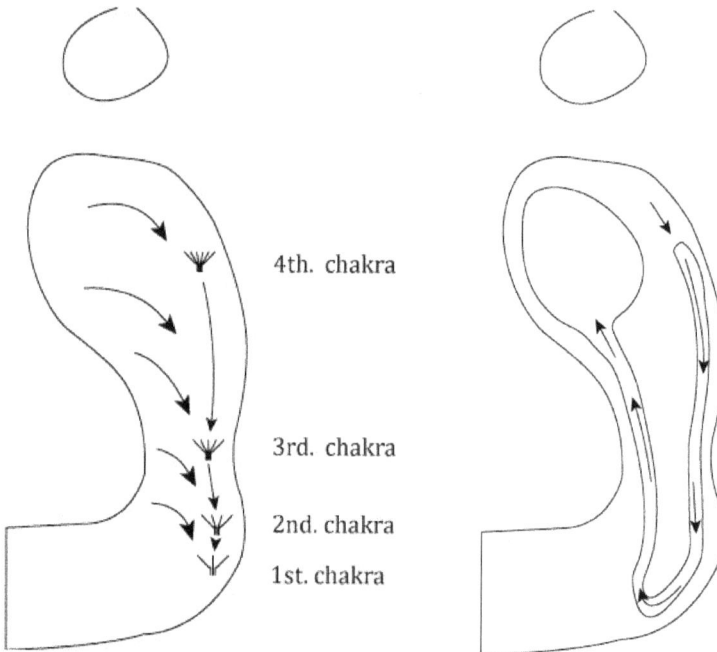

4th. chakra

3rd. chakra

2nd. chakra

1st. chakra

Readers should note that everything will not be explained in these journals. I will explain much but not every detail. I do not always inquire of everything from the astral yogis. My interest is to receive Instructions, not to query.

I am confident of their recommendations. If you have a tendency to doubt, or if you are in the habit of asking questions, restrain that urge. Realize that you can take this information as is. If you need more, intensify the practice and contact superior yogis for assistance.

April 19, 1998

This morning Agastya gave me a technique called slant-pull. Look at this diagram.

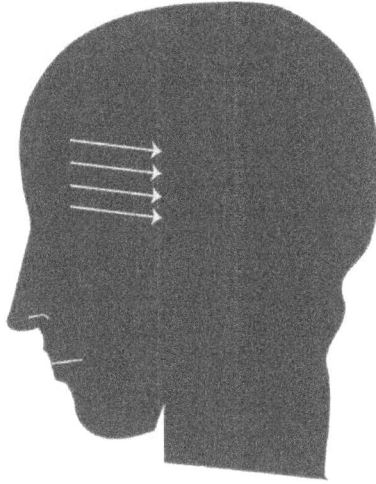

In this exercise a stream of energy is pulled inward in the direction of the arrows shown above. This is related to controlling the intellect's outside-seeking tendency, to make it concerned about matters within the psyche.

While doing this, I was to make the intellect be concerned about the abdomen-slam. Look at this diagram:

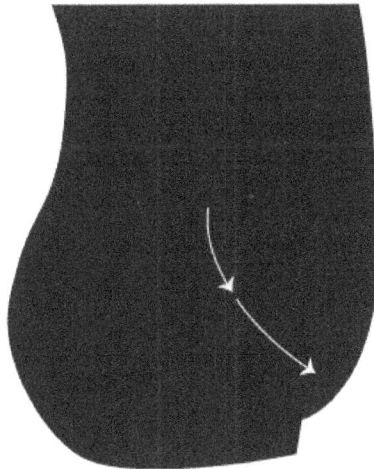

The abdomen slam is an exercise where one slams the abdomen forward. This leads up to an exercise for raising kundalini. In that practice one pushes the abdomen down with steady force while up pulling up the two lower locks; the sex lock and anus lock. Look at this diagram:

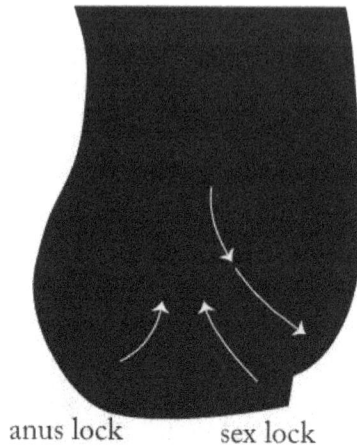

anus lock   sex lock

This pushing down of the abdomen is done after the body is charged with subtle energy just after an intense session of rapid breath-infusion.

The intellect is a psychic organ in the head of the subtle body. It is an actual subtle object. Normally in the materialistic view of life, we regard it as our power of understanding. Actually, it is an entirely separate organ in the subtle head. In higher yoga, one begins to perceive this and by the grace of advanced yogis, like Agastya, one gets to the level of psychic perception, where one perceives the intellect as a subtle object

April 18, 1998

Front kundalini and the three holes for nourishment:

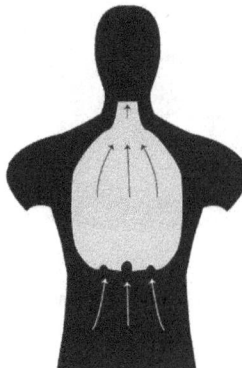

When we eat physical food, we also take subtle nourishment, which is the counterpart to the physical substance. The subtle body uses the subtle stuffs. After death of the physical form when we only have a subtle body and no physical one, we get only subtle nourishment. If we are not adapted to that, if we are attached to gross existence, we feel dissatisfied, as if subtle food were nothing. Thus in the afterworld, in ghostly forms, we fee1 frustrated and try to enter someone's testes to come out again as babies.

When we eat physical food, it travels through the intestinal tubing in the abdomen. Some is absorbed through the intestinal walls. The psychic portion which is absorbed in the subtle body, goes downward through one main tube from which it is distributed through the subtle form. A concentrated oily part goes down into the sexual area of the body.

Yogis are concerned with turning this sexual energy into brain energy in the physical form, and into the higher consciousness energy in the subtle form. Thus they do exercises and mental actions which facilitate the uptake of this energy. This means that they aspire for complete celibacy. The same energy which electrifies the body in sexual intercourse, which is experienced as intense sexual pleasure, is the energy which the yogis use in the brain for increased psychic perception. It is the same energy which is called kundalini.

When raising front kundalini there are many techniques. In this, one draws the nutrients through the three holes which are entrances to suck-tubes. The nutrients are then pulled up under the nose where they evaporate or convert into subtle energy and waste gas. This causes front kundalini to be activated. One feels the front kundalini as a tingling sensation in the front of the gross body. Front kundalini comes up the front part of the gross body. Back kundalini which is more popular among yogis, travels up the back part of the body.

April 19, 1998

Ganesh

He said, "The mode uses the person. The person does not use the mode. Learn how to direct the mode through a channel which helps the practice."

This advice came from Ganesh, while I was on the astral side, speaking to a lady who wanted me to assist her in a pregnancy. Hearing from someone that I was a yogi, and being superstitious, thinking that I could work miracles, this person approached me to check her womb to see if she would have to abort her fetus.

Later I heard that she did abort the embryo. At the time she consulted me, I could not assist her because the consequences in her destiny were preset. Regardless of my supposed miraculous powers, I cannot adjust a preset destiny.

Ganesh made the statement about the mode using the person. At the time I could not see how it applied, and still to this day I do not see how it applied to the pregnant lady or to myself in her association, except that I could have explained to her about using uncertainty as an avenue to gain self-realization.

The mode of energy is such that a limited being cannot thwart or change it. He may, if he can, side-step or avoid it. He should learn how to benefit from it. If one finds that the benefits are unfavorable, one should accept the outcome or cope with it, but one cannot change the way a certain mode operates.

Somehow as human beings we assume a strange attitude where we feel that we should be in a position to thwart nature in every case. That feeling reveals our insanity.

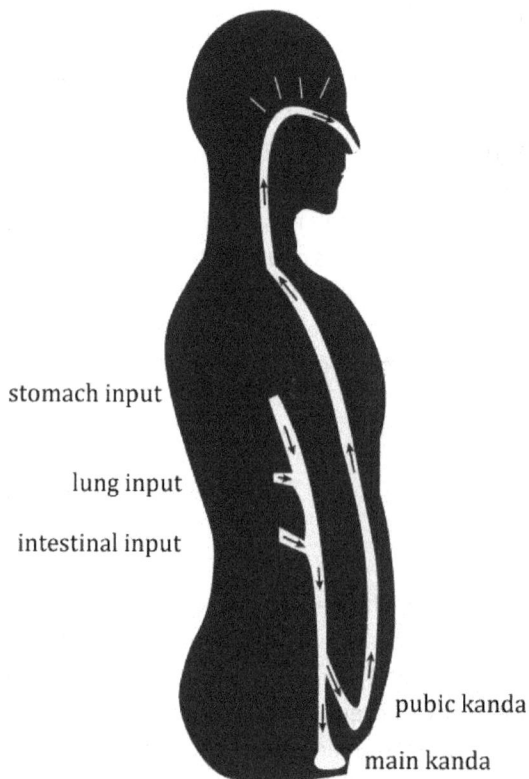

stomach input

lung input

intestinal input

pubic kanda

main kanda

April 26, 1998

This is a technique for controlling the sex kanda. Kanda means a small subtle bag or bulb which holds subtle fluids or gases. These subtle stuffs, if seen, would look like liquid gas.

While doing that technique one should apply the intellect pull-down. That is a psychic pulling of the intellect organ, to move it into a lower position in the subtle brain. It is very easy to locate the intellect organ. One need only think of something or even imagine or remember something. By observing the location of that thought, image, remembrance or idea, one would locate the intellect. One must be sensitive enough to note the location, since as soon as the images vanishes, the intellect will again assume its invisible profile. The location of the thought or idea is the location of the intellect. One should apply a willpower pulling force to that location, even though the organ is not visible. One should pull it down and backwards into the head. One must be confident that even though the image disappeared, the intellect organ is in the location where the image was visualized

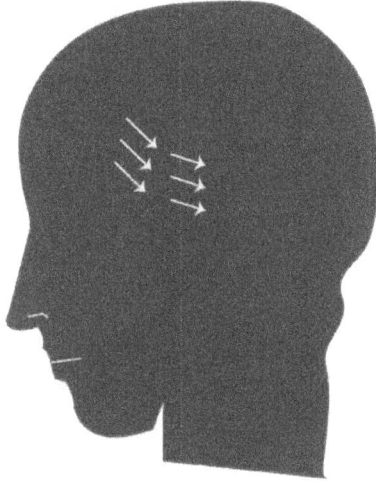

April 24, 1998

Yogi Bhajan said, "Pratyahar means a retraction or inverted expression. For example, sunlight travels many miles through space to reach the earth. This is the sun's expression. If the sun were to pratyahar, it would pull its light into itself. Higher yoga begins with pratyahar. Elementary yoga has yama moral restraints, niyama approved behaviors, asana body postures and pranayama breath-infusion. The higher stages begin when pratyahar is added to the practice."

I studied breath-infusion pranayama from a few disciples of Yogi Bhajan. I attended some of the yogi's classes in 1973. Since then I saw him twice physically, in Los Angeles, California and in Taos, New Mexico. I do not see him frequently on the astral planes either. Recently after he left his body in 2004, I saw him often. Previously he came now and again to check my practice, but those were astral visits, nothing physical. He gave advice.

He is not the kind of guru who stands over disciples, demanding their absolute loyalty. He does not like anyone to bow to him. His idea is that you practice. That is the obligation. Otherwise he does not require honor, worship ceremonies or donations. He is the ideal yogin. He gave me a kundalini pratyahar technique.

He said this, "Yoga practice is private, very personal. You should be attentive to yourself, to your personal energies. It is not a group endeavor. If you are sincere, there will be results. If you are attentive there is consistent and rapid progress. A teacher gives techniques but the student must practice."

My first teacher for kundalini yoga, was Brian. He was Yogi Bhajan's disciple who supervised the Denver Colorado ashram in 1972. Later I was taught by Prem Kaur, another of Bhajan's disciples. During 1973, the yogi came to Denver and gave classes directly. He is a spirited person with radiant energy. Study this diagram concerning kundalini pratyahar:

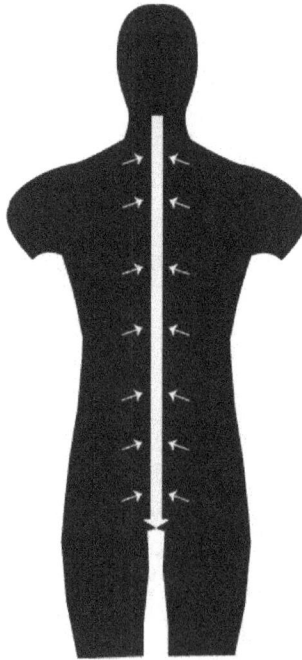

After one does an intense session of rapid breathing, the spinal column will be surcharged. One should pull in the dispersed energy which radiates from the spine. What is the technique for this? First, one must be proficient in surcharging the spine with the subtle energy. Once this is achieved by regular practice, one will have a sense of how to feel that energy radiating while doing the exercises. Then one may practice pulling that energy back into the spine. At first this is done by contracting the muscles which converge on the spine. As one practices, one will sense that the physical contraction causes a retraction of psychic energies in the subtle body.

In the gross body we have muscles, tendons and nerves which we operate by will power. In the subtle form there are corresponding faculties. These become operative in the subtle form of a yogi.

April 25, 1998

Front-kundalini down-pump

In some cases one is inspired to do a certain technique using subtle energy with no physical application. The subtle energy itself, may serve as the guru. In other cases a guru directs either physically or astrally. The guru may be there but one may not perceive him because one's psychic perception may not be keen. In all circumstances when doing yoga, Shiva is there somewhere in a parallel dimension.

This technique is front-kundalini down-pump. Please look at the diagram.

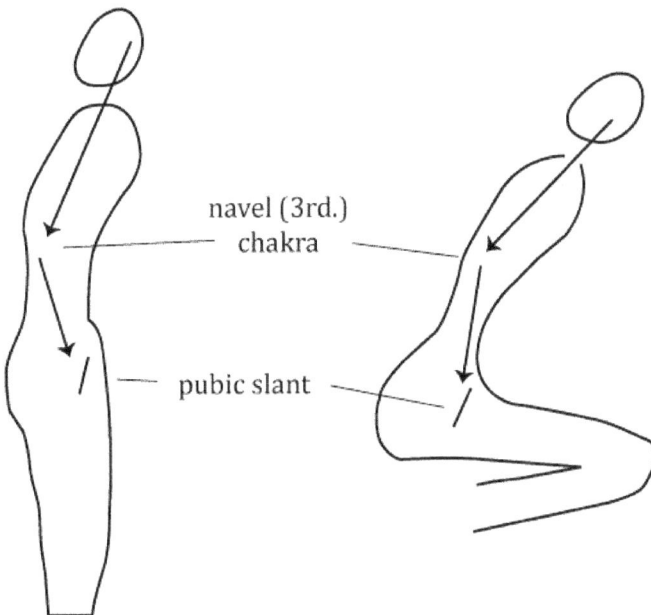

navel (3rd.) chakra

pubic slant

This is usually done from a standing position with hands on the hips. This is done after an intense breath-infusion. After the subtle energy accumulates and exerts a downward push on the polluted used energy, one pulls energy from the forehead, direct it to the third chakra. This is directed to the groin area. One pulls the lower locks upwards but pushes the abdomen outwards.

As soon as one feels that the energy is saturated, one should do the down-draw breath. This is not like the breath-infusion pranayama rapid breathing but it is related. In the down-draw one stands with hands on the hips. One pulls the breath in two or three draws of air into the lower lungs. To restrict the intellect and sensual interest to the inside of the body, the eyes should be closed. One should pull down the air by a sucking action through the nose with short pauses, holding the breath after two or three sucking draws inwards. One should attentively direct the air to the bottom of the lung. When it builds up sufficiently, one should push the abdomen out while pulling up the two lower locks (the anal and sex locks). One should keep the eyes closed and remain observant of the energy distribution in the gross and subtle bodies. All the while one should maintain the neck lock.

If kundalini triggers, rising through the spine or up the front of the body, hold the locks properly. Be attentive to the movement, while holding the breath in the body. If you feel you must release the breath, breathe out quickly. Do one quick down-draw with two or three pulls of air immediately after. Then apply the locks firmly. In this case, as may happen, if one feels kundalini coming up with too much force, sit quickly on your heels or between your heels. Hold the locks tightly until kundalini diffuses. If kundalini comes up with a rapid surge, one may lose control of the standing body because the force of it will penetrate and affect the intellect. That organ may lose track of the body. The body may fall to the ground. Soon after however, when kundalini subsides one will again become aware of the physical body.

The technique is to raise kundalini every day in small amounts so that you get used to it and familiar with the locks for controlling the rising and subsiding of kundalini.

April 25, 1998

As I said, sometimes the subtle energy shows the way by inspiring more advanced practice or a new method. Sometimes a guru does this. Sometimes, it is hard to tell whether the inspiration is by subtle energy or from a guru. If I do not declare a guru on an entry, assume that it may be a guru or indications from the subtle energy.

Abdomen catch-funnel

In the subtle body, the energy from food mixed with breath energy is sent down into the bottom of trunk. It is sent from all sides downwards.

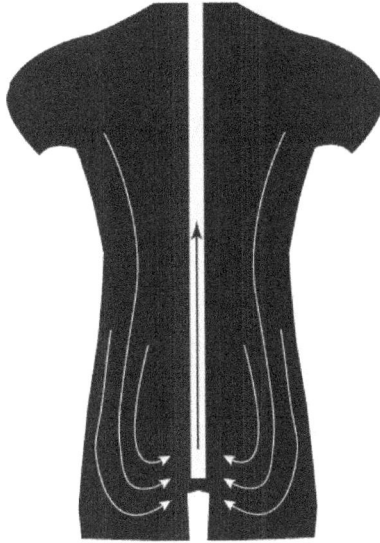

In celibacy yoga, the aim is to pull that energy upwards from the bottom. By using the breath we can suck the energy upward. This is basic in kundalini yoga

April 26, 1998

Agastya

In the subtle world, I saw Agastya to the south.

He said, "Keep this land clean. We drink from it."

With his right hand, he pointed downward to the earth. There were yogis with him. They drank water here and there. Agastya spoke of the pollution of the earth by modern human beings. In the developed countries, people are realizing their irresponsible exploitation of resources. After seeing Agastya, I saw Ganesh way off to the West. Then I saw Shiva to the East. Some yogis were assembled to the North. The same day by Agastya's grace, I discovered a front kundalini route.

Front kundalini is experienced when the front of the subtle body is cleared of pollutants. This occurs by clearing the navel chakra. That is based on eating the right food at the right time and in the right quantity. Eating at night is strictly forbidden but some advanced yogis, do indulge because they fall in the association with worldly persons who become their disciples or donors and who are unable to become reformed from worldly associations. It is a matter of repelling worldly influences.

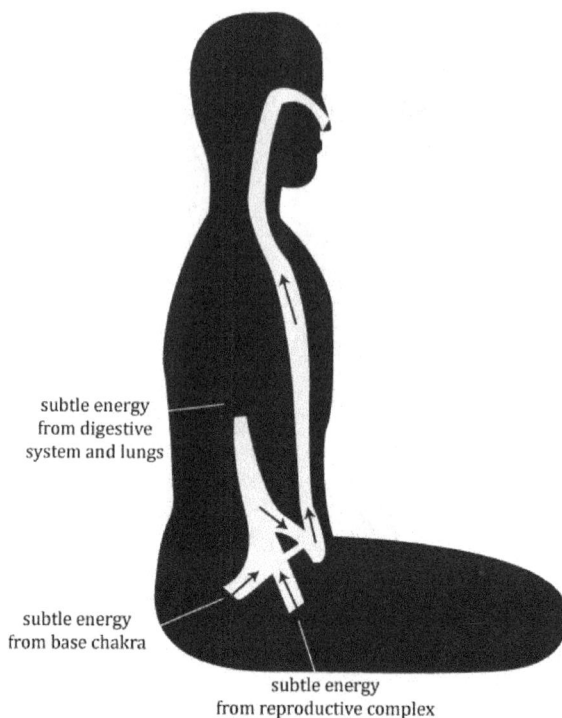

subtle energy
from digestive
system and lungs

subtle energy
from base chakra

subtle energy
from reproductive complex

Agastya instructed me. He said, "Slow stretches cause the development of pranavision. That is the purpose of hatha yoga. This is why in ancient times we developed it to see our way through the gross existence. Be attentive. Dissipation of attention and interference of thoughts, retards advancement.

Remark:

Pranavision is a vision in the subtle energy. It means accumulating fresh subtle energy by doing breath-infusion, getting the body charged with subtle energy by rapid breathing or even by alternate breathing. The result is that one may see inside the body by looking through the charged energy. By doing stretches one can locate the nerves and nadis and see through them. This means peering in the gross and subtle forms simultaneously.

After mastering pranavision, one is taught how to combine that with visual vision. When the two are combined, so I was told by Yogeshwarananda, one can see things as they are. Visual vision means the vision through which one sees materially but which is actually a subtle perception interspaced through the gross body.

Ganesh

I received a mantra for Agastya. This was awarded by Ganesh.

Om Agastyaya namah

This mantra may be used when working with front kundalini. Here is a diagram showing the location at which this mantra is chanted. One may also focus on that location without using a mantra. The mantra is chanted in the body at that location. As far as front and back kundalini are concerned, Yogeshwarananda said that it was elementary.

He said. "The real yoga begins beyond that. Nevertheless that is necessary for beginners. Internally clean the subtle body by awakening kundalini to flush the nadi subtle tubes. Later one may scrap the kundalini and progress further."

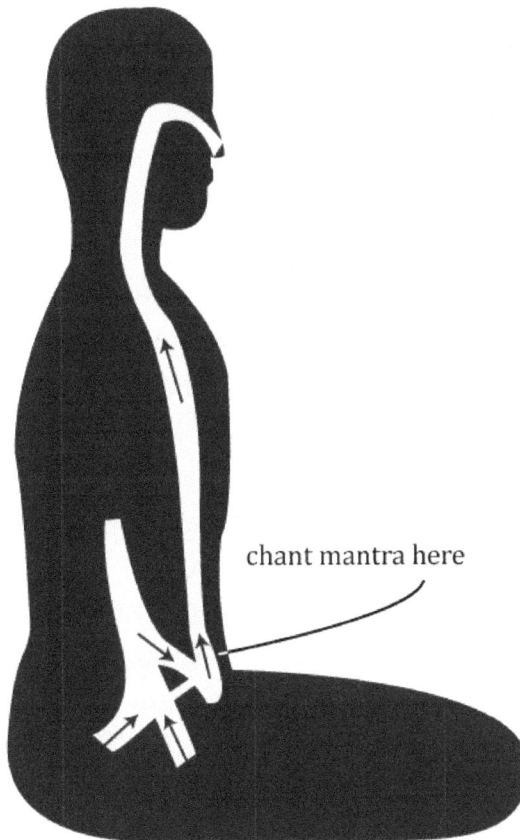

chant mantra here

April 29, 1998

Ganesh / Agastya

This is a frontal kundalini technique. In this one, the intellect organ is in the flow of the frontal kundalini energy which rises up to the lower brain. The intellect however must be pulled down to the lower area of the brain.

In this practice one first arouses frontal kundalini by doing rapid breathing and by pushing the abdomen down and retracting the two bottom locks. When it is pushed down, that is also a lock but it is different from the other abdomen lock when the abdomen is pulled up and under the rib cage. Here are some illustrations which show the difference.

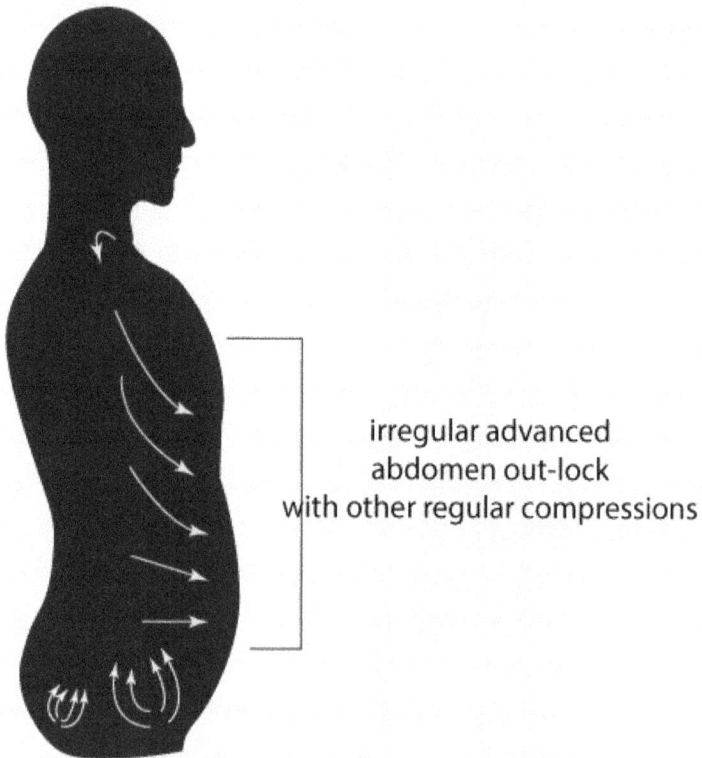

irregular advanced
abdomen out-lock
with other regular compressions

lock compressions (bandhas)

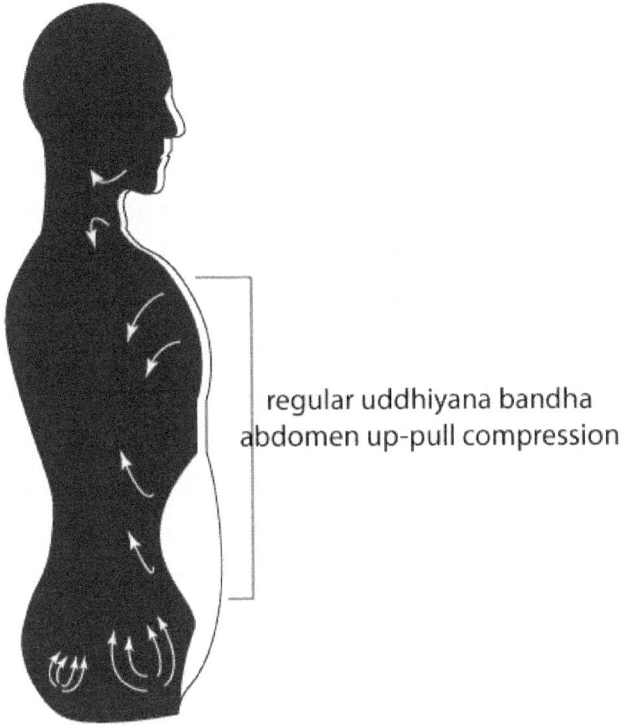

regular uddhiyana bandha
abdomen up-pull compression

lock compressions (bandhas)

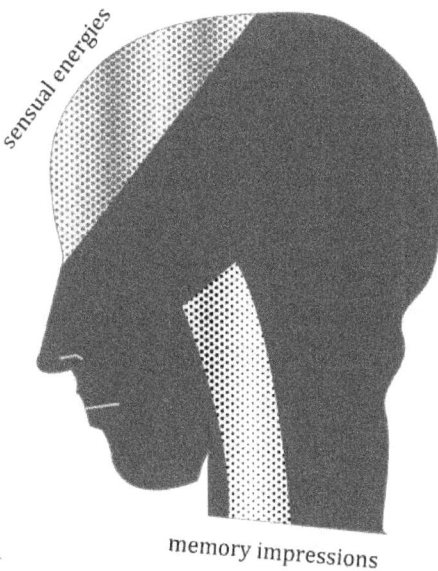

sensual energies

memory impressions

As one arouses frontal kundalini and feels it in the body as a light which is scattered in the front of the body, one pulls down the intellect organ, making sure that the frontal lobe of the mind comes down with it. The frontal lobe of the mind is in the front area of the brain. This part has the sensual energies. It is receptive to the memory impressions which come from the chest area.

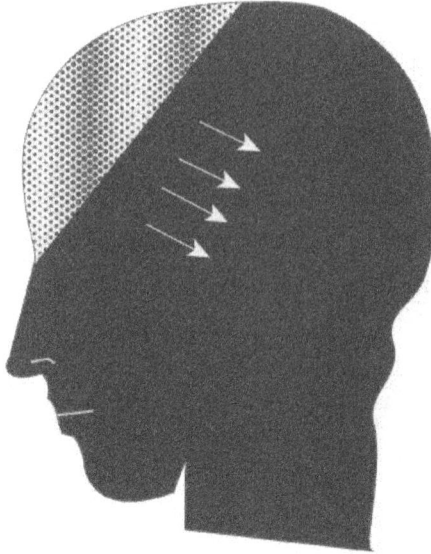

pull back sensual energy

The frontal lobe is part of the intellect mechanism but it is more resistant to being pulled down. This is due to its tendency for going outward.

May 1st 1998

Agastya

Agastya who is a master of the frontal kundalini system gave me a special technique this morning. For this, the pubic floor is lifted slightly and one coordinates a few touch points. There are touch points in every part of the body. In acupuncture which was developed in China and Japan, these spots were identified. In this technique, they are not used for health, but rather for purification of the personal energies. There are also sound points but these are not as effective now as they were, three or four thousand years ago. Those people who use sounds like Om, Aum, Hansa, Hrim and Klim are mainly indulging themselves. These sounds are not as effective today as they were formerly. The environment changed. The gross and subtle material elements do not respond to these intonations as before.

Undoubtedly ancient ascetics made good use of the sounds. The statements in scripture regarding the fantastic results achieved by mantra sound words are true that does not mean that such effects are current today.

Many ascetics are superstitious about sound. They pronounce sounds even though they do not get the results the ancients experienced.

Below is a diagram showing the touch points and the direction in which the pubic slant tube is moved. This tube does not exist in the gross body. It is in the subtle form. In the gross body, its influence is felt however.

The touch points labelled *A* and *B* should be held together by concentration on them simultaneously. These two points are connected electrically in the subtle body. By holding them together, one may intensify the mystic process and gets a sharper clearer realization of the schematic of the psyche.

Even though such a divine personality as Agastya used his last material form some thousands years ago, student yogis need to realize that he is available today. Whatever exemplary austerity he performed in his ancient body, is still available for any qualified ascetic. Agastya may appear to the ascetic, either inside the subtle body or outside of it. His techniques may become self-evident to a student.

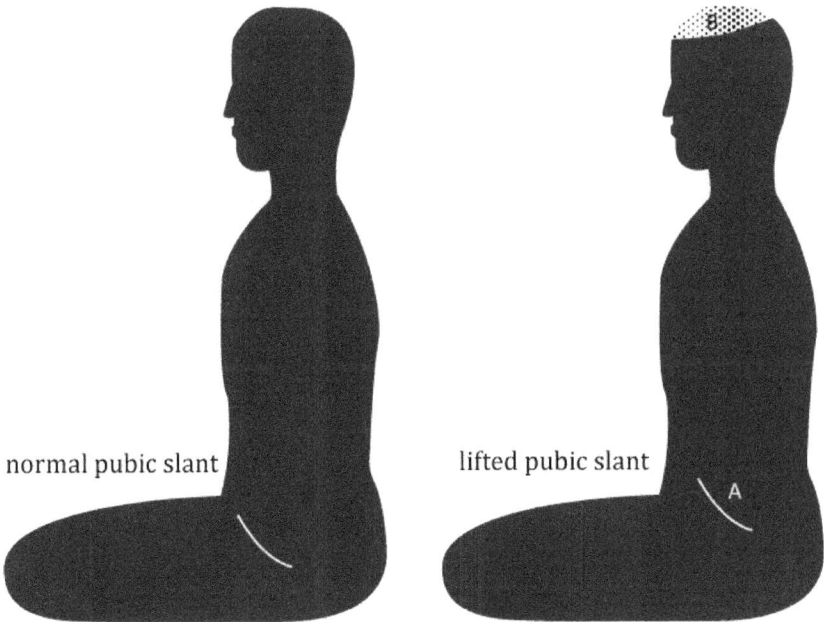

normal pubic slant

lifted pubic slant

Agastya Mahayogin Pita

He gave me this technique to move the intellect down the middle front passage to the groin area. Usually the intellect specializes in outside roaming by scanning the senses for information about objects outside the body. This outside roaming causes the neglect of self-purity. In order to disorient the intellect organ and the senses from outside roaming, one may do any mystic exercises such as this one in the effort to create an inward tendency.

intellect
default location

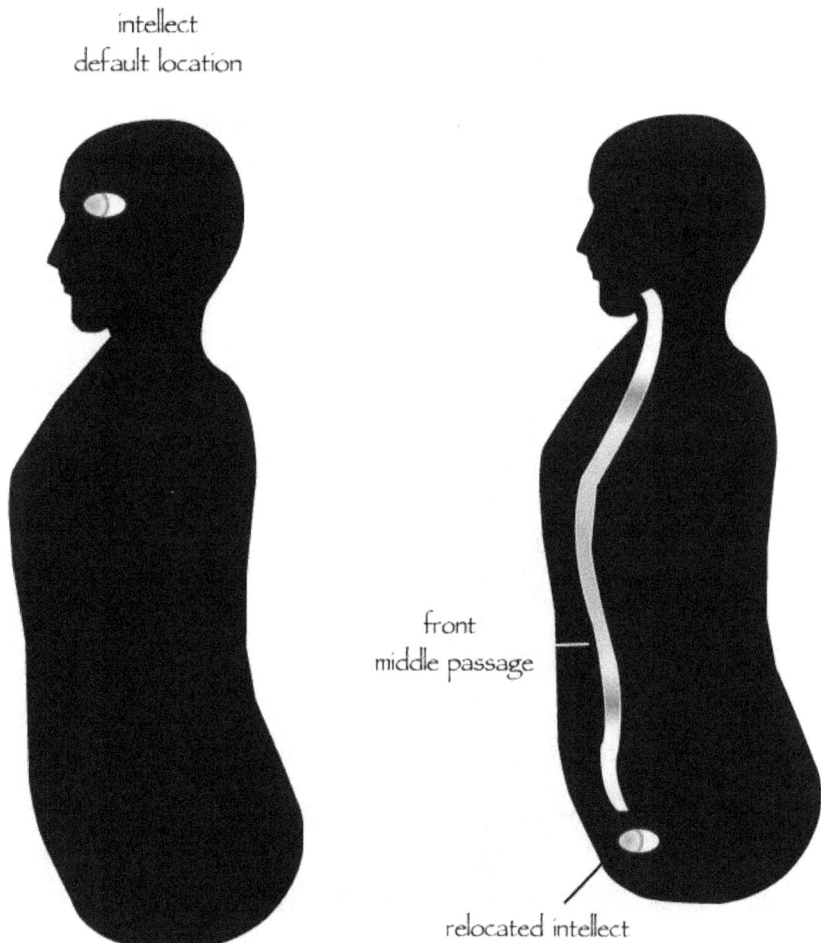

front
middle passage

relocated intellect

In Kundalini yoga, the middle passage is thought to be the sushumna canal which is the central spinal tubing in the subtle body. That is the main middle passage. However, there are other middle passages of importance, such as this frontal middle one. These are passages for subtle energy and for liquid light. As the yogin progresses he develops the perception of these by sensation detection, by visual apprehension and by sensing energy movements.

May 2nd 1998

One persistent problem in yoga is sexual expression. Until it is curbed, one cannot make solid progress. Thus even though it is a constant irritation and a stubborn tendency to root out, it must be faced and dealt with steadily over a long period.

In this technique one meditates on a few tubes which feed the sexual mechanism. These tubes are in the neck and in the higher chest area. It is the same position in female bodies.

At first one should do the exercises described below. While pulling the perineum muscles and the inner thigh muscles, keep the eyes closed and meditate on the higher tube. Do this for one week. Then do the meditation with the lower tube for one week. I did not record the yogin who gave this technique. However by the nature of it, it was Agastya or one of his disciples.

This exercise helps to curb the sex impulse in the subtle body. It stops the tubes which hold sexual fluids from swelling with the fluids. It causes the fluids to move through the body instead of being stored in the groin area and pubic section for sexual expression. This is in the subtle body. It affects the performance of the gross form.

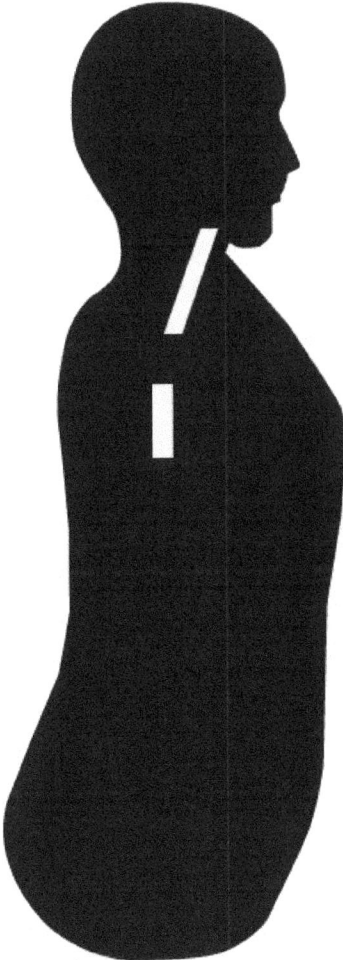

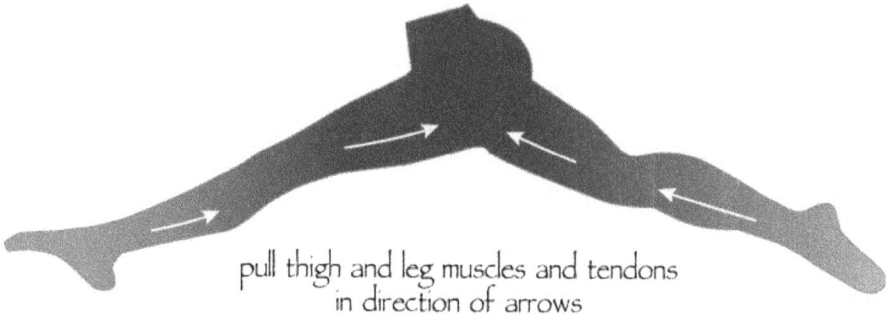

pull thigh and leg muscles and tendons
in direction of arrows

May 5, 1995

Agastya

He said that internal focusing which has no reference to exterior items is a good basis for advanced pratyahar sensual energy withdrawal practice. He gave a technique focus and then said that in these cases there is no minute focal point. One becomes aware of an internal force. This is a type of sensual energy withdrawal because the interest remains confined within the subtle body.

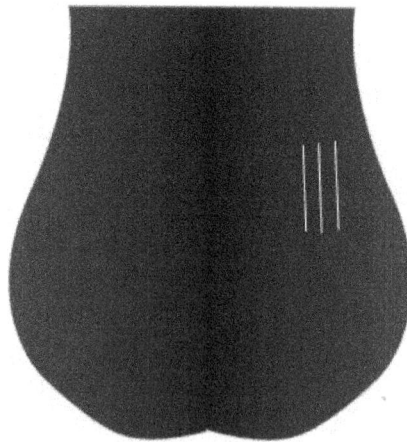

back of body

focus where lines are drawn

A student will discover that as he practices yoga, he will find that there are slight progressions, and small but important events during practice. Then suddenly there may be a summary progression. What an astral teacher recommends may not be explained by him. The important thing is for the student to do as advised based on confidence on the teacher's progressive influence.

Pratyahar is sensual withdrawal from the external world and from internal impressions which are pursuant of the external world. Initially one becomes obsessed with withdrawing from the external world. When that is somewhat achieved, one understands that the external world is not the issue. It is the internal situation of the psyche, the personal energies over which one should take charge.

In the conditioned way of thinking, we use outside references. This means that we correlate even things within the psyche to things which are exterior to it. This is because gross perception is keener and more attractive to the mind. However this outside reference does not help in higher yoga.

May 5, 1998

Agastya

He said, "Always be extremely patient. Be willing to begin a procedure again if the psychic equipment is in disorder.

"Carefully remove the causes of anxiety. Remove, minimize and decrease these. Keep endeavoring. Do not resent disturbances."

On this morning, he gave a technique for mystic meditation. This diagram shows it.

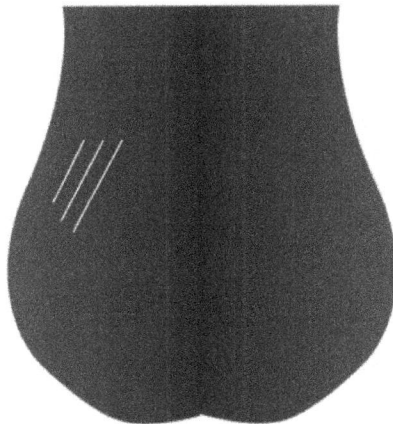

back of body
focus where lines are drawn

Since the disturbances of material nature are perpetually recurring, there is really no use in resenting them. The big part of this is the realization that we are limited. As limited beings we have to expect to be disturbed. As Agastya advised, we should be patient in the execution of spiritual practice. Even if our psychic equipment is in disorder, we should be willing to bring it to order. We must be willing to do this repeatedly. At any time material nature may be up and at it, applying a chaos-producing presence.

Yogeshwarananda had a similar idea. When some aspirants wondered about our limited condition, in being repeatedly degraded and repeatedly conditioned, despite all we might do for liberation, he said that it was normal for us as limited beings to be in such a condition, and that we should endeavor for liberation anyway, just as we perform daily bath and other routine actions for the physical body.

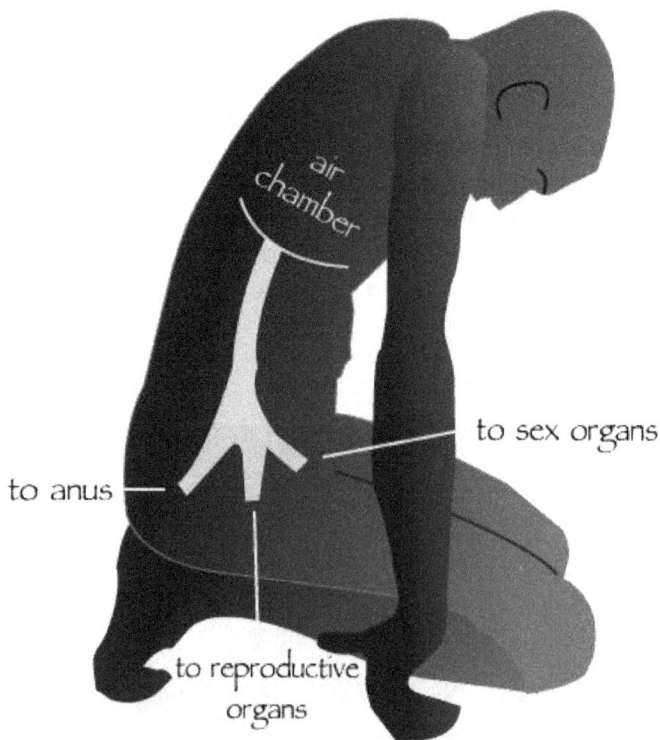

This diagram shows another Agastya technique. It is used during breath-infusion from a standing position while doing down-draw breaths. This is also used from the sitting position when sitting on the heels or floating between them. It may be used in the lotus too. When one holds the breath in after a buildup of charged energy one should push down the accumulated breath force through the tubes shown. If one cannot see the tubes, one should push the energy down mentally.

Do not imagine that the tubes are there. That is not conducive to technique yoga. If you cannot perceive the tubes, have confidence that they are there. Once the mid portion of your body becomes purified, the tubes will manifest in the subtle form. Push down mentally and physically in the direction of the pathways shown in the diagram but do not strain the body physically. Pay attention to your body as you do an exercise. Do not overstrain muscles or tendons.

May 6, 1998

Observe these diagrams:

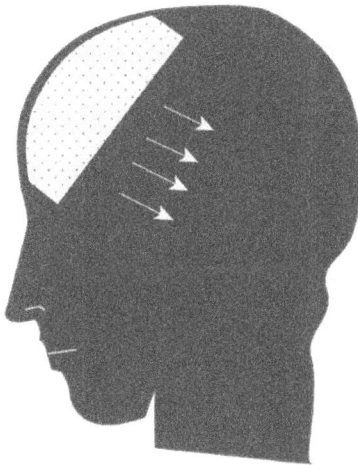

pull back sensual energy

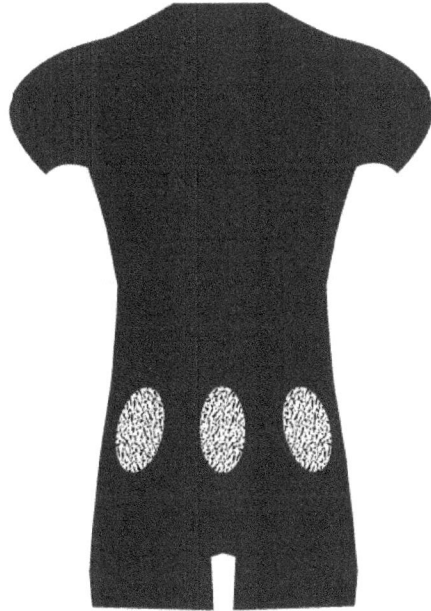

move sensual energies
to each of the shaded areas
in sequence

This is for retraction of sensual energies to do research in certain areas of the body. One first retracts his sensual focus and holds that energy into a zone in the brain. He has to be sure that the energy is confined to that area.

Then he moves the energy to various parts of the body like the abdomen area. This is for knowing various parts of one's psyche. This was given to me by Agastya. At the time of the inspiration I could not detect him.

Agastya

He said, "Spend more time for meditation after the morning breath-infusion exercises. This is the original stomach. It was just a streak of scratched energy."

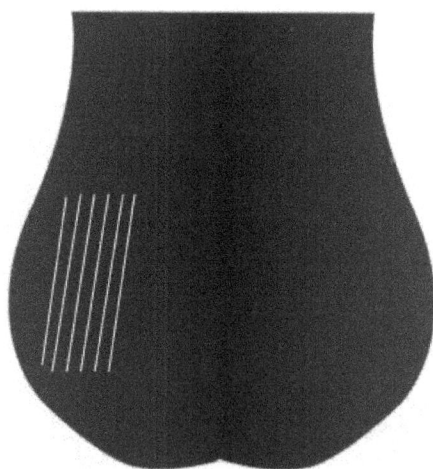

back of body

He added, "Do attention-focus at that location. Stationing the intellect and yourself (core-self) there. Do not project a focus. Go there. When the intellect's external focus is retracted, it feels as if it is lost. But it also feels that it gained an internal affinity for charged energetic subtle force.

Remark:

Sometimes a yogi projects a ray of energy from the third eye. This may originate at the third eye or it may come from the subtle head and then be projected through the third eye. However attention-focus is not a projection. For that, the intellect and core-self go to a locale and experience there. They do not project energy to another place.

Agastya

He directed me to observe this stream of consciousness:

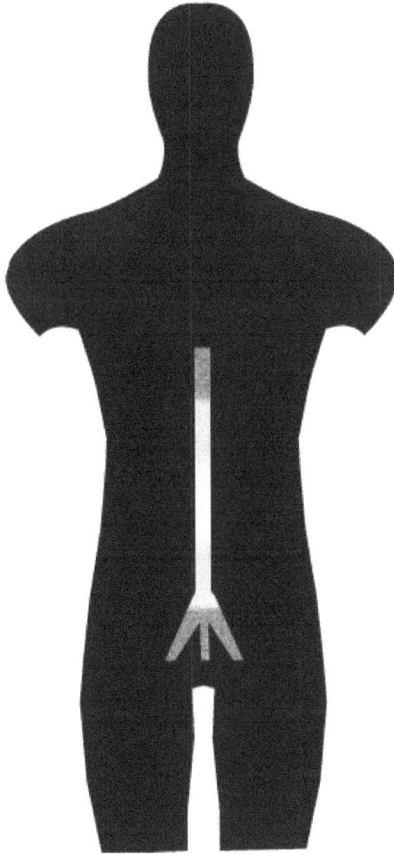

This is in the subtle body. It was a downward flowing stream in contrast to the upward flow of the risen kundalini. Agastya said further, "Retrieve all drifted energy which strayed from your attention. Do this patiently. It takes practice and sincerity. Patiently do this as a loyal servant would serve a great king. This stream of consciousness if cultivated will be a stepping stone to transcendence-contact."

May 10, 1998

Agastya

This is a hook-nerve technique. This nerve is connected to the sex organs. It runs through the thigh. When one does this, one should be sure that the knees are not bent. Even though there will be some strain to keep the knees straight as can be, and even though there will be some pain from the stretched muscles, one should tolerate that. While doing this one should do breath-infusion and then hold the breath, and while concentrating, put the attention where the thigh is connected to the buttocks and sexual organs

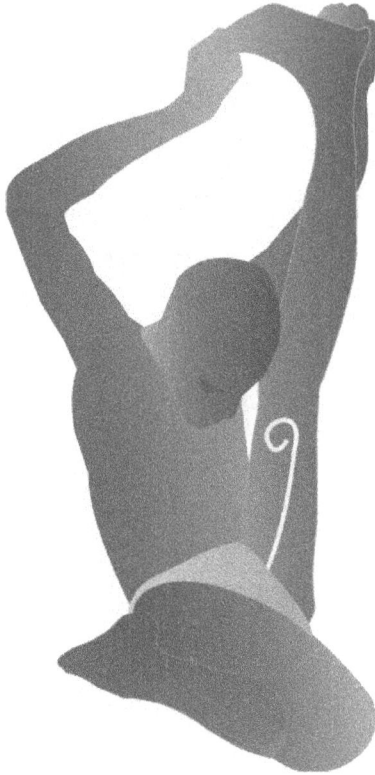

May 11, 1998

Agastya

He said, "Sit in lotus. Show stability."

Remark:

This was an instruction for me to get habituated to sitting in lotus posture. In 1972, I worked with this body to sit in lotus. I used to spend half hour in the posture, locked in a closet, when I was in the US Air Force. Subsequently I could sit in tight lotus, which is called padmasana. Later on after I decreased yoga practice, while I was in the ashram of another society, whose founder disliked yoga, I lost the ability to sit for long periods. However

I am again developing the ability for it. Even though the body I used was forty seven years of age, during the year of 1998, still by the grace Agastya, and other elevated yogins, I can sit in lotus.

The tight lotus is not the only posture which can be used while meditating, but it is the posture that gives the best results. However, if while sitting in it, one is pained in the ankles, knees and thighs, one should practice other postures which loosen the knees and slacken the muscles and tendons in the thigh.

As I sat in lotus on this day, I used pranavision to see within the subtle body and to detect the causal form. Sometimes the pranavision subsided. Then I sense it without vision, by feelings in the darkness of the psyche.

May 12, 1998

Agastya

He had me check on air turmoil at the base of the body. Observe this:

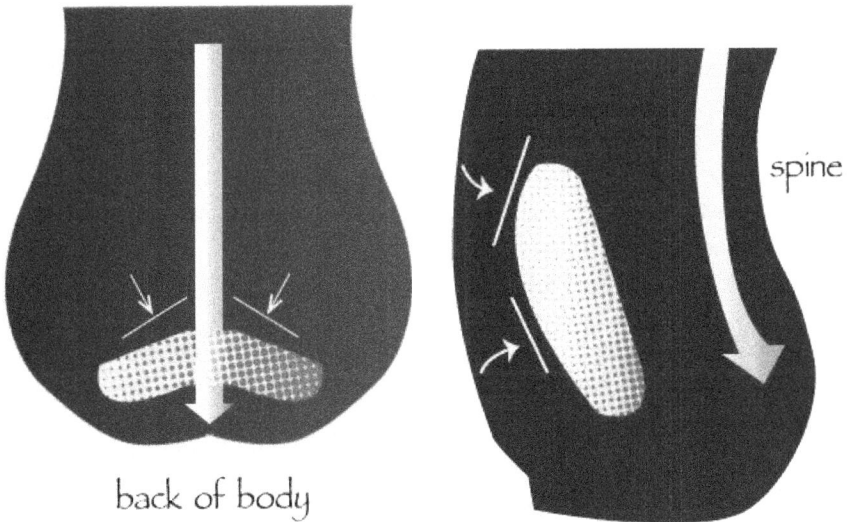

back of body

spine

He said, "After full breath-infusion with sun air or sun-warmed moon air, assume full lotus. Check the air turmoil at the bottom of the trunk. Push it down and around to compact the turmoil, causing it to move up the sushumna central passage in the spine."

Remark:

Sun air means sun-charged subtle energy. Sun-warmed moon air means subtle energy that is charged by the moon and heated by the sun. Air that is charged only by the moon may block the tubes of the subtle body. If one cannot get sun-charged air, one may heat the air slightly with a wood or electric stove. An open flamed gas stove should not be used since the burnt gas has the wrong energy. In the northern hemisphere, the sun might not warm the air during periods of the winter season. Sometimes, the moon alone might be surcharging the air. Such air should be warmed by a wood burning or electric stove. The best thing, of course, is to relocate to the tropics.

Full breath-infusion means a session of breath-infusion in which the person doing the exercises feels that he removed the sluggish energy in the subtle body by pushing it out with fresh energy. If there is sufficient subtle air pumped through the subtle lungs, it will go throughout the subtle body to replace and push out the stale dulling energy.

Part 2

Agastya

He said, "The lotus posture is important to cut off the foot nerve and steady the body for attention-focus. This, with the movement of the intellect downward, is the preliminary preparation."

Remark:

There are some postures which are preparatory for sitting in lotus. These concern stretching the ankle, knee and thigh. There are many such poses and movements which can be combined with breath-infusion. Here are a few:

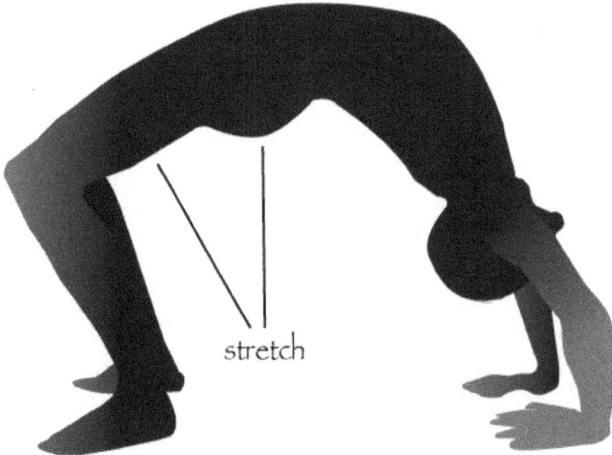

stretch

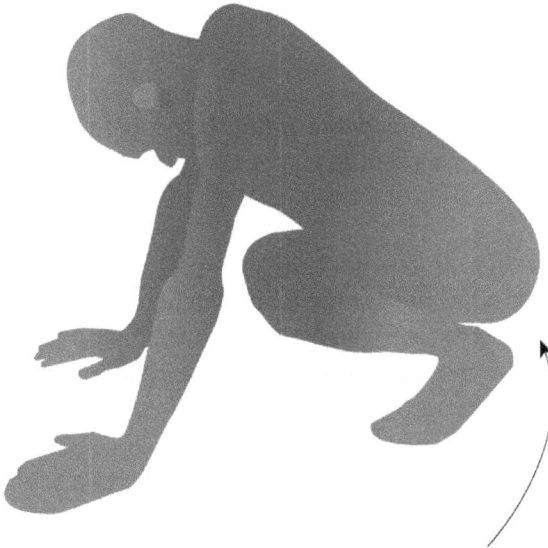

bounce buttocks up and down

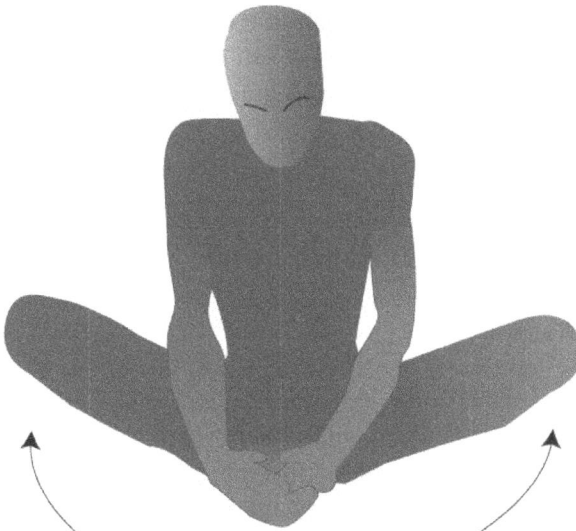

move knees up and down

The pulling down of the intellect has to do with making it concerned with the psyche. In the conditioned stage, the intellect maintains an external interest and neglects the interest of the psyche. This tendency must be reversed. One should pull the intellect down so that it develops interest in the internal behavior of the subtle body.

May 13, 1998

Agastya

He said, "A good yogi bears the brunt. By proper self-criticism he finds his portion of the fault. He rectifies it."

Remarks

Agastya said this after I considered what might be my part in the attraction of people who come to me for instruction but who cannot progress spiritually because they are destined only for cultural objectives. The question as to why a person cannot progress spiritually in a particular life is answered by one word: Destiny.

Providence is all-powerful. If someone was destined for cultural upliftment only, no one can adjust that. Some come to a yogi and utilize his time and energy all to no avail. They benefit by converting his attention into cultural improvement.

Yogic attention, though meant only for yoga progress, can be converted into cultural development. In any case, my purpose is to avoid such culturally determined people. What is my fault in the matter? Why is it that I cannot successfully avoid such people? I must bear the brunt of their counterproductive association. By a program of self-criticism, I would find the portion of fault that lies with me.

May 13, 1998

Agastya

He said, "Face the air."

Remark:

This instruction was given while I did breath-infusion. At the time and place, at which I did the exercises, I faced the south side since Agastya was present it that direction. He directed me to turn to the west, from which direction fresh air blew. This type of instruction is a spur of the moment one. On the next day I might face the south again or some other direction. Each day, one should sense the refreshing direction. The hard and fast rule is: Do whatever causes success.

May 14, 1998

Agastya

He said, "There are two methods, either energy concentration or energy stabilization. Centration concerns intellect stabilization. The best method is stabilization but it cannot be done if the intellect is disobedient and sticky towards the sensual energies and memory. First the core-self should look down to find any subtle energy turmoil. While doing that, the intellect should be moved to the turmoil location. Leave the intellect there for a while. If it drifts, relocate it in the turmoil energies again. Do so without any quam or complaint. Keep it at the turmoil location. This brings stabilization in the beginning of intense absorption. The lotus posture is important, as I told you formerly."

Remark:

Here is an example of getting a direct instruction from a great yogin in the astral world. In this case, I was on the physical side. Agastya was on the astral side. However, even when I operate the physical body I can hear and see astrally.

In meditation, energy concentration is preliminary. It all depends on one's level of advancement. For some persons, energy concentration is a big achievement. The scattering of the personal energies, occurs both within and without the psyche, but it is promoted mostly by external objects which the psyche desires and perceives. Both, the psyche and the external environment are involved. Since the external environment cannot be adjusted, it is best to find the internal faults and correct those. As soon as one executes that self-correction, one makes sufficient advancement whereby material nature shows some respect for one's wishes. Nature eases the pressure and allows one some exemption from cultural involvements.

Energy concentration means retracting the sensual powers and refraining them from mundane interests. After this is achieved to a degree, one works for energy stabilization or containment.

The personal energies are mostly moving within the psyche just like atoms moving within a container of air. The atoms are never still. They move randomly with intentions to revolve electromagnet relationships to each other and to breach the container. The personal energies are ever seeking a sensual outlet. Thus, there is a need to stabilize them so that they no longer seek the outward expressions with the gross and subtle material energy

Consider that any repression will eventually result in an expression. What then is the point of repressing anything? One represses something to control it and to reconfigure it in a desirable way. Of course if the repression is not done effectively, it will fail. In the end one will express the energy forcibly in an impulsive and undesirable way

Stabilization occurs when the restrained energy loses tension, then it becomes content not going outward, not making sensual investigations externally, not maintaining a pleasure-seeking attitude. That condition is not reached merely by restraint. To the restraint must be added sincerity and constructive purpose. Some persons cannot afford such a sincerity of purpose for yoga, but they have sincerity for cultural improvements. For those who can have sincerity of purpose for yoga, there must be in their nature an inborn tendency for neglect of cultural improvements along with a sense of righteous duty for supporting the same cultural life for the sake of order in human society.

By transcendental irony, Krishna identified the cultural improvements as being his work and his psychological discipline, mat karma, mat yoga. That is described in the Bhagavad Gita, the discourse which convinced Arjuna to get involved in cultural corrections.

However for yoga, we must eventually forego such cultural interest, even the global cultural concerns. But we can only do so with God's permission and by his awarding an exemption from such service. Somehow by the grace of Balarama, I was given an exemption. Once when I followed him and Krishna, Balarama said, "You had better go. Sit with Bhava (Shiva). If you follow us you will be hurt. A boy like you with frail limbs has no business on battlefields. Sit with Bhava and learn yoga, fight internally."

Energy stabilization only occurs when the energies in the psyche are relaxed where they have no interest in extrovert behavior. Some feel that they may view things intellectually and that will be sufficient, but no, we must deal with the emotional nature and with the super-subtle mundane energy which is lodged in the causal, subtle and physical bodies. That too must be adjusted. Hence the need for asana postures, pranayama breath-infusion and psychological analysis to discover and root out hidden faults.

Agastya instructed that I see the masters of the lotus posture. He spoke of yogis like Yogeshwarananda, who earlier, told me to do some more loosening postures which help to stretch and relax the front muscles of the thigh area.

Agastya

He, said, "Do not allow the lifeforce to enthuse the intellect while pushing the intellect away to use the given energy externally. Look back into the lifeforce until it stops pushing."

Remark:

This action of the lifeforce represents an external struggle as well. It is also a struggle with others who are lifeforce dominant, and who, as servants of the lifeforce, want the yogi to act in a materialistic way.

From within the subtle body, the lifeforce may enthuse the intellect with impulsive energies. Once this is done, the intellect will endeavor for fulfillments in the subtle and gross worlds. Most of this enjoyment is highlighted by sexual intercourse which may occur on the physical and subtle planes simultaneously. Or it may occur in dreams on the subtle level only. Thus, unless one can regulate the contacts which the lifeforce has with the intellect organ, one cannot stop the impulsive actions.

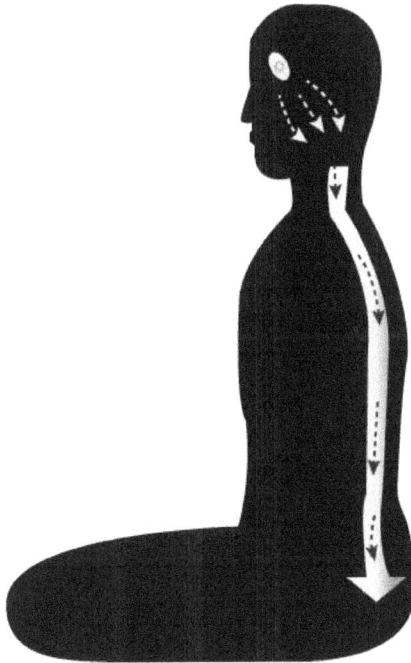

The intellect is goaded by the lifeforce. Even though the intellect seems to be a directive power, it is mostly goaded from behind by lifeforce energy.

Servants are regularly seen to be going in and out of a palace but that does not mean that they are unsupervised. They are sent on missions. Similarly, even though the intellect seems to be the big actor, it is goaded by the lifeforce, which is the operational controller of the material body. However, for the purposes of this yoga, the natural system of lifeforce motivation should be changed. A big event is to give up the association of all people, believers or nonbelievers, theists and atheists, who are driven primarily by their lifeforces.

May 17, 1998

Agastya

Penis Pranavision

This is used while doing breath-infusion. It may be used by females for vaginal pranavision. In this case the penis, being disoriented from sexual intercourse, and being stationed in its urination function, without a lust impetus, can be used for a positive purpose of developing pranavision. So long as the penis is regarded as a sexual organ, there can be little progression in yoga. One has to get away from that view and regard it by its urinary function, overlooking and foregoing the sexual one. In the females, the sexual and childbearing functions are considered. The idea of childbearing is primitive and is particular to earthly situations. It is not useful in the subtle world, where anyone can appear (be born) without having to pass through a woman's vaginal passage. Female ascetics have to free themselves from the birth-delivery function.

An ascetic should not feel that he can rid his body of its sexual construction. Rather he should be willing to yield to sexuality while simultaneously relying on sexual neutrality.

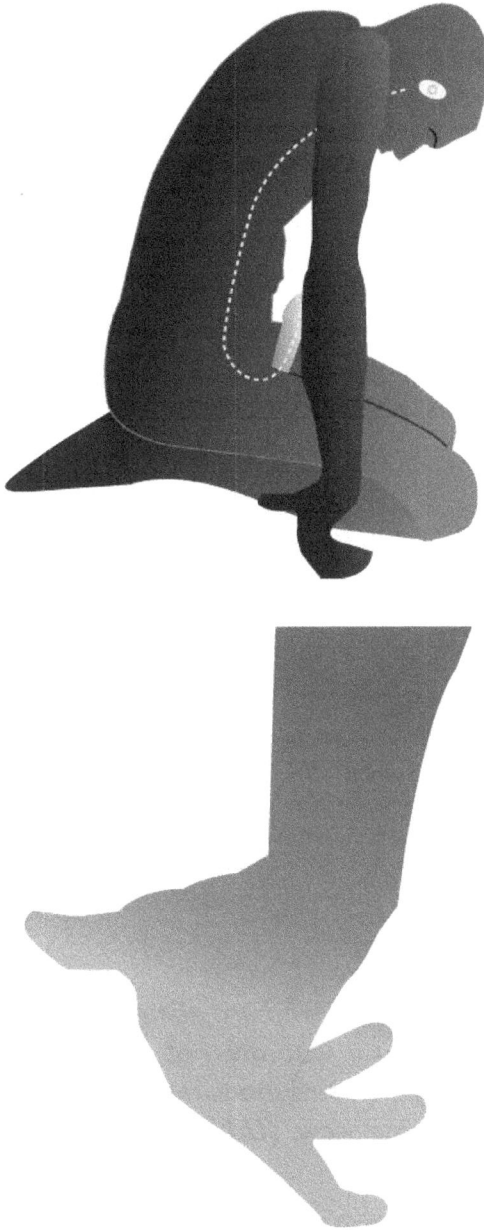

While performing this technique, one should have the soles of the feet together with buttocks raised slightly, pressing on the fingers as shown in the diagram. The subtle energy which is compressed into the lungs by rapid breathing, is directed through the head of the penis or entrance of the vaginal passage. If this pranavision is developed, a partner-tantric yogi can see into the body of his partner during sexual acts. These acts need not be physical but might be experienced through the subtle body only. By looking through the penis, he may also see the spirits who transit from a male body into a female one for developing baby forms. A female ascetic has the special advantage of seeing how an ancestral spirit develops an embryo in the womb. This gives a yogini a review of what she did to acquire the present material body.

May 17, 1998

Agastya

He said, "Anyone can start yoga, but it is a task to get to a point of no return."

Remark:

I read a statement in the Uddhava Gita:

त्यागो ऽयं दुष्करो भूमन्
कामाना विषयात्मभिः ।
सुतरा त्वयि सर्वात्मन्न्
अभक्तैर् इति मे मतिः ॥ २.१५ ॥

tyāgo 'yaṁ duṣkaro bhūman
kāmānāṁ viṣayātmabhiḥ
sutarāṁ tvayi sarvātmann
abhaktair iti me matiḥ (2.15)

tyāgo = tyag — renunciation of results; 'yam = ayam — this; duṣkaro = duṣkaraḥ — difficult to accomplish; bhūman — O infinite Lord; kāmānām — of cravings; viṣayātmabhiḥ = viṣaya — sense enjoyment + ātmabhiḥ — by those spirits who are absorbed in; sutarām — especially; tvayi — to you; sarvātmann — O soul of all beings; abhaktair = abhaktaiḥ — by those who are not devotees; iti — thus; me — my; matiḥ — view.

Translation

O infinite Lord, for those who are absorbed in sense enjoyment and especially for those who are not devoted to you, who are the soul of all beings, this renunciation of cravings is difficult to accomplish. This is my view. (Uddhava Gita 2.15)

In relation to this Agastya said that one has to get to a point where one is self-compelled to complete yoga.

May 17, 1998

Shiva

He said, "Be sure to record that."

Remark:

I had an experience that I did not intent to record. It was this:

By pranavision, I saw through the male orifice, the tiny astral hole in the center of the subtle male organ. This was part of my research of the personal energies in the subtle body. It is recommended by Yogeshwarananda that one should investigate every part of the body, seeing various parts of it. However, somehow, there was a dimensional switch.

As I looked through the orifice, I found myself looking into the womb of a. woman through her orifice. In any case, these things happen in mystic practice. After that Agastya, who observed what happened, said, "Do not do that again. One should not peer upward through the body of a female. Pranavision must be controlled. Restrict it to your personal energies. If you find that somehow you switched into other dimensions, switch back immediately."

Then he said, "I wish to show the first part."

By mystic vision I saw this:

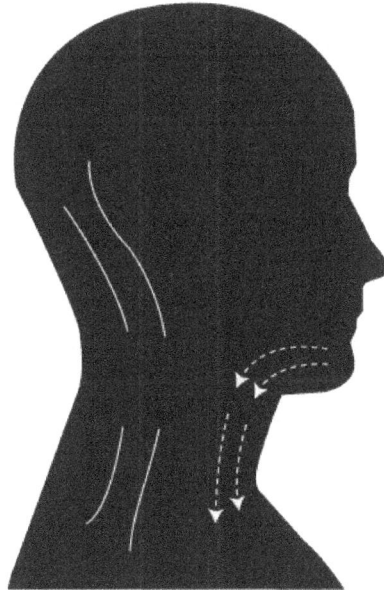

All cells under throat and in neck
have magnetic force
drawning down into body

Then he showed this:

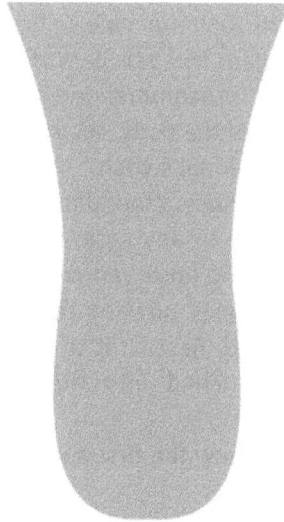

This shows that the sexual function is first triggered in the mouth. I asked him about the air. He showed this:

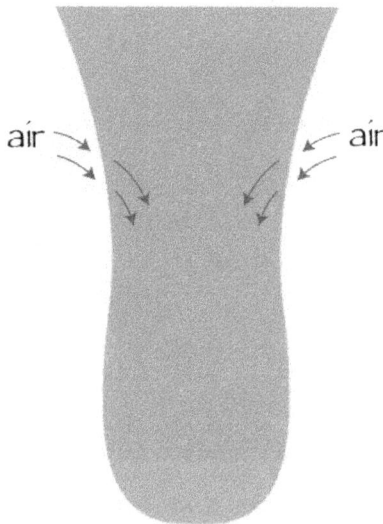

That shows air in the mid-region. I asked him about the semen tube. He said there is a check valve which develops underneath. The diagram below shows the viewing tube I used when I looked under the woman's orifice. It was more like an environment with rivers, mountains and scenery, a landscape but it is mostly a nutrition place

viewing tube

May 17, 1998

Agastya

While I did rapid breathing, he instructed that I lower the back into the buttocks area. This is done psychically not physically. It is possible on the mystic plane. While one does breath-infusion, he or she should be attentive to the practice, keeping the eyes closed for the most part to concentrate within the body, to observe the subtle energy movements and displacements. One should be sensitive to advice given by yogis who use astral forms and who might be in the vicinity.

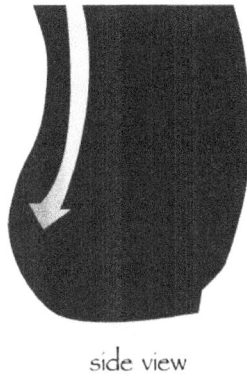

side view

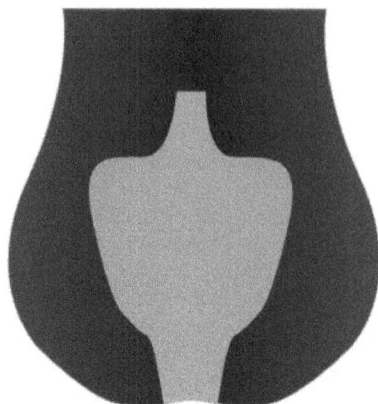

back of body

May 18, 1998

Agastya

Just after midnight, he said this:

"Because they are not existent here, particular rare types of subtle energy (prana) were introduced here. This is similar to rare soil or fruit brought from an island to a continent. A particular advanced yogi or siddha perfected being transposes it. Eventually it disappears. More may be imported if you require it."

Remark:

This was in reference to special subtle energy that I was allowed to breathe into my subtle body, to allow it to have a particular mystic insight.

May 18, 1998

Lahiri Mahasaya

He said, "Lotus posture is special. It requires empowerment for its performance. It cannot be done correctly without the blessings of higher yogis. I got help from Agastya. "

Remark:

I received assistance for performance of lotus from many yogins. I began by taking help from Rishi Singh Gherwal. Later I took help from Vishnudevananda and Shivananda. I got assistance from Lahiri Mahasaya and Babaji. In the early years of practice in this body, I took assistance from

Shivananda because he kept track of me when I took this new body in a location which was distant from India, in Guyana. That assistance was received subconsciously.

It is a habit of yogis, that when they leave a body, they congregate with other yogins in the astral world. If a yogi is resistant to transmigration through mundane life forms, he does not readily nor eagerly take an embryo in a female body. When however a consequential force acts on a particular yogin, he may not resist the tendency to enter a womb. Then he must take help. Usually at that point, just before he would become an embryo, he may ask a superior yogin for protection. This means that the superior yogin will keep track of him while he is in the woman's uterus and will try to inspire him to take up yoga again as soon as his body gets out of her womb and becomes detached from her maternal influence, which is normally bewitching.

Because of the bewitching force which operates in her psyche to make her child feel dependent on her and to cause that person to forget the past life, a woman may be rated as being alluring.

Any yogin who does not get coverage from a superior soul and who takes a body is more or less doomed to become materialistic. Shivananda agreed to give me protection. He shielded my body for the first sixteen years. It took me that long to recover from the bewitchment of maternal force.

At the age of sixteen when I broke away, I could not objectively determine who assisted me. Later on, I met my first meditation instructor, an American yogi named Arthur Beverford. His guru was Rishi Singh Gherwal, an accomplished hatha yogi, a contemporary of Paramhansa Yogananda. Rishi Singh wrote some books on hatha yoga. He translated parts of the Mahabharata concerning great yogins like Markandeya. He wrote about great yogins in the Himalayas.

I will share some information from Arthur Beverford. After Yogananda, that great publicist of the Babaji technique lineage, departed from his body, his followers claimed that his body remained incorruptible for a number of weeks. Rishi Singh GherwaL was in California at the time. Hearing this, he went to the place where Paramhansa's dead body was kept. After viewing the body, he stated that the claim was invalid. Such a statement by a reliable samadhi yogin, puts to question the credibility of the incorruptible claims. It may be that his followers wanted to establish Paramhansa as a person who was comparable to Jesus Christ who supposedly resurrected his dead body after nearly three days of interment.

In my own history, as admitted above, it may be questioned as to why it took me sixteen years in this body, before I broke loose from the maternal influence. The answer is that such a birth influence is powerful because it is supported by the genetic energy in the new body. In fact after those sixteen years, I just began to recover, like an intoxicated man who arises after several days of sleeping under the effects of a narcotic or alcoholic beverage.

May 18, 1996

Agastya

He said, "This is an offer for sexual smacking. Are you hungry?"

Remark:

Since ancient times, even before Rama, the son of Dasharath appeared, Agastya was known for his sense of humor, on one side, and his seriousness on the other. He chided me for an incidence. At one point I positioned his sculptured form next to that of another authority who became famous recently. Agastya said to me in the astral world, "Why should I sit with a phony yogi."

This is his humor. The serious side of the comment is this: Many persons become authorized spiritual teachers without expertise in yoga. To make matters worse, the unqualified teacher may have a large following. He may sit on a high seat and explain technique yoga, even though he is not proficient.

The teacher's assumption is that since he did it in past lives, he can recall details. However, if one practices and checks his statements, one can realize that his lectures are either drawn from pure intellectual analysis of information left by actual yogis or from ancient books which give sketches of the austerities. These teachers cheat the audiences. They undoubtedly practiced yoga in a past life but they forgot. They do not have the power to recall the details. Yet, they dishonestly make a claim about remembrance. Agastya told me that he did not want his sculpture to be placed next to that of a phony teacher.

Agastya warned me not to indulge in sexual snacking. Just as a person might take a large meal, and then during intervals take snacks, one may take a large indulgence of sexual intercourse and then take small ones in the form of flirtations and sexual thinking. To seal my celibacy and not to disturb it, Agastya warned of sexual snacking, smaller sexual engagements which are subtle but which are just as destructive of celibacy.

He said further, "It is a serious offence, this sexual snacking. Many phony ascetics were, by this, led back into a woman's womb."

This is funny. There are three ways to be led back into a woman's womb. The first method is penetrative sexual indulgence with her. The second is by coming out of a male sexual organ in a rush of sexual energy during intercourse as a mere urge within a man's semen. The third way is by coming out of the female part in an infant body, being pushed out forcibly while crying for pity.

When Agastya warned me about sexual snacking, I saw some women with sexually revealing clothing. He wanted to bar me to protect the celibate efforts and accelerate yoga progression.

May 18, 1998

Agastya

He said, "How did you conquer food snacks?"
I replied,"
"Initially I ate medicinal food at snack time. I absorbed more air by doing breath-infusion before snack time."

He remarked, "Do something similar to counteract the sex snack. Use the penis pranavision as the medicine but do not peer through it into another matching body."

Remark:

This conversation means that it is possible to completely curb physical or subtle sexual flirtations. Initially by isolation or by forcibly stopping the physical eyes from making contact with sexually-revealing forms, one may curb the physical exposure but that will not cease flirtations on the psychic plane. Agastya, in concern for my full success in celibacy, advised that I use certain techniques to purify the sexual energy in my psyche. The matching bodies are those of the opposite sex which have an attraction to mine, which have a sex appeal to my form and which are willing to engage in subtle sexual maneuvers with my subtle body. There are many such forms. If possible each should be avoided.

May 22, 1998

Agastya

He said, "Accumulate a series of small high energy absorptions which last for a short period. After sometime you may experience the longer absorptions. These come from three processes, namely,

- Take intellect to meet the lifeforce
- Regulating the lifeforce to meet the intellect when the lifeforce upswings

- The core-self goes to the lifeforce and stays with it. After this action the intellect may follow the core-self at a standard mystic distance in reference to the core.

In all such cases, polluted subtle energy must be flushed out. One must have the proper diet for consistent purity."

Remark:

This instruction has to do with my being practical. Since I cannot spend hours doing pranayama in preparation for high energy absorption, I should work with my present schedule and be satisfied with small periods for absorption. In the year 2000, the year of this remark, Yogeshwarananda explained that it takes a certain amount of pranayama breath-infusion to cause withdrawal of the senses from social concerns. In turn, a certain degree of withdrawal brings spontaneous concentration. So much concentration causes deep absorption. If one does not practice sufficiently, he cannot get the desired results. I will explain Agastya's instructions for small absorptions.

- Take intellect to meet the lifeforce

This is a mystic act of taking the intellect organ in the head of the subtle body and carrying it down to the base of the spine to meet with the lifeforce, to remain in its proximity. Since this is a mystic action it is difficult to perform. However, if one practices regularly one may do it. Generally the intellect does not move from its position in the head of the subtle body. But it can move if the soul either drags, pulls, lifts or forcibly moves it in some way. Normally, the lifeforce comes to meet the intellect or the lifeforce sends sensations which goads and motivates the intellect. That natural process can change if one first expels the dark energy in the subtle form, replacing it with crystal clear subtle force. To do this one must practice breath-infusion and use the correct diet, eating at the right times to bring about efficient psyche energization.

- Regulating the lifeforce to meet the intellect when the lifeforce upswings

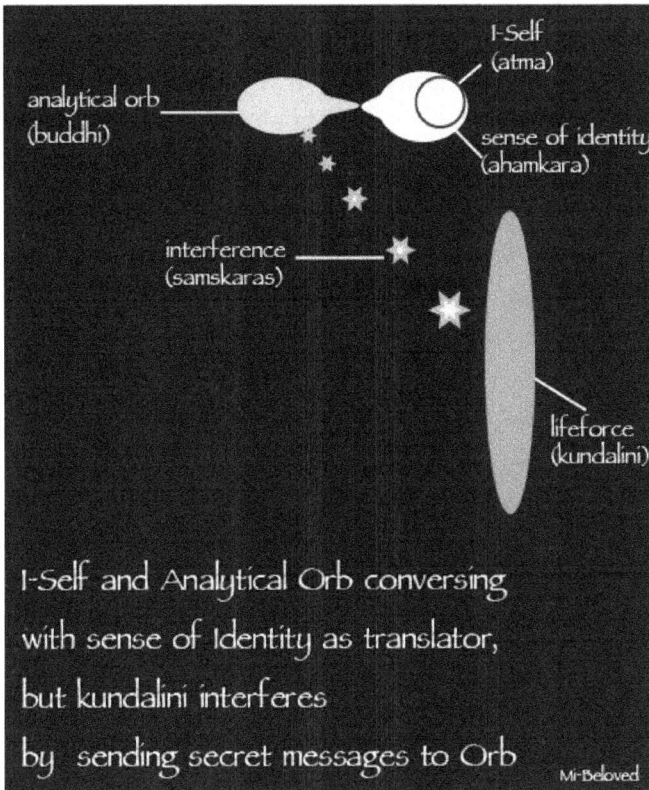

I-Self
(atma)

analytical orb
(buddhi)

sense of identity
(ahamkara)

interference
(samskaras)

lifeforce
(kundalini)

I-Self and Analytical Orb conversing

with sense of Identity as translator,

but kundalini interferes

by sending secret messages to Orb

Mi-Beloved

The lifeforce usually upswings indirectly by sending polluted energy to goad and motivate the intellect to act. This indirect upswing serves the cultural purpose but it does nothing for spiritual upliftment. When the lifeforce is purified, and when the channels which it uses are cleared, it directly upswings. Instead of sending out heavy polluted subtle energy, it moves in a translucent or crystal clear brilliance and travels up through the nadi subtle tubes in the subtle body, going up the spine in search of the intellect, which is in the subtle head. Sometimes, it does not have enough force to ascent the entire spinal column. It may ascend a certain distance and then collapse to the base

After repeated attempts, a yogin, by purification, may bring the kundalini up suddenly but even then it stays up for the most for about 30 seconds or 3 minutes. Then it collapses downward. Gradually by consistent practice, and by being sincere, not avoiding the disciplines, the yogi may keep it shining day and night, giving off its brilliance towards the intellect through nadi channels.

The intellect and lifeforce may be compared to a separated husband and wife. In cultural life, these two meet in the pleasure room of the lifeforce. This pleasure room is not where the lifeforce usually resides. It is nearby, at the pubio-coccus circular nerve. The two meet there during sexual intercourse, otherwise the lifeforce stays away from the intellect and the intellect does likewise.

sexual climax experience

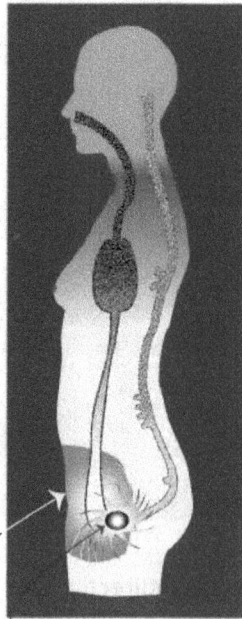

buddhi intellect orb relocated to sex energy and kundalini lifeforce explosion at sex organ chakra

For kundalini yoga, the lifeforce and intellect should meet in the office of the intellect, which is in the central brain. In some yogic lore, when Shakti is united with Shiva, success is attained. Shakti represents the lifeforce. Shiva represents the intellect. Thus when the wife and husband are united in the location, in the subtle brain, and not in the wrong location, in the sexual area, the two live in ecstasy.

kundalini lifeforce

explosion in subtle head

buddhi intellect orb is affected

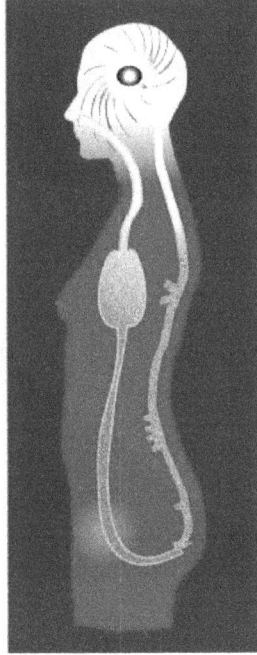

- The core-self goes to the lifeforce and stays with it. After this action the intellect may follow the core-self at a standard mystic distance in reference to the core.

Just as a coach which is hitched to a horse remains at a set distance from the animal depending on the length of the connecting shaft, the standard distance between the core-self and the intellect remains the same in most circumstances. The core-self has the ability to enter into the space which the intellect occupies but that occurs on a higher existential plane. When the core-self relates to the intellect, it does so with the help of the ego-identifying sense. This identifying sense (ahamkara) is the sense of "I am doing this or that." It is the sense of "I exist."

Even if the intellect is reluctant to vacate the subtle brain, if the spirit is can relocate itself, the intellect because it is linked at a certain distance in reference, will follow the core-self despite its reluctance.

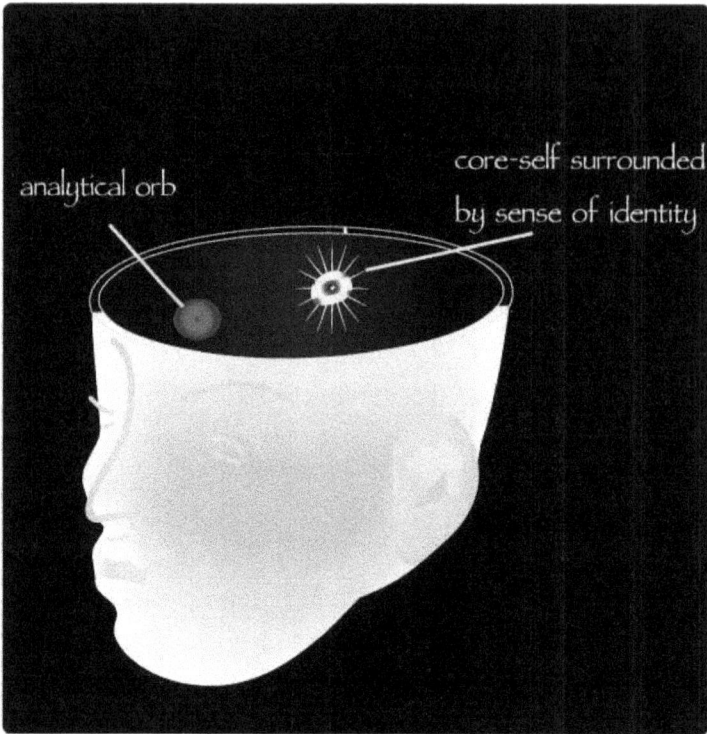

The core-self is attracted to the lifeforce during the pleasure of a sexual intercourse. It goes there forcibly with the identifying sense and the intellect. After the sexual pleasure climaxes or reaches its greatest intensity, the core-self, the identifying sense and the intellect, enter a discouragement since the lifeforce which is like a battery, exhausts its potent charge and becomes energy-less like a well-lit room which suddenly becomes pitch black.

For this meditation, the core-self goes to the lifeforce and the intellect follows. If the lifeforce is properly charged, and was not discharged by a sexual intercourse, the core-self will see, sense or feel the lifeforce as an energy or as a crystal clear light. When the intellect comes there, remaining at a certain distance from the core-self, it too will feel the energy of the lifeforce. In turn, the lifeforce will feel the radiance of the intellect. They may become united like a husband meeting a wife after a long separation. This is sometimes compared to Shiva meeting Goddess Durga after they had not seen each other, eye to eye, for several million years.

In these experiences it is important to be on a diet which facilitates technique yoga. One must eat at the right time and do pranayama breath-infusion as recommended by a competent yogi.

May 24, 1998

Agastya

A hand/sushumna middle passage locator

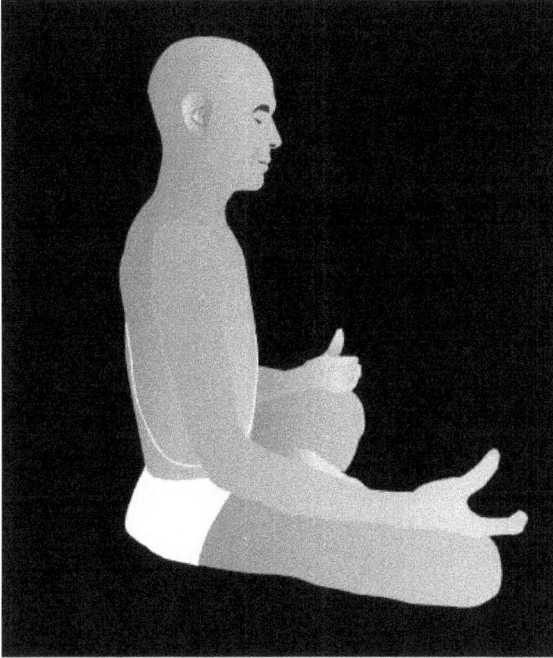

He showed a special mudra hand posture, through which one may find the sushumna middle passage in the subtle body. In most people, this passage is clogged. For neophyte yogis it is clogged some of the time. They do physical postures, breath exercises and mental procedures to keep it open. Initially it cannot be opened permanently. It opens and then closes repeatedly, until one gets a high level of efficient practice.

May 26, 1998

Agastya

He said, "It is the quality of the psychic material nature. There is no room if you are removed from the passionate energy. Get far into the clarifying subtle force. Situate yourself there. "

Remark:

So long as we remain in association with the passionate energy of material nature, we will be inclined in a certain way and will be motivated to do certain pleasant and unpleasant things. If we prefer not to be induced by that energy we should move ourselves from it and move into the higher, more clarifying power, which is known as the sattva guna or the clarifying force. It is called clarifying because it reveals the disadvantages and flaws of the enticing energies. It does not force one to act blindly as one is impelled by passion which sponsors a lack of understanding of consequences for irresponsible actions. In passion there is some clarity for advantages and opportunities only. That mode does not show the liabilities.

In the Shiva Purana it is explained that initially, when there was just a handful of beings manifested around and about this planet, Shiva was reluctant to take a position in the passionate energy. Most of the other supernatural people became annoyed at him, because unless one becomes enthused passionately, one cannot reproduce in this creation. They knew that unless Shiva started the passionate action, they would be discouraged from it as well. They yearned to delve into the passionate force. Since Shiva remained in the clarifying energy, he was resented. From the clarifying position, one cannot further this material world, because it is the passionate energy that does that. This situation is perplexing.

May 25, 1998

Shiva

He said, "Use the lingam diagram, as if you sat on that organ."

Remark:

Shiva gave a penis inversion technique, which would cause the sexual thrusting power to remain within the psyche and not to seek expression beyond it. This is the sublimation of vulgar sexual drive.

There is more than one method for achieving this. In this one, the sexual thrusting or pushing power is sublimated. In the male body, this sexual power is divided up in many ways. Part of that expression takes the form of being able to thrust the male organ into the female one, for without the ability to do that, the male semen fluids would fall outside the female body. This thrusting power is different to the muscular power of the organ, but the two forces are related.

In this inversion practice, one sits in lotus. The sushumna passage acts as the penis itself, going upwards through the spine. The base of the body which is the base of the kundalini power acts as a female vaginal passage, through which the male organ was inserted. The head of the body acts as the uterus in which the semen is injected. Here are some diagrams

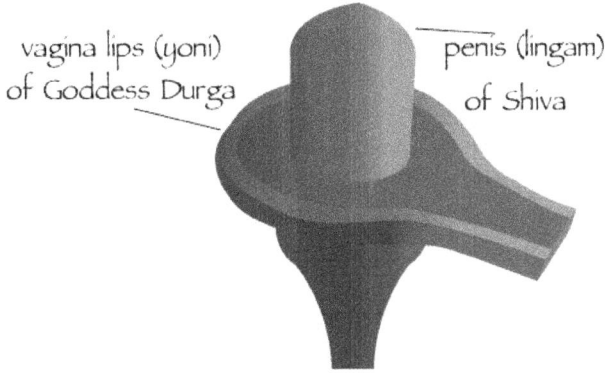

vagina lips (yoni) of Goddess Durga

penis (lingam) of Shiva

Shiva lingam inserted into yoni of the Goddess (Devi)

cross-section of female torso with yogi superimposed

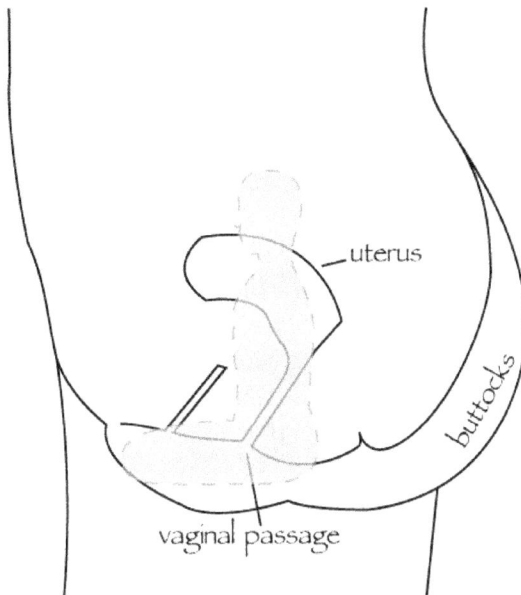

uterus

buttocks

vaginal passage

May 26, 1998

Agastya

He said:

Locate the out-pouring energy. Take steps to curb it. The vision will develop no further without conserving it.

Remark:

There are many spiritual seekers who wish for a guru who can touch and give spiritual vision. The idea is that to be a guru one should have a vision-granting ability. It is expected that such a guru will bless the disciple with divine nature and insight.

Most of this is invalid. It is mostly a fantasy in the minds of childish people who want rapid spiritual achievement without having to endeavor for it. Agastya explained a basic point which should be learned by all aspiring yogis. It is this:

The potential for divine power is present in the disciple. It is not something the spiritual master has to bestow. Divine power is being used by the disciple at all stages, but it is directed into the material energy. When it is withdrawn from lower involvement and conserved, the spiritual insight develops. It is the same power but the focus and nature of it changes. It is the same power but so long as we direct it into the material pursuits, it denies spiritual insight. By consistent practice at sensual energy withdrawal and by a lack of interest in this world, we conserve it. Then it develops in the spiritual direction as desired.

If we need anything from a yogi, it is the encouragement and motivation to maintain the spiritual disciplines. If we have the practice, everything else will follow. If for instance, one desires to turn water into steam, one should place the water above a fire. If we need spiritual life, all we need is a valid practice.

An argument against this may be presented in the case of Arjuna, who was granted supernatural and then divine vision by Krishna. However, that argument is flawed. Arjuna was qualified for the bestowal in a special way. It fact in the Gita, Krishna mentioned Arjuna's unique position as His friend and endearing devotee. Krishna even said that even the deva supernatural rulers, and even the great sages did not get that vision which was granted to Arjuna. We must understand that it was Arjuna's divine vision that opened. At first when Krishna provided the revelation of the Universal Form, Arjuna could not see the apparition until Krishna opened Arjuna's supernatural and spiritual eyes.

Krishna will not do this for any and everybody. In fact, in the Anu Gita when again Arjuna requested Krishna to repeat that miracle, Krishna declined stating that he did that previously by special yoga technique and he would not repeat it for Arjuna.

Part 3

Agastya

A swelling- of-the-organ technique

He gave me an exercise which sublimates the muscular aspect of the sexual organ. Generally the organ, when it is without lusty interest, is flabby without erect muscular aspect. When there is sensual impetus, it is aroused with an influx of lusty blood. This is operated by feelings of enthusiasm.

According to Yogeshwarananda, the organ discharges harmful chemicals when its sole function is urination. Otherwise it operates in passion for sexual affairs or renders pain when it is diseased. Passionate energy in the organ has usefulness for progeny generation but when one's body engages with another for such generation, a strong electrical charge is developed. If the mind interprets this as pleasure, the usefulness of passion is converted into a psychological obsession. That ruins the energy by repeated indulgences without respect to progeny generation.

Apart from the thrusting force in the male organ, there is the swelling force which takes away its flabby aspect. This enlargement may arise at any time, even inappropriately when there is no opportunity for sexual intercourse nor for responsible child care. In that way it may inspire the body to crave sexual participation. In this technique, the swelling aspect is sublimated. One should do exercises which stretch the muscles under the buttocks, where it connects to the thigh.

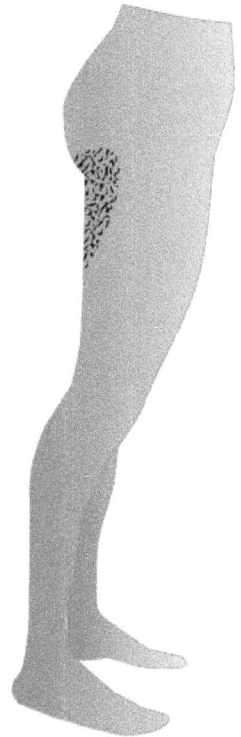

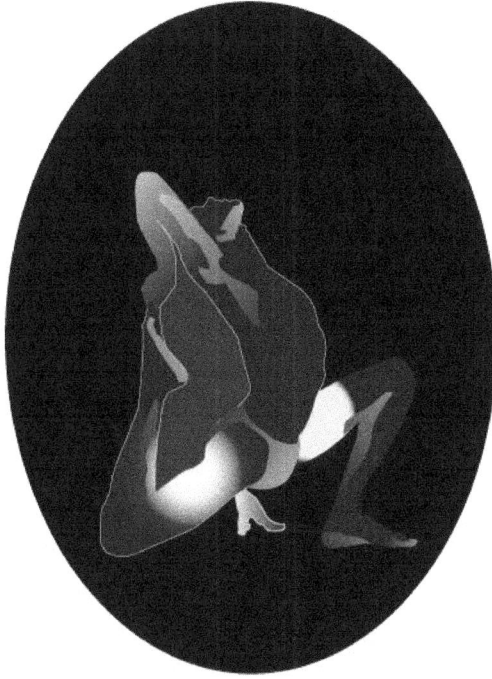

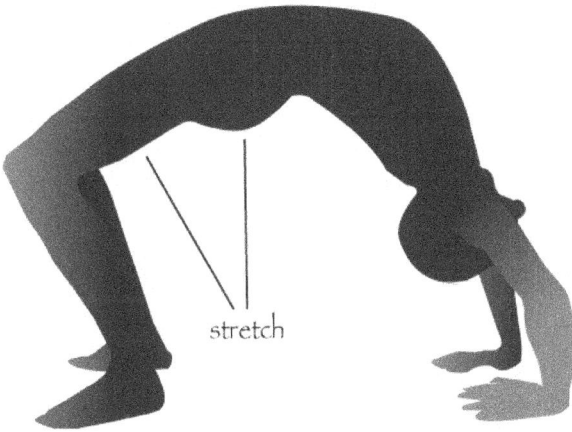

stretch

May 27, 1998

Agastya

He said, "Why can they not do it?"
I replied, "It is not their essential nature."

He responded, "The correct term is localized subtle energy or prakriti all-pervading universal energy. It is not their essential subtle level. Or it is not their familiarity with the universal energy"

Remark:

He made these comments in reference to persons who attempted to improve diet and restrict the on-going greed for food. Later he told me that some are reborn repeatedly in many material bodies, and still they move no further in the cultural or spiritual direction.

May 30, 1998

Shiva

On this day, Shiva showed a tantric practice which is used with yogini women in the astral world. Some yoginis may help an aspiring yogi. Some may ruin him. Some enter and possess the body of the yogi. One may see them enter early in the morning while doing breath-infusion practice. Breath-infusion rapid breathing is very important for the development of subtle vision. I introduced some friends to it. Due to the dulling influence which prevails over their minds, I am not successful with many of them. One may try it for a few times and then reject it. This is because they want a process which gives instant success. They instinctively desire a process which will give them something immediate.

In that technique, the male sexual organ is interspaced in the female one of a yogini woman who is expert in yoga tantra technique. There may not be such a woman in one's physical proximity but that does not matter. There are many on the astral planes. They are very willing to help a yogi to advance with his celibate practice through terminal sexual connections. Since they want to advance further, if they need a limited amount of sexual intercourses to complete the study of sexual effects, they may engage a male yogi, who can transcend sexual activity.

Besides this, it is possible to do this technique more safely without a partner. If one checks the technique which Shiva gave me on the May 25, 1998 entry, one will see that it is possible to do the techniques without a partner. Sometimes such a singular tantric process does not give the satisfaction one expects, but if one persists with sincerity, clarity will come in the practice.

The technique shown to me by Shiva is done while the male subtle body is interlocked sexually with a yogini who has some expertise in sexual yogic perception. That expertise means that she is not so excited about sexual contact actually. She is enjoyment-neutral and regards it the way a scientist regards experiments in a laboratory.

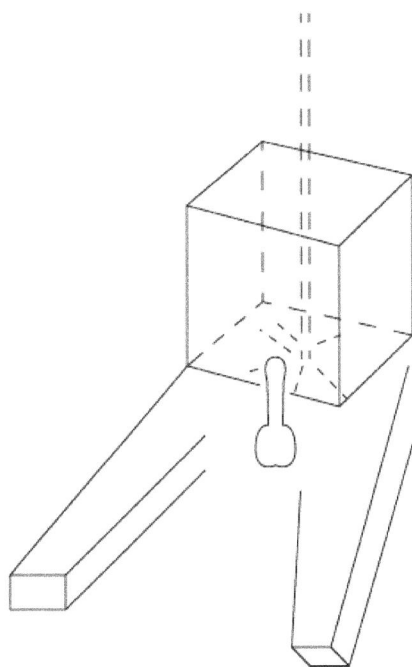

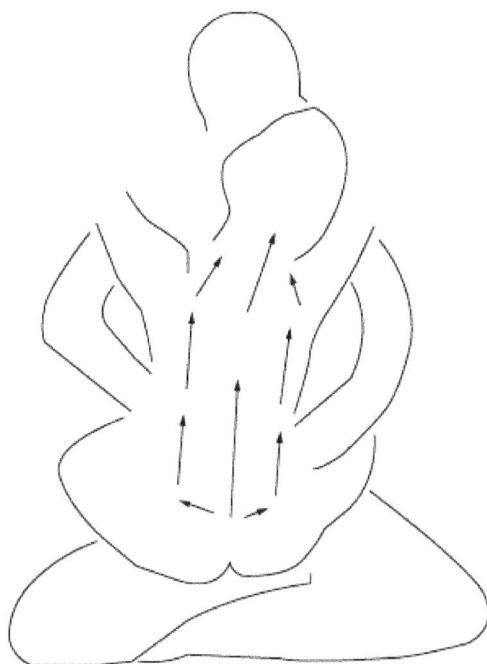

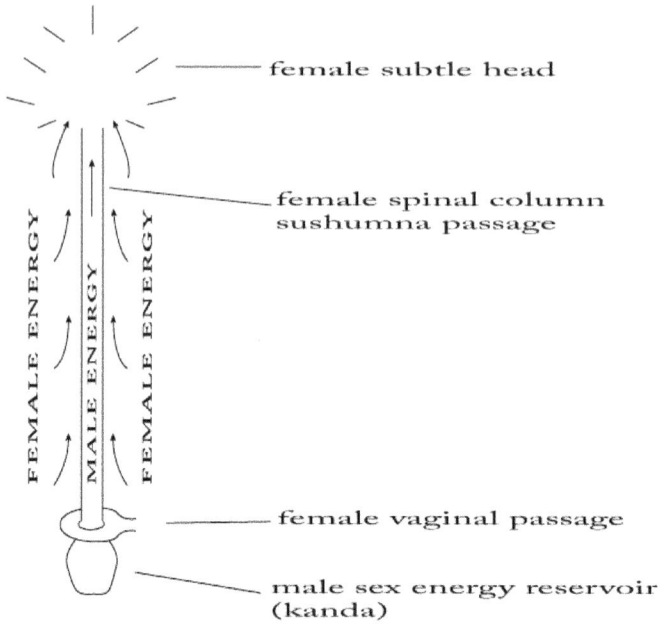

female subtle head

female spinal column
sushumna passage

FEMALE ENERGY

MALE ENERGY

FEMALE ENERGY

female vaginal passage

male sex energy reservoir
(kanda)

Arrows show direction of travel of sexual energy which is transferred into female subtle body. A similar configuration applies to the male subtle form.

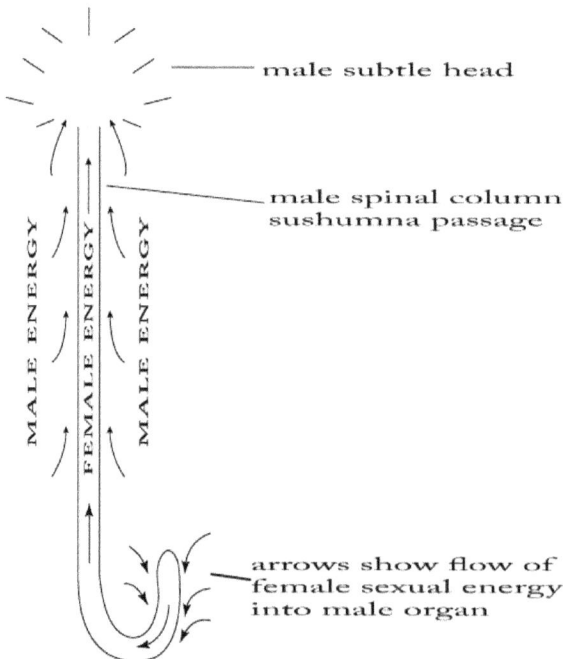

male subtle head

male spinal column
sushumna passage

MALE ENERGY

FEMALE ENERGY

MALE ENERGY

arrows show flow of
female sexual energy
into male organ

Normally in sexual intercourse, the energy burst occurs in the sexual organs, in the pubic area primarily. In that area, during climax there is a burst of subtle light. But in this practice, the energy burst occurs in the head of the partners instead of the genital areas. Thus the intellect organ does not move down into the genital place, rather the kundalini energy moves up into the subtle head, which is the location of the intellect.

In conventional sexual intercourse between a male and female, there may be simultaneous or non-simultaneous burst of energy. The same may occur in the tantric practices, except that the energy burst occurs in the genital area in the normal intercourse. This is the distinction. If for Instance, only the male experiences a burst of energy in a normal intercourse, he will experience a thrilling pleasure which is actually a burst of kundalini light in his genital area. To brighten the light the female may move her body in a seductive way while the male has that climatic experience. However, the more the light brightens, the greater will be the darkness after the climax is over. This darkness will occur both at the kundalini position in the lower spine and in the head where the intellect is located.

If alternately, the female has a climax experiences, she will feel that burst of energy in her vaginal area, especially around the organ called the clitoris. But similarly in that case, if the male moves in a seductive way while she experiences this or if she is stimulated in some other way, there will be a bright flash of light or a more intense pleasure, followed by a dullness and tiredness.

Sometimes there is a feeling of unfulfillment which manifest as if the experience should be repeated. In that case a female who is impulsive and who cannot suppress the need may attempt to have another climax, but this is like puncturing a tube a second time.

At the first puncture, some of the air escaped. At the second, more will leave, thus depressing the tire even more. The darkness in consciousness is actually a darkness but it is experience as mental and emotional depression. In the proficient tantric practice, this depression does not occur. Usually however tantra is done imperfectly with part of the energy going into the brain and the remaining portion going down to the genitals. This practice is difficult to complete in the perfect way because usually nature wants the energy to go downward. If we study nature carefully, we will understand that nature requires that water or any liquid move downwards, unless such a liquid is put under a pressure or unless it is evaporated. In cases where it evaporates, it usually condenses and falls downwards anyway. If it is placed under pressure, as in the case of artesian wells, for instance, the rise upwards is followed by a quick descent anyway. Thus nature usually endorses the downward flow of liquid energy.

Yogeshwarananda prohibited us from indulging in tantric yoga. His opinion is that it has no usefulness. He says that ultimately all yogis, if they advance, will have to be solitary. He stated that eventually all the sexual organs will have to be relinquished, especially if one wants to go to the causal level of existence. He was not in favor of mutual tantric sensuality. It may be questioned as to why I included sexual information in these books, as if to violate his order.

The reason is: If we are to live up to his expectation, we may have to deal with the tantric issue to get beyond it. After all, as good sons, we must live up to his expectations sooner or later but we may also have to pass through or advance beyond the need for partner involvement.

I feel that one should strive for self-tantric. For instance, my guru for kundalini yoga, Yogiji Harbhajan Sing Sahib Urdhvaretacharya never advised me to do tantric yoga. He advised others, but he never advised me. All the same he transmitted the techniques into my psyche so I know them and can teach them with his permission. The meaning then for me, is that I should be a self-tantric only, thus complying with the rigid demands of Yogeshwarananda. A summary study of what is required for self-tantric was published under the title of *Kundalini Self-Tantric*.

I took risks in many books to discuss sexual intercourse. The purpose of this is to help those ascetics who must be involved before they can get beyond it. I am hopeful that you understand my view in this. I took the risk to describe the influence of lust. Give me your well-wishes by studying this carefully so that you can get beyond this.

Sexual intercourse is a bewildering experience. Even Shiva is sometimes heard to express wonderment at the power of it. But it does not make sense that since we were stymied by it, we should try to get something out of it by having intercourses for purpose of getting the sexual energy of a partner into our subtle heads. If you review this idea very carefully you will agree that it is not rational. In any case, there are angelic worlds where people do just that. They endure such sexual experiences for many years on end continuously without a break. This may be regarded as sexual unity between soul mates. However ultimately it is a pointless. The secret to success is to cause your kundalini energy to come into your subtle head and to make progress beyond that, so that one can go with the mahayogins and those who have moved on to Siddhaloka and Satyaloka. Sticking around angelic places just to be sexually interlocked with a person of the opposite sex is not an intelligent choice.

Sex stymied us because we are pleasure-starved beings. As soon as we unlock ourselves from these lower dimensions that will come to an end. Poor people always hanker for wealth while those who are familiar with money do not chase petty luxuries.

May 31, 1998

Agastya

He showed the kakutasana posture (rooster posture):

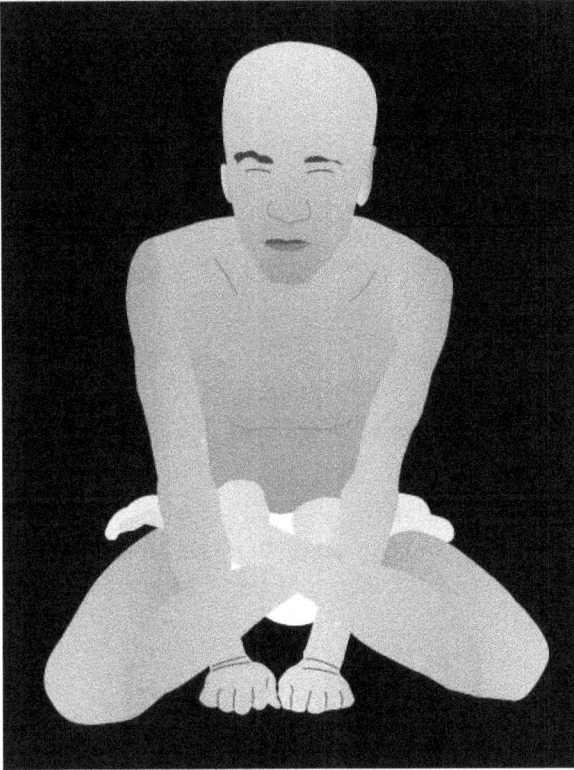

Assuming that posture, I did breath-infusion while mentally concentrating the subtle energy which collected at the knobby at the back of the head.

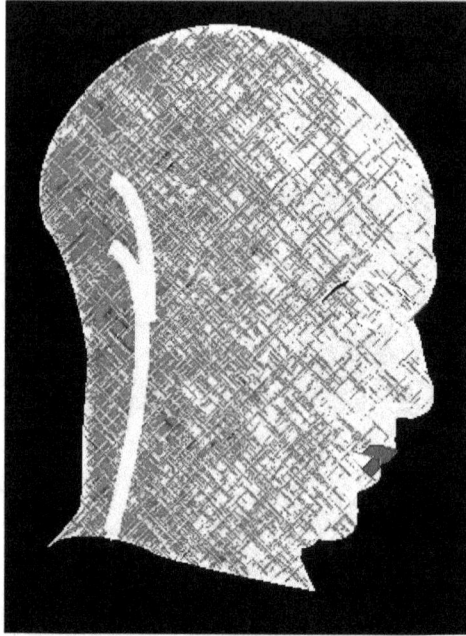

In assuming any variation of kakutasana posture, one might have difficulty pushing the hands through the feet and thighs. It is easier to accomplish if one has silky pants or if one's forearms are moistened with water or rubbed with oil.

May 31, 1998

Agastya

I asked him, "How did they get ahead of us, Yogiraj?

He replied, "They did not my son. They live in this area eternally. This is just before Deviloka, Goddess Durga's territory, which is just below Shivaloka. Be sure that you touch of one of them, otherwise you cannot pass beyond. You will be forced back instead. Ask Ganesh about this."

I replied, "I will touch one."

He said, "Touch here."

Remark:

This refers to Chandikaloka, a place where there are only females, who by nature have a masculine attitude. They instinctively dislike males. Agastya instructed me to touch one of them in the back of her thigh just under her buttock. In that way I discharge a sexual energy which created friendship with them to allow me to pass through their realm

Dimensionally speaking, after this world, there are several places; one is Chandika's realm. She is a parallel goddess to Devi, Shiva's reputed wife. Generally a human being cannot pass through the place. He or she has to be an advanced yogi to traverse that location. Information in the Srimad Bhagavatam states that in a jiffy Krishna took Arjuna through several of these places, all by Krishna's supernatural power. Ordinarily, Arjuna was not capable of venturing through those places with such ease, even though he reached the Swargaloka places by his yogic achievements.

With the help of great yogins, like Agastya and Yogeshwarananda, one may pass through many such places which are normally inaccessible to human beings

June 1, 1998

Agastya

A zone-crossing technique

He gave me a technique that even in his absence, would make my subtle body cross the Chandika territory. The idea is that in the future if I should require to traverse there, and if he was absent, or if some other powerful being did not assist, I could cross and perhaps take another yogi or yogini across. This technique is as follows.

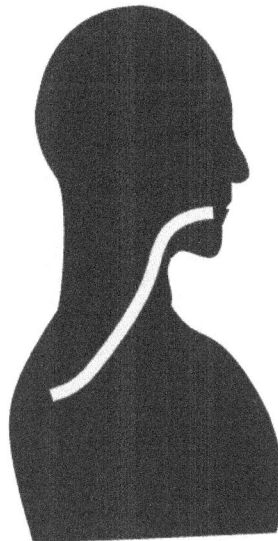

One should find this tube in the astral body in a certain dimension of that form. One should travel through the tube repeatedly until it remains manifested in that body and until one is able to keep that body in the dimension where that tube is plainly sensed.

The astral body can manifest in more than one dimension. Its capacity is different in each dimension. Even though there is one subtle form, it has various similar and dissimilar dimensions. In that sense, there is more than one version of that form. One should be familiar with the dimensional changes, otherwise one will be fooled into thinking that some phases of the subtle body are a spiritual form.

Agastya / Buddha Shakyamuni

A thin higher dimension absorption with eyes turned up.

Remark:

To achieve this, I took assistance from Agastya and from Shakyamuni Buddha simultaneously. A thin higher dimension absorption, is not as complete as the broad one achieved by the Buddha. However this thin higher dimension absorption comes after much practice in squeezing bandhas, which are bodily locks done in hatha yoga, in addition to taking the proper diet at the proper time. One feels the bottom subtle energy streaming up as a thin stream of crystal clear energy. This hits the intellect like a laser beam. The senses which are offshoots of the intellect organ turn to that energy and become introspective of their own accord. The eyes turn up of their own accord and have no urge to see externally.

In that state, one realizes the intellect as a distinct organ in the subtle head. One realizes that it is possible to control the intellect and to stop its outward-seeking tendency.

June 3, 1998

Agastya

He said, "For a personality outside, there is an inside. Go down and away from the manifestations. Then there is no argument, no comment, no neglect, just an absorption of attention elsewhere."

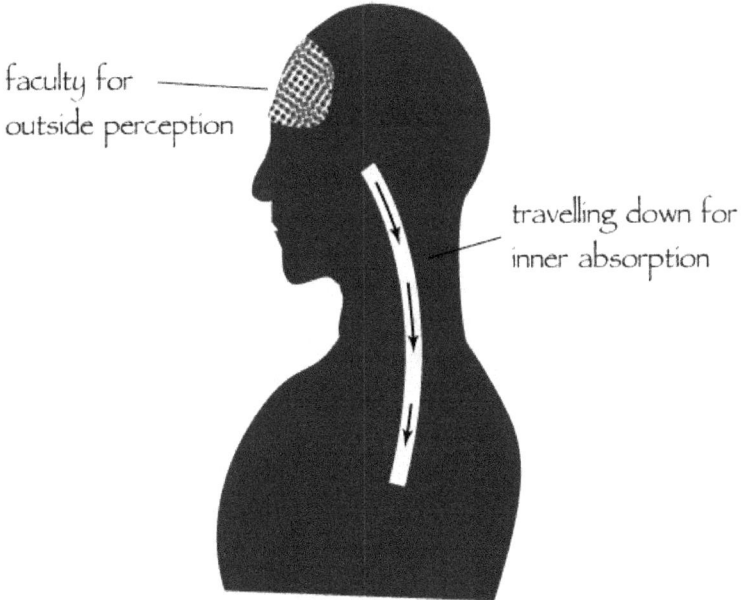

faculty for
outside perception

travelling down for
inner absorption

This is a technique for escaping the influence of powerful yoginis or other witches who by supernatural power, may harass a yogi for one reason or another. Some want sexual intercourse. Some want to argue over technical points. Some want to fight to prove that they can defeat males. In order to escape one may enter the causal body, in which there are no interactions.

Sometimes it becomes necessary to temporarily abandon the subtle body. One may somehow become transferred into a parallel world. While there one may forget one's existence elsewhere, just as we assumed this gross body and forget existences we had in other places. If one goes to a parallel world and it is not to one's liking, one may abandon the subtle body or the phase of the subtle body which exist there. By that mystic action, one would escape from that place. Most persons who would be transferred to a parallel world would not remember anything about any former existence. Unless the subtle body can resume its existence in relation to this world or some other realm, one would unknowingly become restricted to that parallel dimension, regardless of whether the status there is favorable or unfavorable. There are many people, millions of them, who in this current existence, are not well-situated. They are stuck with a mediocre or bemeaning culture, but they have no recall of any other existence. They have no power to transit from this place.

Modern astronomers in cahoots with physicists state that there are parallel worlds. They feel that our universe is one of many parallel cosmos, and that a person's appearance here may well be by a whim of time, alternated with a similar appearance of another double elsewhere, little do they know that their speculations are true. There are many parallel worlds. They are an infinite number of them. As soon as one develops the psychic perception, a parallel cosmos may be manifested in meditation and in conscious dream states.

Agastya

He said, "Set it with an up-breath-infusion pull. Let it pass through the intellect as raw energy. If it is already formed, it will diffuse while rising. The intellect will get its quota of energy, and will be satisfied. Deal directly with the subtle energies. They are the motivators.

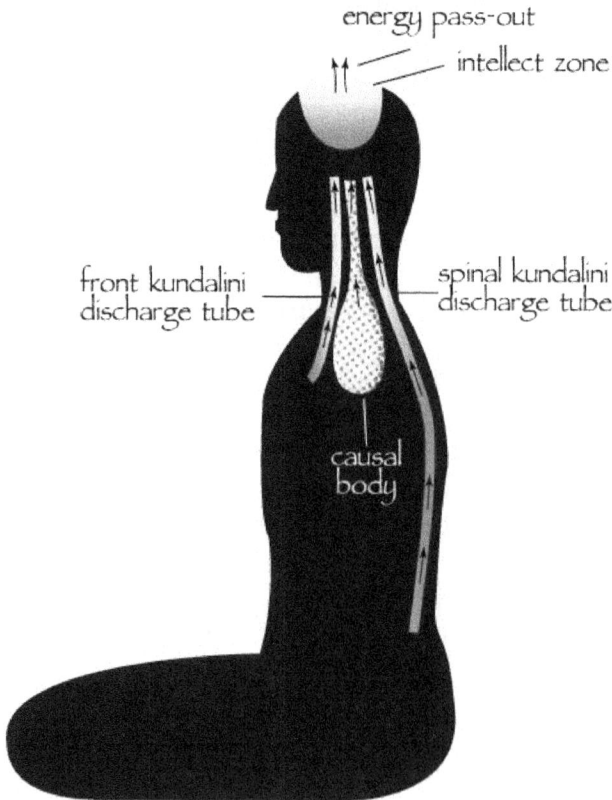

Remark:

This has to do with lifting resentment energy and other negative forces which forcibly entered the psyche of a yogi. He must eliminate it because it affects spiritual advancement by reducing the ability to complete the required disciplines.

Generally the dulling energies come from two types of interaction. One type is from disciples or fellow yogis. From disciples one takes resentments which are envy and false expectations. From other yogis one takes in bad energies from arguments about methods of practice. Such discussions are unnecessary, since a method reveals itself by its productive or nonproductive effects. Thus if a yogi is confident of a method, he should practice to test its worth, instead of pursuing others for conflicting arguments.

The other types of interaction comes from performance of karma yoga. This is actually the main topic of the Bhagavad Gita but some say that the headline is bhakti yoga. In the Gita, Krishna said that he taught two applications of yoga, as karma yoga and jnana yoga but there is a tit bit of information on other yogas. In any event, in the performance of karma yoga, one must take some resentment, since that carries with it bad feelings from the persons disciplined. Yudhishthira and his brothers, who included Arjuna, took much resentment before, during and after the battle of Kurukshetra, a war which Krishna encouraged them to wage. Thus even under Krishna's direction, one may be targeted by resentments for karma yoga. It is a question of how to expel that negative energy.

Even though Krishna assured the Pandavas about not getting reactions, they could not avoid resentments. Perhaps Krishna in his definitions of reactions did not include social resentments. In any case, Yudhishthira practically fell apart. He broke down emotionally and cried at the end, not finding peace of mind. He was so full of the resentments absorbed that he entered a manic depression. However, Krishna, the ultimate yogi, the Supreme Being, directed a senior yogi, Bhishma, to pull Yudhishthira out of it. Bhishma was a seasoned yogi and master statesman, who was the least affected by the hazards of karma yoga. He spoke in a way that dissolved the resentments, which lodged in the Yudhishthira's mind.

However, in inSelf yoga, we do not ask opponents to take away the resentments. We look for an ongoing method that is not dependent on the presence of helpers. We are disinclined from bothering other advanced yogis except to get advice on how to deal with it ourselves. Since we are not in the political field and since we reduced cultural involvements, we deal with small amounts of this negative energy. Thus we can eliminate it if we have effective methods like the one given to me by Agastya

Most problems in this area come from teaching others. Since I reduced the number of students, the resentments decreased. For the most part, I live free of negative darts from others. This is by the grace of Babaji, who instructed that I not have disciples. Conversely, Shiva insisted that instead of taking disciples, I should give information. Thus I began these journals and completed other related books. From this literary contribution, some persons could know about yoga and its intricacies.

June 6, 1998

Agastya.
He said, "Disregard the core-self. Deal with the energy pressure from prakriti. Agree to that. Work to that. Ease the pressure. Or sidestep that and evade."
Remark:

This was advice for me to disregard anyone who pestered me. I was to see that the material energy, prakriti, creates and supervises the harassment. Sometimes it is not wise to ignore the prakriti. One may then agree to its proposals and work to assist it. Sometimes the core-selves, the souls, serve as agents of the prakriti. Thus one may have to obey anyone of them when the material nature uses them to give directives. In any event, one must have a clear perception about the action-motivator. According to the Bhagavad-Gita, all or most of the material activities is being conducted by the material energy.

Here a verse:

मयाध्यक्षेण प्रकृतिः
सूयते सचराचरम् ।
हेतुनानेन कौन्तेय
जगद्विपरिवर्तते ॥९.१०॥

mayādhyakṣeṇa prakṛtiḥ
sūyate sacarācaram
hetunānena kaunteya
jagadviparivartate (9.10)

mayā — with Me + adhyakṣeṇa — as supervisor; prakṛtiḥ — material nature; sūyate — produces; sacarācaram — moving and non-moving things; hetunānena = hetunā — by cause of + anena — by this; kaunteya — son of Kuntī; jagad = jagat — world; viparivartate — operates

With Me as the supervisor, material nature produces moving and nonmoving things. By this cause, O son of Kuntī, the universe operates. (9.10)

Here is another verse:

प्रकृत्यैव च कर्माणि
क्रियमाणानि सर्वशः ।
यः पश्यति तथात्मानम्
अकर्तारं स पश्यति ॥१३.३०

prakṛtyaiva ca karmāṇi
kriyamāṇāni sarvaśaḥ
yaḥ paśyati tathātmānam
akartāraṁ sa paśyati (13.30)

prakṛtyaiva = prakṛtya — by material nature + eva — indeed: ca — and; karmāṇi — actions; kriyamāṇāni — performed; sarvaśaḥ — in all cases, yaḥ — who; paśyati — he sees; tathātmānam = tathā— as regarding + ātmānam — self; akartāram — non-doer; sa = saḥ— he: paśyati — truly sees

He who sees, that in all cases, the actions are performed by material nature, and who regards himself as a non-doer, truly sees. (13.30)

When Agastya spoke of disregarding core-selves and dealing with material nature, he showed a technique. Student yogis should notice that in most cases of these instructions, certain mystic acts were done by me upon recommendation by a great yogin. This is different to get information, forming an intellectual review of it and going on with one's life. This entails actions within the psyche for purity of the subtle body.

June 6, 1998

Agastya

Tiny thread-to-base chakra

This tiny thread shown to me by Agastya, was to be connected by willpower from the intellect organ in the subtle brain to the base chakra.

What I was shown is based on practice. It is not based on desire to see what is fantastic. The need may be there but if there is no consistent practice nothing will be revealed. When there is no clarifying subtle energy, the subtle body remains dark, murky and cloudy. In that condition such visions cannot be derived.

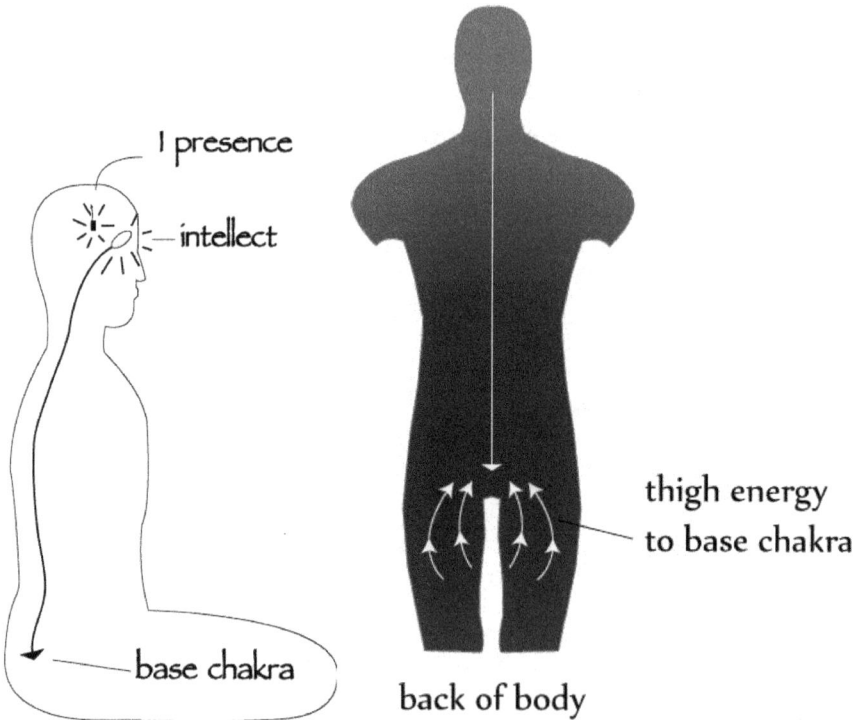

I presence

intellect

base chakra

thigh energy
to base chakra

back of body

June 6, 1998

Agastya

A neck technique for removing bad energy

Bad energy enters the neck from certain subtle beings and from other entities who have psychic power. Some of this may be avoided. Some of it, being mandatory, must be accepted. One should know how to remove it. The important thing is not to redirect it since everyone within range must bear a portion of the negative aspects of this existence.

In this technique, one may use any standard draw-up posture. One contracts upward the back of the neck and pulls up the bottom locks tightly, so that one feels a complete drying out of the liquid hormones in the physical body and the subtle fluids in the lower part of the subtle form.

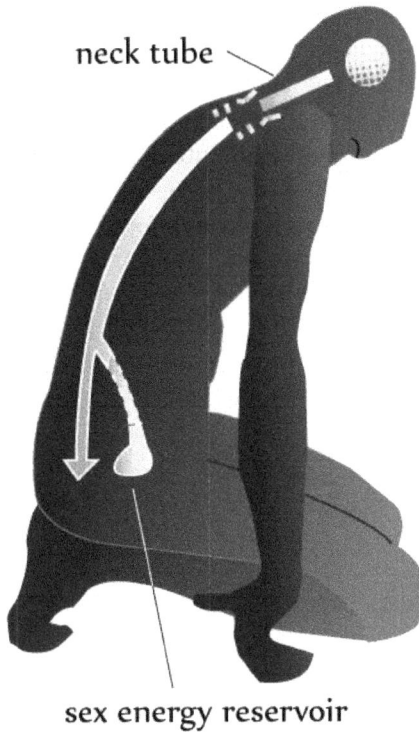

neck tube

sex energy reservoir

A draw-up posture is one in which one does pranayama breath-infusion to quickly pull the physical and astral fluids which usually pool or settle in the groin area.

June 7, 1998

Agastya

Removing energy which was projected from a woman's thigh.

This technique applies to removing sexual force which enters a male body from a female thigh. Any of these techniques may be used by females to remove sexual energy which enters from a male.

In this procedure, one sits between the heels, draws the thighs together and does breath-infusion to withdraw the energy that penetrated. This technique does not involve the person from whom the energy was derived. It involves the victim only. This is an example of a self-tantric practice. It demonstrates that one can dissolve sexual energies without having a partner, thus satisfying the request of Yogeshwarananda that we desists from sexual contacts.

By extracting the energy from the thigh, one frees himself or herself from having to have a sexual intercourse with the person from whom the energy was derived. Instead of going into the second chakra to enliven the sexual organ with passion, the energy goes into the head of the subtle body and exits through the top as utilized subtle force.

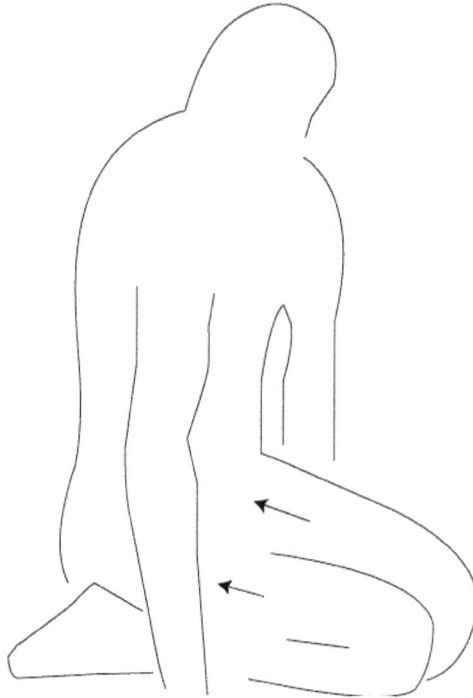

June 7, 1998

Agastya

He said, "Only 85%, son. 95% is incorrect. It may be 95% of what is perceived. Some which is too subtle evades observation."

Remark:

Agastya Yogiraj made this remark when I considered the percentage of retraction of my sensual energy. Pratyahar is the containment of sensual energy. He said that I contained only 85% thus losing 15%. This is a good grade but it is not sufficient for success. It does not take one to super concentration which leads one to full absorption (samadhi).

Agastya

An under-brain cove.

Agastya showed me a cove where one could hide from psychic disturbances. If known, such places are used by yogis to hide from disturbing psychic energies which enter the subtle brain and interrupt efforts at meditation and spiritual research.

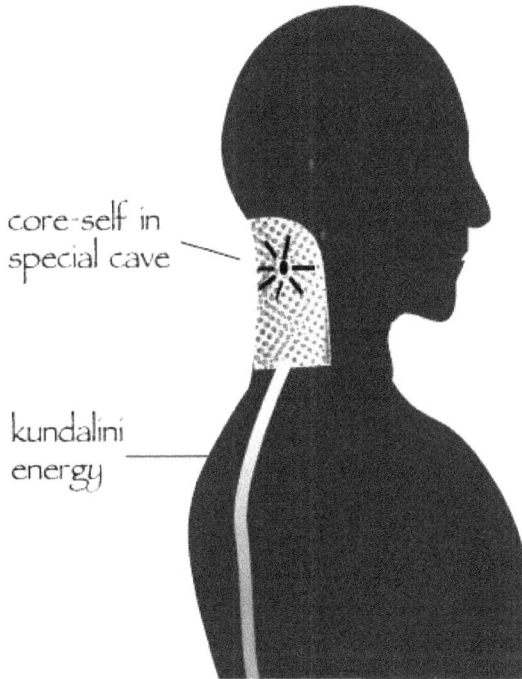

core-self in
special cave

kundalini
energy

A center pull-in chest-lock.

This technique was discovered while practicing postures and breath-infusion. Since it developed out of the techniques Agastya gave me, it should be credited to him. It is said that subtle energy shows the way. This means that if one sticks with the disciplines, the purifying energy will act as a self-revealing force. Such things become self-evident but that does not mean that one is not obligated to the yoga masters. One remains obligated for anything which develops during a practice which was introduced by the teacher.

Some spiritual masters insist that their disciples appraise them formally. If the disciple does not, the teacher deprives association. Usually, that teacher trains his fanatical disciples to shun anyone who does not offer glorification. In my experience with advanced teachers, they do not demand glorification. If a student realizes his obligation, they do not stop him from expressing it but they do not demand recognition. Spiritual masters who are themselves staunch students of great teachers, remain as students of the said masters. Their teaching of others does not budge them from the practice. They are not distracted by the glorifications offered by indulgent disciples.

This technique in the diagram below helps to remove resentment energy which entered the chest region.

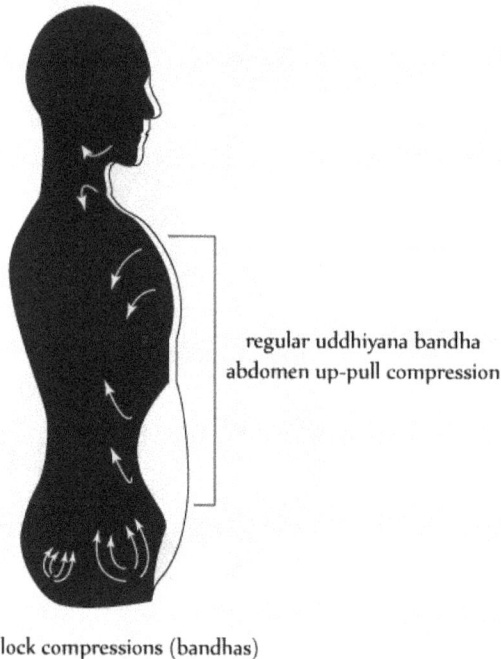

regular uddhiyana bandha
abdomen up-pull compression

lock compressions (bandhas)

June 8, 1998

Agastya

Sexual energy chest suck-in

This technique gives one the ability to pull in mandatory sexual energy which one must receive but which if absorbed through the subtle pubic area, would disturb celibacy.

This technique is effective if the donor of the sexual energy does not insist on a pubic reception. The donor is the person from whom the energy projected.

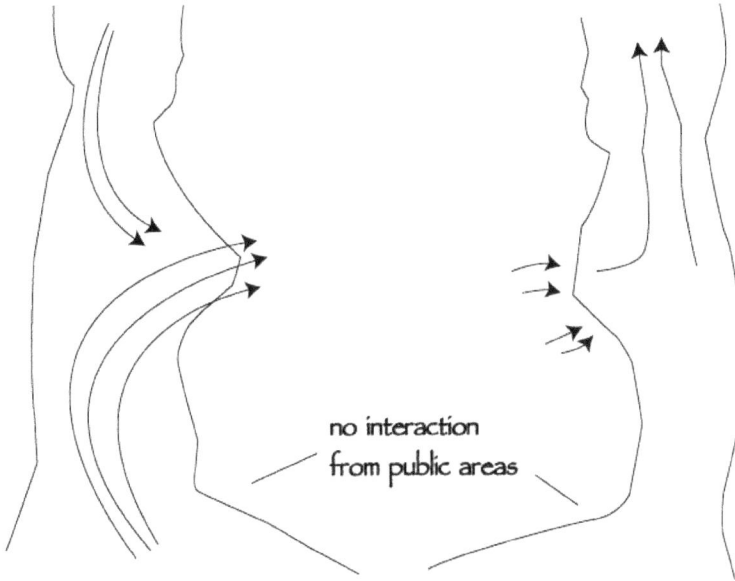

no interaction
from public areas

June 8, 1998

Agastya

He said, "While falling back into the whole energy, contact me on the open front."

Remark:

The open front area is the brow or third eye chakra, when it is pulsating, being fully open or dispersed. Falling back, refers to the core-self falling back into the sensations which are in the subtle chest.

That same day Agastya advised me to avoid persons who pressure me to assist in social development. He said, "Be careful in doing that since it consumes time which could otherwise be spent in yogic practice. These socially-involved persons will perpetually be involved. That is their instinct. There is no need to assist them. In relating to them you weaken celibacy. Social affairs are summarized by sexual indulgence."

After I was told this, I got verification. I assisted a lady to meet a lawyer. She needed legal advice. While entering the door of the lawyer's office, one of the lawyer's secretaries, a seductive woman, came to me. She invited me to tour the ornate building. Seeing the sexual energy bursting out from every part of her body, I politely declined the tour. However some of the energy still entered my psyche. Later that day, I did the chest suck-in technique which Agastya showed me.

Sometime after on the same day, I listened to an Indian musician's recording. I studied tabla notes. However, all of a sudden, Agastya spoke in my consciousness, He said, "It is very sensitive. Protect it."

He spoke of the mind. When one listens to music, the mind becomes attached to the melodies. Later, the mind re-composes the music even when one does not desire it. This is counterproductive for meditation. It is the same with videos. If one is serious, he should stay away from music, television and videos.

June 8, 1998

Brahma

He said, "If you deal with the subtle energy, everything will be sealed."

Remarks

I used techniques to lift low-frequency subtle energies. Agastya gave me one for pulling the brow chakra disc downwards to the base area. Brahma explained that if a yogi could get his lower subtle energies exchanged for higher ones, his yogic development would be firm. The yogin would complete higher meditation (pratyahar, dharana, dhyana and samadhi) and reach the perfection desired.

A yogi is not so sure where he will be in perfection. Unlike other transcendentalists who propose a definite destination, a yogi has a wait-and-see attitude. His mind set is this: When I reach perfection, then I will see it.

Someone is sure that he will go to a Christian heaven. Another says that he is sure he will go where Mohammed resides. While yet another says that he is going to merge into Brahman. Another person says that he will go to Vishnu's Vaikuntha. A yogi cannot be sure until his perfection actually occurs. He is more concerned with the outcome of his perfection, rather than a belief in a set result.

As soon as the yogi can purify the energy of his subtle body and reach the causal plane, he will experience actual perfection. He will know who the presiding deity will be.

In the beginning of kundalini yoga practice, a yogi tries to stir up and thus energize and purify the energy of the subtle body. Later he actually changes that low grade energy for a higher quality of subtle energy. Thus his mystic perfection increases proportionately. It becomes more direct and accurate. I will give an example which occurred on December 16, 2000, the day when I made notes for this entry. Two days prior on December 14, 2000, I connected electrical circuits to a water pump which was embedded in a pond. During the day I saw a friend through my subtle body. I saw his subtle form wave and call out to me. I waved in return and greeted him with my subtle form only. I did not perceive his physical body.

Due to being attentive to a physical task, I did not proceed with my physical body to check and confirm the subtle experience. The day after, on December 15, 2000, I called that friend by telephone. He immediately said that he saw me on the previous day. He claimed that he waved and called and that I ignored him. I then made some excuses about being busy.

These excuses were truths. Indeed, I was under the pressure of time. However this shows clearly that subtle bodies are seen by an advanced yogi. Such a yogi may see something psychic and not see the physical counterpart of the same psychic object or action. At a certain stage the subtle body becomes so perceptive, operative and predominant, that the gross form becomes irrelevant. This is sometimes described as the jivanmukta liberated-while-using-a-physical-body stage, where a yogi is freed from the gross concept, through having mystic perception. While I was aware of what my and my friend's subtle body did, the friend was only aware of physical movement. He did not sense the subtle interaction when I waved with my subtle hand and replied to his greeting with subtle words.

June 8, 1998

Brow chakra disc pull-down

In this technique, one feels the brow chakra disc after doing a session of breath-infusion. One pulls it down into the central head, away from the brow area. This may done while lying on the back of the body or even in any other position. One pulls until the energy from the brow chakra feels flattened.

This technique developed naturally. It was discovered while doing breath-infusion. As for the posture, the yogi should assume whatever pose facilitates a particular technique. One day, a certain posture best serves the purpose. On another day, another posture, may give results. One should act to intensify the energy movements.

Pull down sushumna knob

In this technique, one first becomes aware of the sushumna passage. One pulls down the sushumna knob from the neck area. One reduces its height, gradually shrinking it to the base

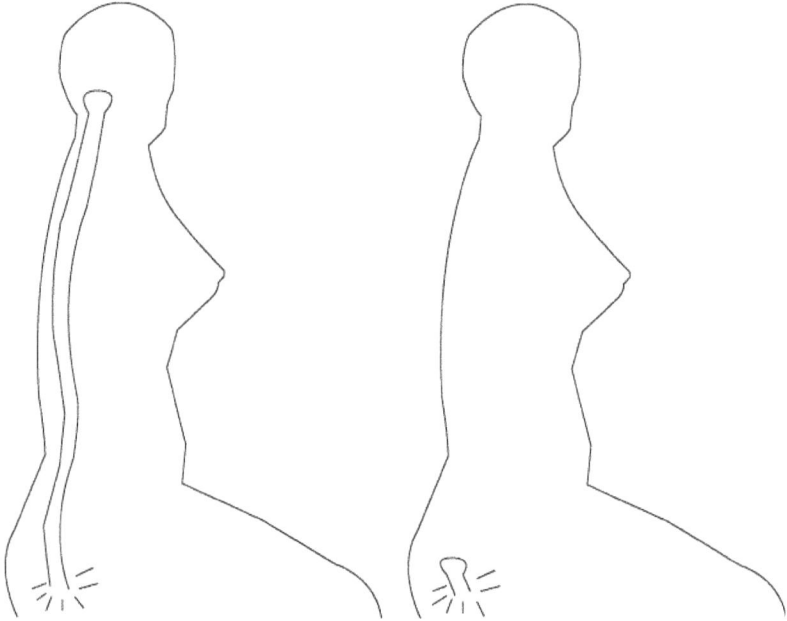

This practice is done in preparation for the elimination of the sushumna passage, for its absorption into the causal form. Eventually all the subtle bodies, as they dissolve out of existence, are merged back into being indistinct causal energy,

The subtle body is not eternal. However the yogi takes steps to dissolve his. To do this, he must first purify it. He has to train it to absorb only clarifying energy. That is a non-heavy, non-opaque type of subtle force.

At first one has to purify the subtle form. Some feel that the subtle body can be eliminated without first purifying it, but that is not possible except when the universal dissolution occurs. To regress the subtle form now, a yogi has to purify it and then energize himself to the causal plane, from where he may withdraw attention from it, while pointing his interest-sense into the causal zone.

June 9, 1998

Agastya

He said, "Progress is not linear. It develops with digressions and progressions between stages."

Remark:

On some days spiritual focus is easy, otherwise it is not. There are many progressive and non-progressive influences, such as supernatural power, natural power, clarifying energy, passionate force and dulling power. Even though some factors are beyond the yogi's control he should consistently maintain the practice.

June 9, 1998

Agastya

He said, "Always perform for one side, then for the other. Even if one side is performed with ease, and the other with difficulty, complete both sides."

Remark:

When I got that instruction, I did this posture:

on sole of foot

sit on heel

foot is turned in

June 9, 1998

On this day, I met Yogeshwarananda's spiritual master, who was known as Atmananda. He was not well known because as an ideal yogin, he lived in isolation in Tibet. He was as Yogeshwarananda described him, a Vaishnava. His value was that by his touch, Yogeshwarananda's head became clarified. The organs in the head of his subtle body, became perceptible of the chit akash. The details of this were explained by Yogeshwarananda in his books.

When I said that I met him on this day, I meant that I met that guru's subtle body. It was a clear perception. At that meeting I could understand that he was Agastya in a previous existence. Somehow he still has a subtle form as Agastya, the ancient ascetic, who is an associated of Shiva, and who is legendary.

Recently I took help from Yogeshwarananda, but while he got a complete revelation of his subtle and causal forms in just a few days, and that formed as a permanent experience for him. I get that understanding and vision gradually over a period of years. In comparison, Yogeshwarananda performed more preparatory disciplines before he met Atmananda. Such is the difference. Unless the lives of two ascetics are identical, one should expect the same progression for each.

June 10, 1998

Agastya

He said, "After a time, after a period of sincere practice, the lifeforce does as required. This is why it is not tasted anymore."

Remark:

There might be a question as to why Atmananda appeared to me through his old configuration of Agastya. Why initially, he did not appear as Atmananda. The reason is simply this. In my case, my practices in this era are prompted by my practice during the time of Rama when I practiced in the forest near Kishkindhya in India. Since then though I repeat the practice, I do not advance in each birth. I merely recap what I achieved before. I fall back and advance, fall back and advance repeatedly. At the time of Rama I was a student of great yogis who included Agastya and Matanga Rishi,

In each life, Agastya comes at a certain stage. He supervises my redevelopment. My subtle body is familiar with the Agastya configuration. That is the form which appears to me in each redevelopment.

Agastya explained the above; that after repeated efforts to control good intake, the lifeforce's resistance decreased. It did as requested, not desiring extra meals. I used to take a 9 a.m. snack which I tried to eliminate. I tried for months to get rid of the need. My method was this:

When I felt the urge to eat, I would do some breath-infusion to fill the gross and subtle bodies with air and subtle air respectively. I would wait about 15 minutes, then I would eat. However I would only eat something light like a liquid. Usually it was popcorn and milk. Gradually after I did the exercises, I felt that I did not need to eat. The strong appetite which was there before I did the exercises, would not be there after I completed a full session of rapid breathing. Feeling this, I took advantage and stopped eating at that time.

At first when I stopped eating I felt nutrients circulating within the palate mouth area. I could taste hormones circulating in that area but after, even that taste went away. At that stage, my subtle body was divested of heavy energy around the spine. I saw lines of clear energy, directed into the spine. This is called the pine tree technique, because it takes a shape which is similar to certain pine trees.

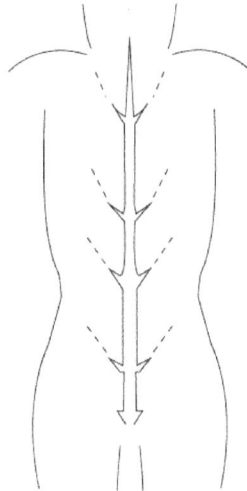

June 11, 1998

Agastya

Brow chakra retraction into the intellect

This is a vision energy retraction.

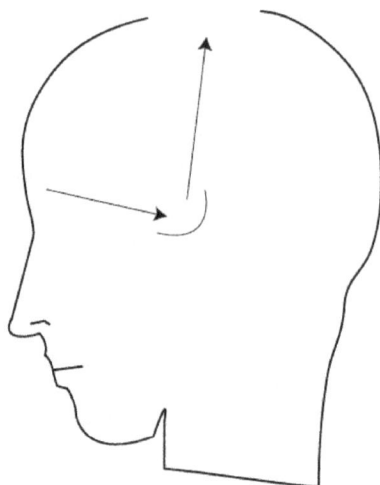

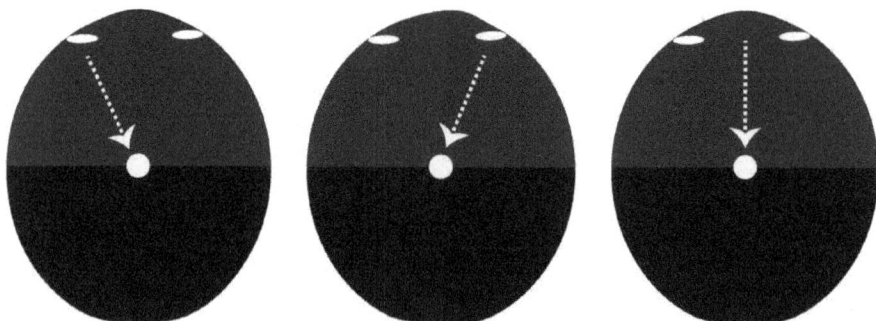

The vision energy may be retracted from the left eye or right eye or from the central position.

June 11, 1998

Agastya

He said, "Use that energy to help the focus. You can pull it into the focus without being diverted."

Remark:

Some negative energy entered my psyche. That was a mandatory intake. Agastya Yogiraj advised that I accept the energy without trying to protect myself from it. Then I was to pass it through the focus of my current practice.

Many advanced yogis do similar mystic actions, whereby they accept a negative charge which cannot be avoided but they are not affected adversely. It does not cause a lag in practice. In some cases however one is affected but one does not take that seriously. One understands that it is unavoidable. One cheerfully accepts the lag in practice.

Agastya

An eye vision pratyahar

Control of the brow chakra is related to retracting or pulling in the eye vision. There are different kinds of vision. For example there is subtle energy vision, which is the ability to see directly through subtle energy without using any apparatus like an eye. There is chakra vision, which is vision through an energy whirl. However if one wants to retract the outward going power, he should retract the eye vision. This is the energy that funnels down the optic nerves. If this energy is retracted, the intellect organ is strengthened and one gains more insight.

Here are diagrams:

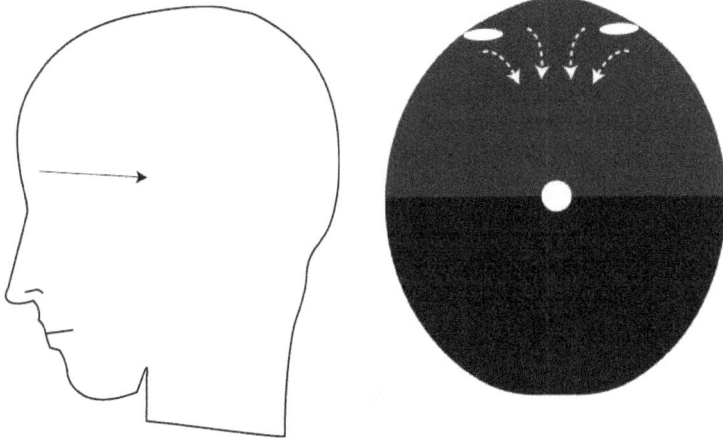

June 12, 1998

Agastya

He gave me a technique for pulling in the frontal energy. This frontal area is resistant. When one wants to retract all the energy which seeks to find fulfillment in the external world, this frontal area greatly resists one's efforts,

Here is a diagram:

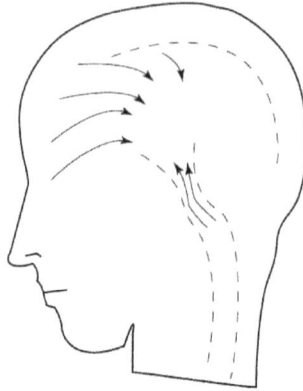

June 12, 1998

Agastya

Cylinder blood takeout

With this technique one sorts between blood and hormones. Hormones are a more concentrated fluid. Their primary collection is in the trunk of the body in the genital area.

In the subtle body, there is a gland which is called the kanda. This kanda is seen as a small bulb from time to time, either by pranavision, chakra vision or subtle eye vision. With the blood takeout technique, one pumps plasma to the physical heart chakra. In working with hormones one focuses differently. Usually the hormones are moved from the kanda to the brain.

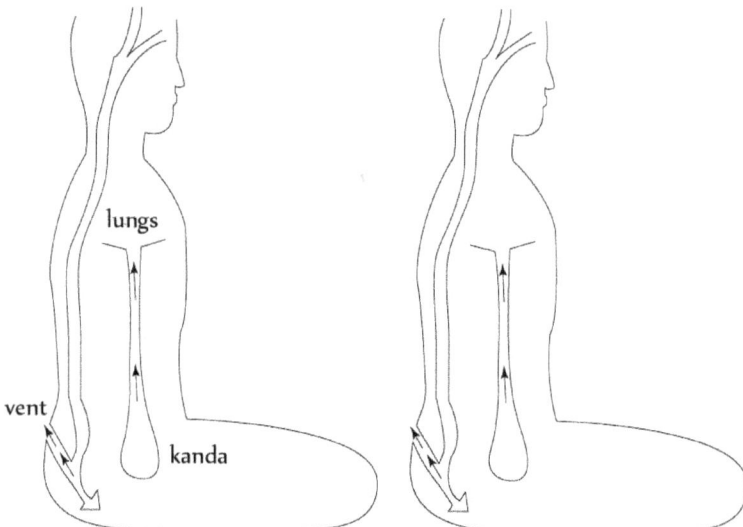

Part 4

June 13, 1998

Agastya

Lung-down lock-down tube

This is a tube which goes down into the lungs. By looking down through this tube one perceives where the causal body is located. One gains insight about the lungs. One views a nadi passage that leads from the central chest into the base of the body.

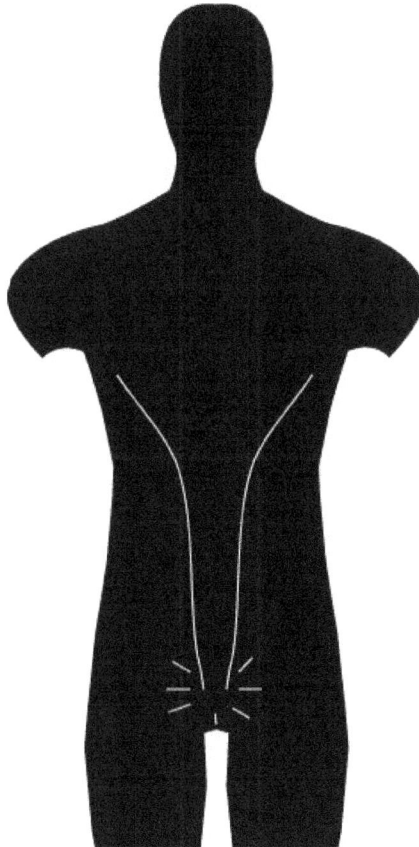

Agastya

Funnel draw-up.

Agastya gave me a technique for drawing up negative energies which accumulate at the bottom of the body. Some of these energies enter the psyche as psychic charges which come from others and which attach to some part of the psyche, and then go to the base area, and remain there. Some others enter the body through the mouth in food or through the lung by air. Food and air have subtle counterparts which carry negative or positive charges. Some undesirable energies cannot be checked. A yogi should know how to eject them. If he ignores them and allows them to accumulate, they will in the course of time, cause loss of advancement. Too much of such energies causes a yogi to completely give up the disciplines and to begin acting just as if he had no yogic interest. One should be industrious; ridding the psyche of such energies. A lazy yogi cannot achieve success. The negative forces will overtake him.

This funnel draw-up which is shown in the diagram below, is very similar in configuration to the pine tree technique given before. Preferably one should do this in the lotus padmasana posture.

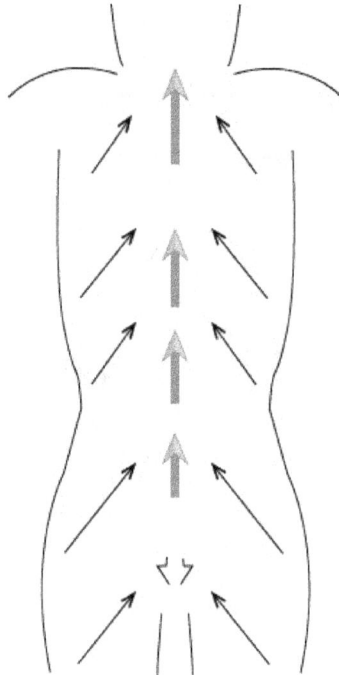

June 14, 1998

Agastya

<u>Funnel free-fall within clear subtle energy</u>

This technique is one in which, without using its intellect, the core-self moves itself.

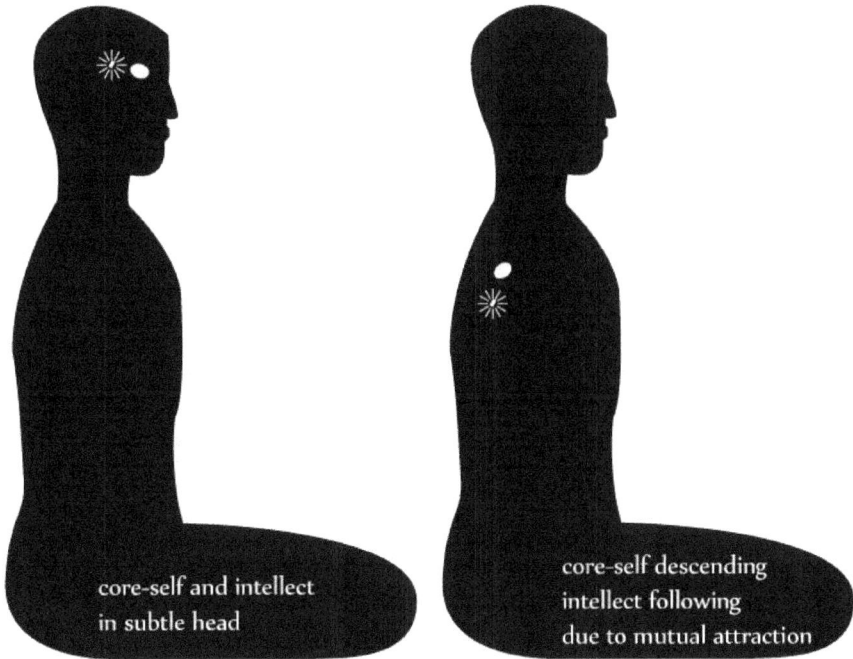

core-self and intellect
in subtle head

core-self descending
intellect following
due to mutual attraction

June 15, 1998

Shiva

He said, "Although you think it is a repeated experience, record it for others. It is novel. The quality of concentration and the precision of focus increased."

Remark:

This *Yoga inVision* series is sponsored by Shiva. As I stated elsewhere, Babaji instructed that I accept no disciples and make no attempt to establish myself as a spiritual master. Since then I changed the course of how I deal with persons who want to learn yoga. In any case, Shiva instructed that I record experiences. I do not record everything. I publish the more pronounced ones. In this case, I felt that it was a repeat of something I already explained. Shiva instructed that I record it anyway. Here is that technique:

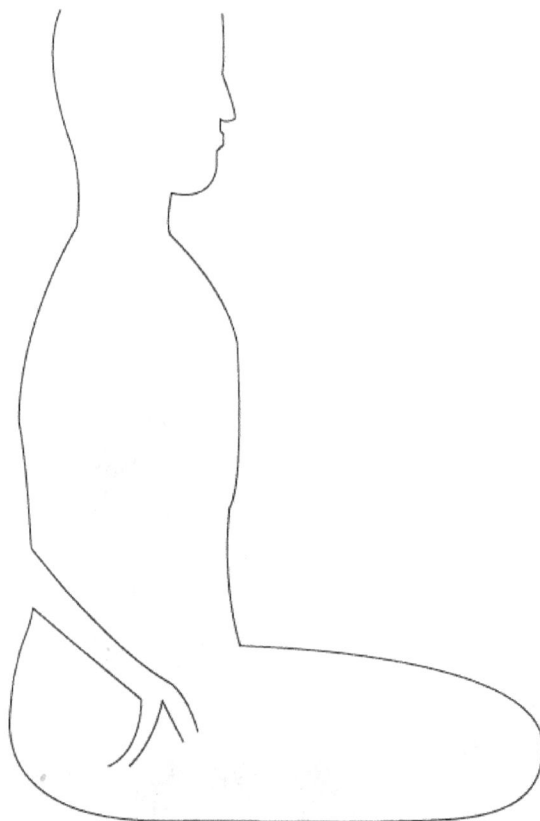

vent nadi tubes

June 16, 1998

Jesus Christ

He said, "I will help you with the other venture. As a child you wanted to be a carpenter. Here is the chance. I regret that your body did not get the formal training."

Remark:

This is an unusual entry. I forgot this entry until I read my notes on December 22nd of 2000. When this was said I already decided to stop working at a Christian church and to be employed independently as a handyman carpenter. I did not remember the carpentry desires of this body in infancy.

At that time, I did small projects like repairing benches, driving nails through boards which fell away from dilapidated buildings in the shanty where this body lived. I used to paint benches and walls with thick messy slow-drying oil paints. I had no formal training in carpenter. I had absolutely no opportunity.

There was a friend of this body, when it was about 12 or 13 years of age. His father was a cabinet maker. I used to watch the man cut out, plane and sand very thin boards for lining the glazed portions of cabinets but I never got the opportunity to learn this. Such is this life. A limited entity should be satisfied with it.

In any case Jesus Christ was aware of my desire. He intercepted my thoughts on that day to state that he would help me in the venture of having a carpentry business. This is proof that deity contact may work for a yogi-devotee. Since the day when Jesus said this in my consciousness on June 16th of 1998, most of the persons who hired me for carpentry-related work, were Christians. In fact, the person who desired that I be successful was this Jesus Christ himself. Then the minister of the church where I was employed, wished me well even though he was reluctant to accept my resignation from the maintenance janitorial job I conducted there. The same minister referred me to a church member who owned a construction company. That builder emphatically said that I would be successful. Thus far, their affirmations proved fruitful.

I can say now that not a day passed that I did not remember Jesus Christ. I usually worked for Christians. They always mentioned Christ and his influence in their lives.

June 16, 1998

Agastya

He stated, "That destroys the hope of celibacy. He installed motivations which will produce sexual actions in the next life."

Remark:

A man I knew went to Europe with three ladies. One of the women was his wife. The others were friends. Agastya explained that travelling with women in that way would destroy efforts at celibacy.

This is how it works. We have subconscious desires from past lives. These motivate us in this or a future life. The desire-energy, being forceful, inspires us to act even if present circumstances do not permit fulfillment.

At present we set the tone for new desires which will be activated in a future life. At that time, we may forget how the motivations was formed, but regardless they will force us to act for appropriate or inappropriate fulfillments.

The man had no idea that the excursion with the two women and his wife set into motion consequences for other lives when he will become obligated to espouse the two who in this life were mere friends.

June 16, 1998

Agastya

Down-push technique

This one is used to remove negative energy. After an intense energizing session of breath-infusion, one may do this in the posture shown or in the lotus posture. The negative energies will go downward leaving the body through the bottom or travelling up the spine and leaving the body through the back of the neck or the top of the head.

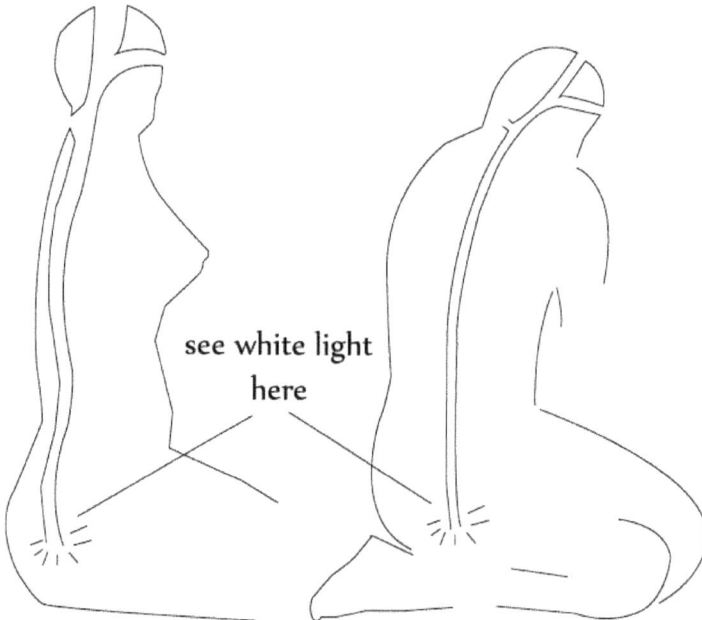

see white light
here

December 7, 1998

Shivananda

He asked, "What did your friend want?"

I replied, "He asked about the sexual desire of his disciple."

Shivananda responded, "Yes, he is a little more than a dirty old man. What has he to do with siddhas? What have the siddhas to gain from him?"

Remark:

This occurred in the astral world. A friend met me there and asked about his female disciple who had a liking for him and who wanted to meet him for sexual intercourse. As he spoke to me, Shivananda heard the conversation and made this remark.

Many become gurus, either by appointment or by self-declaration. Many of them are not aware of subtle activities. Sometimes, such a person meets me in the subtle world but in his physical consciousness he is unaware of the discussion. He has no astral recall. Many authorized and unauthorized spiritual masters fool the followers. A person who is not aware of the subtle body should not become a spiritual master and should not suggest or advocate that he can free anyone from material existence. This depends on self-honesty and freedom from the love of fame.

December 9, 1998

Shiva

He said, "Forget him. Keep track of the orbs."

Remark:

This was an instruction for me to forget trying to help that friend of mine who is a spiritual master. I was to keep track of two mini-orbs of sensing energy in the intellect organ; the orb of vision and the orb of taste. This has to do with the intellect-control part of yoga practice (buddhi yoga).

If I spend time with friends who act as gurus but who do not have mystic perception and who do not even know subtle activities, I could in effect be sabotaging my progress.

December 12, 1998

On this day I got a realization about a Rudra form which I purchased In Guyana. At first I thought that it was the form of Shiva. On this date however Babaji Mahasaya revealed that it was his form.

He showed a procedure for drawing up energies which were related to the vision and taste orbs.

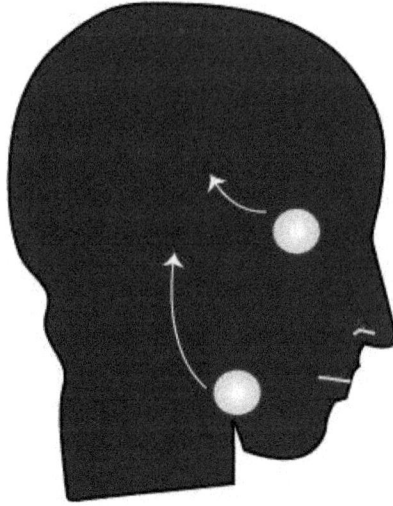

A dream with symbolism about Babaji Mahasaya

In the dream I was in a place where everyone was panicky, running here and there to get out, to avoid being trapped. I looked for an escape by some stairs. Two boys tried to follow me but disappeared after a while. I continued looking. I found a shaft and saw a man in a canoe down there. He used a body as if he were from the South Islands like Tahiti. He came up through the shaft suddenly. He appeared before me. He instructed that I follow him.

I went down the shaft after him and sat before him in the very narrow canoe which had two seats. Without an engine, without paddles, he began to move the canoe in this very deep water. I could not trace how he moved it. I wondered.

In response, he said, "The power is based on this." He pointed to his thighs and to my thighs as well. He said that he helped others before assisting me. He did this repeatedly for those who wanted to escape and who could see down the shaft.

Remark:

When this dream was over, I realized that the person who came was Babaji Mahasaya. The shaft represents the cleared kundalini channel, the sushumna nadi. The thighs represent the stage in celibate practice when the energy of the thighs no longer service sexual expression.

Babaji Mahasaya personally helps the aspiring yogis who reach a certain stage after seriously practicing the disciplines.

December 13, 1998

Babaji Mahasaya

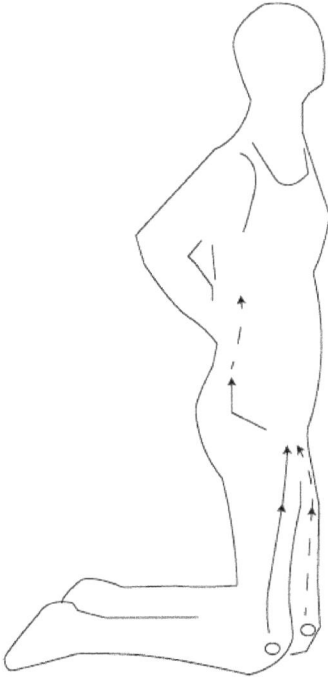

He showed me how to pull some sexual energy which was lodged in the knees. This is done while doing breath-infusion.

December 14, 1998

Babaji Mahasaya

He gave me a technique of pulling back some orbs or bunches of energy through the back of the head in white light energy. There were three orbs of energy, a vision orb, a taste orb and a sexual-energy orb.

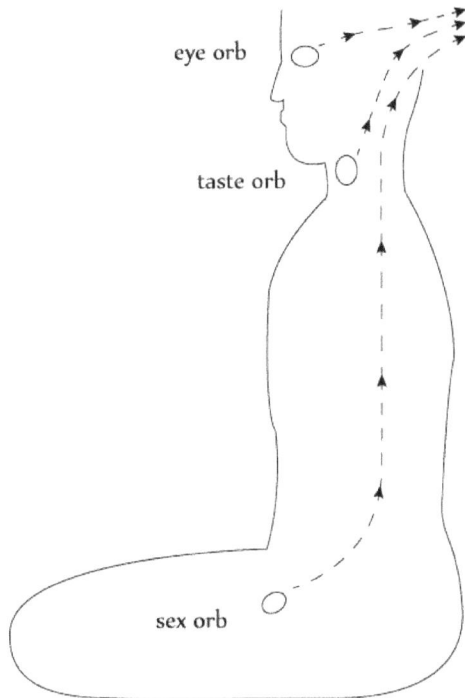

He said. "Since asana postures are so serviceable, they should be respected and done with due care. They release the sincere yogi from certain lower tendencies. Give asanas the proper attention."

Remark:

Babaji gave a mystic technique on that day. This one is done in lotus posture. It is done after an intense breath-infusion session. One pulls up the taste energy and the sexual energy orbs. This is sensual energy withdrawal within the body.

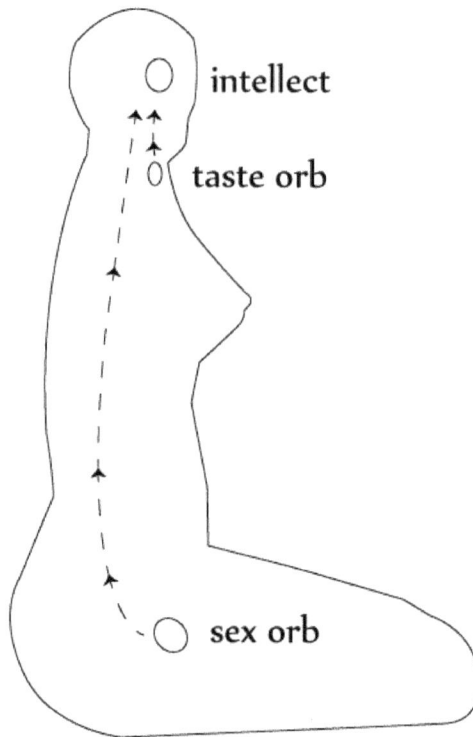

intellect

taste orb

sex orb

December 16, 1998

Babaji Mahasaya

He said, "Without exception, flirtations are filthy. One cannot realize this except after the thighs and knee caps are stretched. The worldly moralists speak against flirtations only when such things affect their prestige. Their view is incorrect.

When the thighs and knees are not properly stretched, when the waist is improperly curved, and the back is slumped like an ape's, the lotus posture is not possible."

Remark:

This is for the practice of celibacy yoga. It depends on the type of body one assumed at birth. Some bodies are genetically unresponsive to celibacy or are highly resistant to it. Even if he took a bad body, a yogi should keep endeavoring. If he becomes lazy, he risks taking a yoga-resistant body again in the next life.

December 15, 1998

Shiva

He said, "It is good that you reached a stage to qualify for his association. I am proud for having directed you."

Remark:

Shiva is much greater than Babaji Mahasaya but here he expressed appreciation. It is because Babaji mastered particular techniques which are relevant to the bodies we take in this modern era.

December 18, 1998

Babaji Mahasaya

He said, "Many of the recently perfected yogins are more difficult to contact than the anciently perfected ones. Those who are securing their perfection now, are not as relaxed as those who have traveled further already."

Later on that same say, Babaji Mahasaya said to me, "Stay with us friend. Do not go away."

Remark:

I was being pulled away mentally by some thoughts which came from some worldly friends who were pretense spiritualists. Babaji reminded me to stay with the mahayogins and not to respond to diversions.

December 19, 1998

Babaji Mahasaya

He said, "See the kundalini in all parts with orbs in each area."

Remark:

This has to do with vision of kundalini energy in the various parts of the body which are between the neck and the anus. In each of the important organs there are orbs of energy which serve as chakra distribution centers.

December 19, 1998

Agastya

He said, "Keep the channels separate. When they mix there is unwanted activity, Use the Hanuman hand posture which he gave yesterday. Keep ida and pingala apart."

Remark:

Hanuman, that mahapranayama yogin, gave me a sitting posture to use for meditation. This is with the body in lotus posture, with the hands on the lap, with palms upwards, with fingernails touching each finger correspondingly.

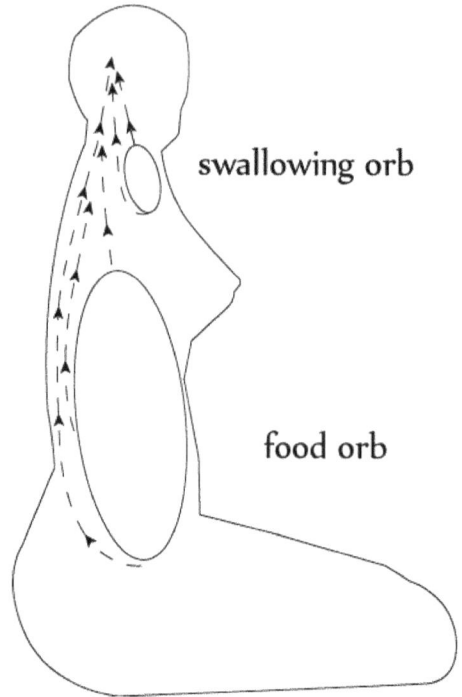

swallowing orb

food orb

Once Shiva explained to me that when sitting in padmasana lotus posture, one should not let the hands touch but keep them separate. Here however, Hanuman said that if they touch it should be the nails only.

Agastya explained that if the two channels of the body interact, there will be an unwanted exchange of energy which may disrupt meditation.

December 24, 1998

Brahma

He showed me a food orb in the abdomen area. It should be retracted in the pratyahar sense withdrawal process. One should note that the orb in the abdomen area is very large. However, if one tries to retract it, he will retract the essential energy within it. It will shrink and shrink and become concentrated as it is pulled-in mentally.

December 26, 1998

Babaji Mahasaya

In the subtle world, he initiated me so that I could formally begin subtle body yoga. This occurred two days prior, on December 24, 1998. This allows me to begin the process of doing yoga in the subtle world, so that if I leave this body before developing a yoga siddha form or before eliminating kundalini shakti, then at least I can complete the austerities in the subtle world, without having to take another physical system for the purpose.

These exercises begin with physical practice in which the subtle form may do techniques which the gross one is unable to complete. For instance, on this day, Babaji showed me that when I do an intense session of breath-infusion and when the subtle and gross bodies are fully charged with fresh air and fresh subtle energy respectively, I may stand up applying the locks and doing the slower draw-breath. At that time the gross spine is stretched up but the subtle spine is stretched way up, beyond the gross one. Physically it would appear as if the gross spine was stretched up just a little but on the subtle plane, the subtle form would have stretched very much. See these diagrams below where the subtle body stretches are shown with dotted lines.

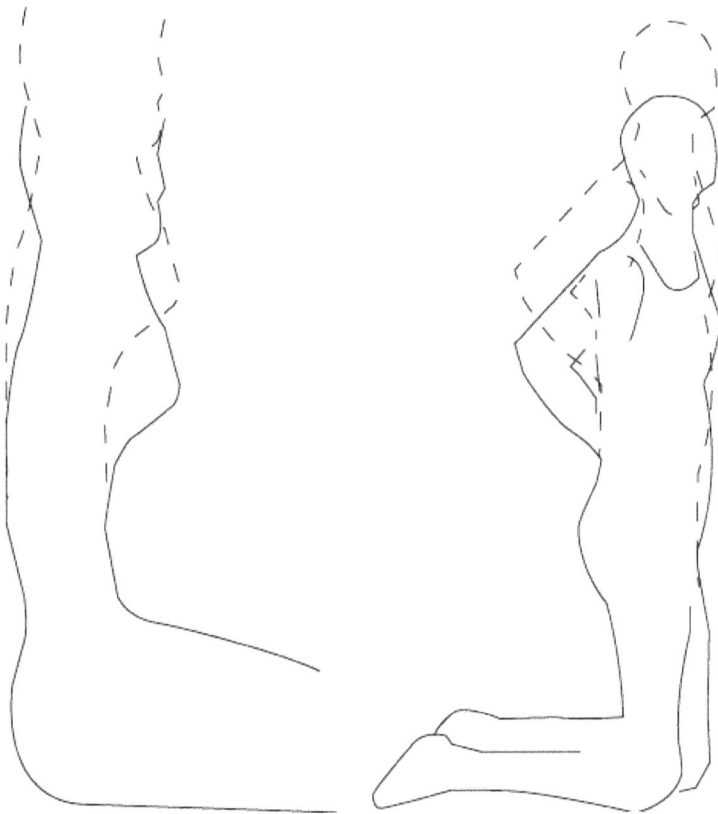

December 26, 1998

Matanga Rishi Yogiraj

He said, "Keep the channels separate. See this admixture. Still, the various grades of subtle energy separate out on the causal plane. Any mixing is symptomatic of involvement. Control thought development by keeping the various types of subtle energy separate. If there is leakage, find it, close it off. Thought can be generated only from the mixture of the two channels."

Remark:

This advice is relevant only if one performs effective mystic techniques. One must be able to see subtle energy, either visually or by pranavision. In pranavision one senses and sees through microscopic dots of pranic force. These may be multi-colored or crystal-clear dots. These are minute, active, gyrating and moving, all clustered together.

December 28, 1998

Vishnudevananda

With him I had a discussion about the effect of hatha yoga on the evacuation process. We discussed the importance of taking one meal daily. Vishnudevananda made the point that the two systems, that of digestion and that of evacuation, take energy from one circuit. He said that if the energy is being used for evacuation, there will not be enough current for a thorough digestion.

The idea is that the main meal should be once per day. The digestion and evacuation systems should each get their proper quota of energy, rather than operate in competition with very little energy shared between them.

December 28, 1998

Babaji Mahasaya

He showed me same subtle nerves in the intellect. There were two nerves made of light energy. When they interacted, thoughts flashed in the intellect. Babaji said that when the two nerves are relaxed, there is no thinking. When they are tensed, thinking occurs impulsively.

cross section of subtle head

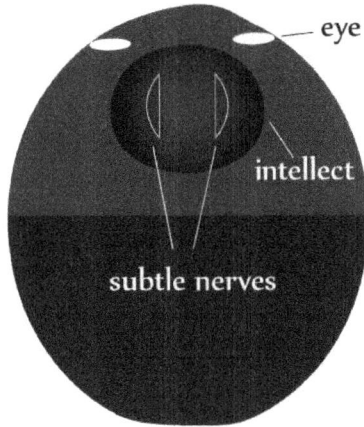

December 29, 1998

Shivananda

He explained to me that yoga and anxiety go ill together. A yogi has to design his life in such a simple way that there is no daily stress from a job or business. He wanted yogis to realize that they should make sacrifices, even to become poor for the sake of maintaining yoga practice.

December 29, 1998

Babaji Mahasaya

He said, "Just as those who derive little or nothing from it, have little or no faith in it, those who get much from yoga should give much back to it. One should give to yoga by keeping a steady practice."

December 31, 1998

Balarama

He showed me Yoga Ma. This is a female deity who is expert at the final forms of hatha yoga postures. Sometimes, this deity is said to be Sarasvati Ma. Sometimes it is another mahayogini. I was in lotus posture doing a meditation when Balarama showed me. She was walking by a river in the subtle world. This lady has a tall body. She wears a green fabric over her breast. She was wearing a skirt. Her midribs and navel were exposed. She carried a clay pot perfectly balanced on her head. Somehow or the other, as I sat in lotus physically, my subtle form transferred to where she existed. Waking and walking towards me, she reached where my subtle body sat. Suddenly she jumped into it. She sat in a miniature tiny form high in the chest of it.

I began to pull sexual energy from the kanda of the subtle form. It entered her through her subtle sexual organ. Such a practice might seem odd, especially since Balarama's name is attached to this entry. However in tantric yoga there are some constructive terminal sexual encounters which are mandatory for advancement in practice.

This deity is also known as Tara.

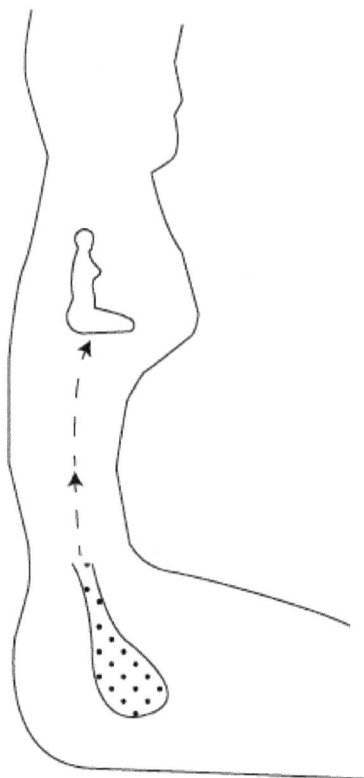

January 1, 1999

Ganesh

He said, "Let the devi mount the energy. That allows transfer of the interest."

Remark:

Ganesh spoke of the same sexual energy and the same Yoga Ma. He told me to permit her to mount the sexual energy that was drawn up as in the previous diagram. His statement about the transfer of the interest, meant that the sexual interest of my psyche would be transferred to that deity. Then it would be eliminated. She would absorb it to the extent of extinguishing it.

January 7, 1999

On this date, I endeavored to change the genetic habit of my physical and subtle bodies for holding physical and subtle reproductive hormones. Sometime thereafter, in the year 2000, I accomplished this. In celibacy yoga, one tries at first to channel the energy upwards. This is called: kundalini yoga. After one advances one practices techniques which prevent the body from storing sexual energy.

January 8, 1999

On this date, I had a realization that nutrition is the support of sex desire. Nutrition is promoted by departed ancestors who require bodies. Some ancestors live in our subtle forms and share in the performances of our physical bodies. They influence what we eat. They select sex enhancing foods and cause our bodies to desire these. As one advances and becomes loyal to yoga by a steady practice, one gets a proportionate freedom from their influence. Otherwise no matter what one does, one eats the wrong foods at the wrong times.

January 8, 1999

Valmiki Muni Mahayogin, an ancient yogi, explained that greed leads to more responsibility. For a yogi greed is undesirable.

Greed results in responsibility. Since the sincere yogi simplifies his life and prays and works for a reduction in responsibilities, for him greed is a threat. If the responsibilities are not reduced, the time for yoga practice would not be increased. Without that increase one cannot advance rapidly enough to get out of the material world.

January 11, 1999

Ganesh

He showed me how to retract the pranic energy from the ear lobes. The energy in each lobe was in the form of a grape with a frosty grey-brown color. I pulled it in the base chakra.

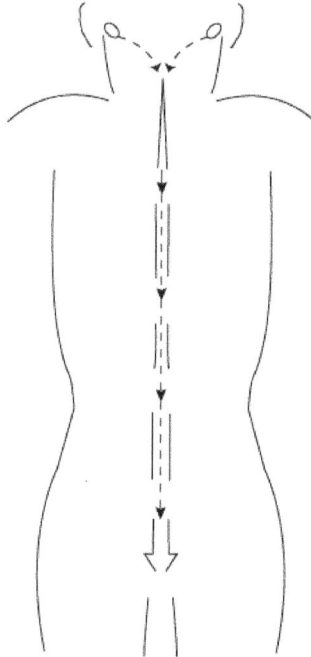

On this day, I had the realization that certain yogis help one with heavy subtle energy. Others assist with lighter subtle force. For instance Gambhiranatha helped me with the higher, more subtle potencies.

January 12, 1999

Vasishtha Yogiraj

He instructed, "Compress this. Join this to this."

Remark:

This was an instruction to compress the lower chakras upwards to the throat. I was to join the sexual energy whorl to the throat.

These refer to two systems. The spinal chakra system is one of the kundalini lifeforce and mixed subtle energy. The sex energies are hormonal liquids. Both are joined at the throat. That portion of the sexual energy which is pulled into the spine unifies with kundalini force. Some of it comes through the center of the body. A portion moves through the front of the body up to the navel.

January 13, 1999

Shiva

He showed me ear lobes which are connected to the kundalini energy and the ones which are in the intellect organ

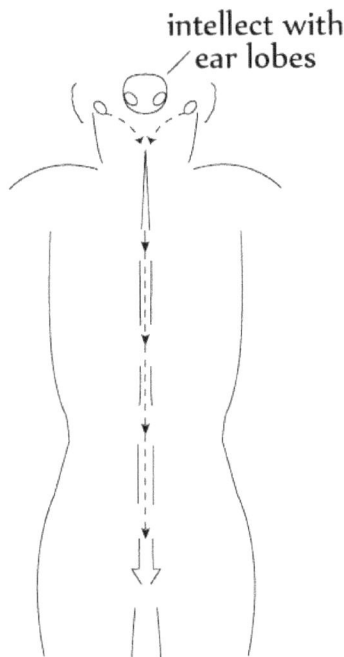

intellect with
ear lobes

February 1, 1999

Babaji Mahasaya

He showed me a way of cleaning the lower back. This is done while doing breath-infusion One pushes the air through the middle back area.

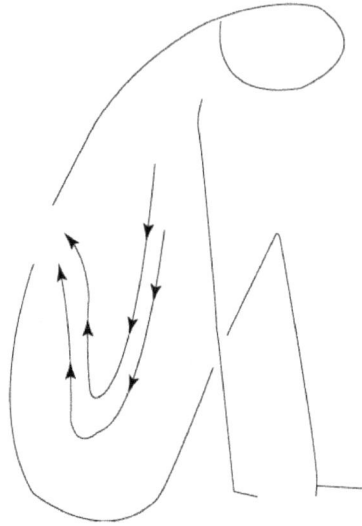

Babaji Mahasaya

He said, "Keep retracting the intellect. Restrict its interest within the psyche. Gradually its habits will change."

He showed a technique for retracting the intellect into the top of the causal form.

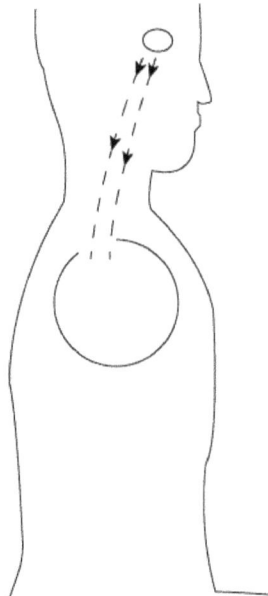

February 4, 1999

Babaji Mahasaya

He said, "What do you observe?

I replied, "As some aspects of the psyche are retracted, they disappear.

He remarked, "Repeatedly draw the aspects in. Be satisfied with the practice. Have confidence. When the gross senses cease their pursuits, subtle ones will develop internally."

February 11, 1999

Shiva

He showed how to infuse light into the kanda bulb in the subtle body. In more advanced stages, this kanda is eliminated. One should endeavor at one's level. When one advances one can cease some practices while instituting newer more relevant ones.

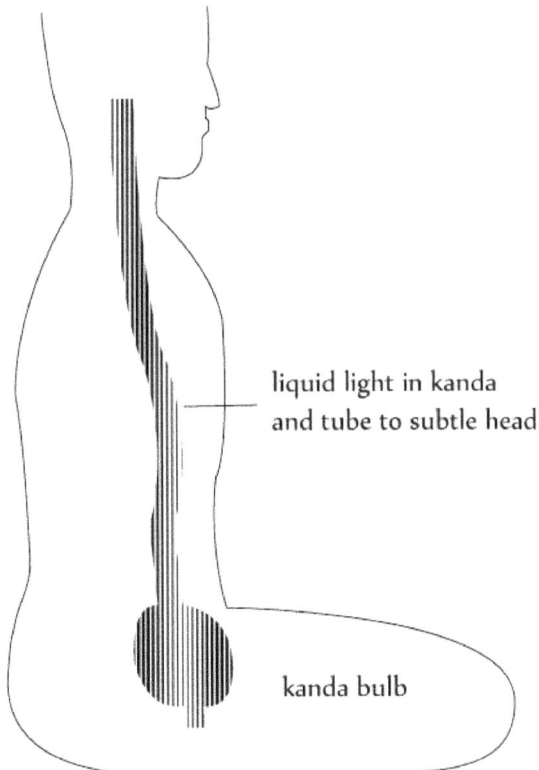

liquid light in kanda and tube to subtle head

kanda bulb

February 13, 1999

Shiva

He showed me some light gathering techniques. This is the gathering of subtle light or kundalini energy which is so energized that it is a form of light. It may be a combination of subtle energy and kundalini-generated light, with intellect light. This is subtle phenomena which is perceived either by pranavision, intellect visual vision or by both simultaneously. This practice is done immediately after an intense session of breath-infusion. One should not try to do these practices without first doing breath-infusion. If one fails to observe this rule, one will of necessity imagine everything. That is not mystic perception.

Very advanced yogis may not need to do pranayama to develop a pranic charge but others should practice and not pretend.

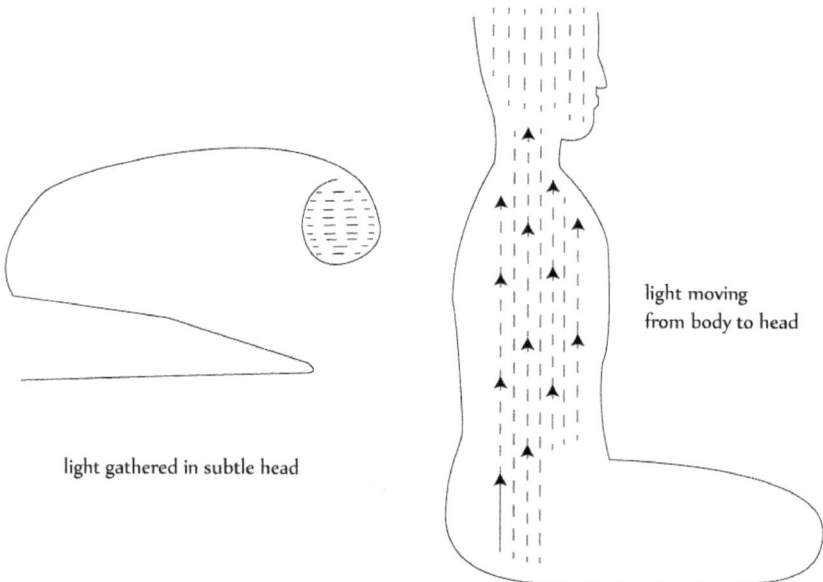

light gathered in subtle head

light moving from body to head

February 16, 1999

Shiva

He instructed me in doing a special posture in which the subtle body's kanda, is cleared of polluted energy. In this posture in the subtle body, one sees gas and light in the kanda. By doing breath-infusion one voids the gas and light through the subtle tube that passes under the nose.

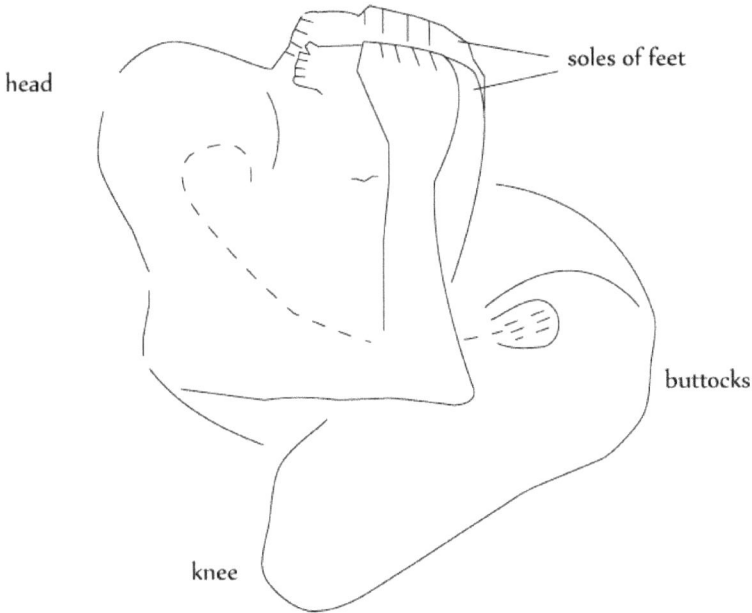

February 16, 1999

Babaji Mahasaya

He said: "Use this to draw subtle energy through the others; thus create and centralize the sushumna."

Remark:

I was supposed to use the brow chakra to help draw up energy through the subtle spinal column. Sometimes the sushumna subtle passage appears to be nonexistent. One can create it by doing an intense session of breath-infusion in various postures. However one should keep the energies centralized.

One should energize the brow chakra by doing breath-infusion while focusing the mind between the eyebrows. While doing this one should use the first and middle fingers to apply gentle pressure on the eyes. When that is applied one sees light at the center of the eyebrows. If one does breath-infusion sufficiently while applying that pressure, a greenish and then yellowish circle of light will form between the brows. This is the energized chakra. One can then use that chakra as a pulling point to pull subtle energy through the central spinal passage.

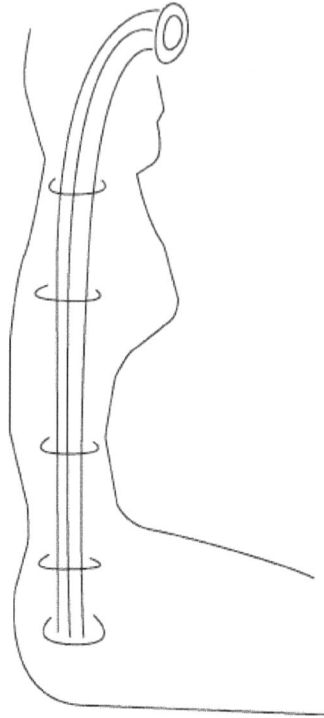

February 17, 1999

Shiva

He gave a sushumna blow-out practice.

Remark:

Before doing this one must practice the transfer of the brow chakra circle to the spinal chakra force. This is done while sitting in meditation after an intense session of breath-infusion where the brow chakra central power is taken down into the spinal column to mix it with the kundalini energy there. After repeatedly doing this for some months one can do the sushumna blow-out practice. The blow-out is done in the posture below while doing breath-infusion. After the psyche is surcharged, one should turn about inside psychologically and peer down through the spine, as if one is peering down a tube.

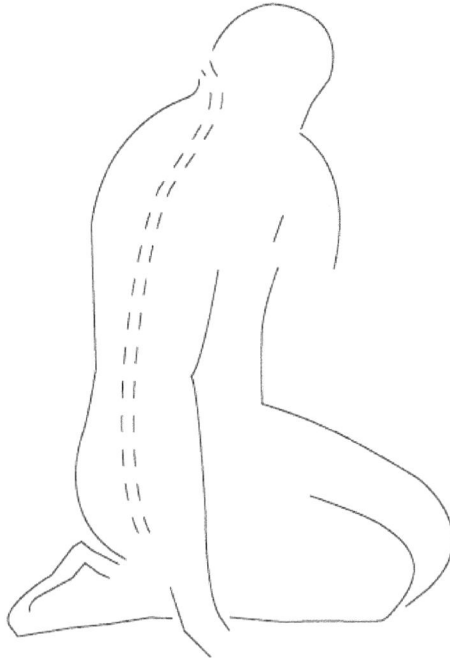

After subtle body is charged with breath energy one should, without touching the hands to ears, cuff the hands and place one near to each ear.

February 20, 1999

Ganesh

He gave me a technique for tracking light which emanated from the intellect organ and shines through the front and back of the body

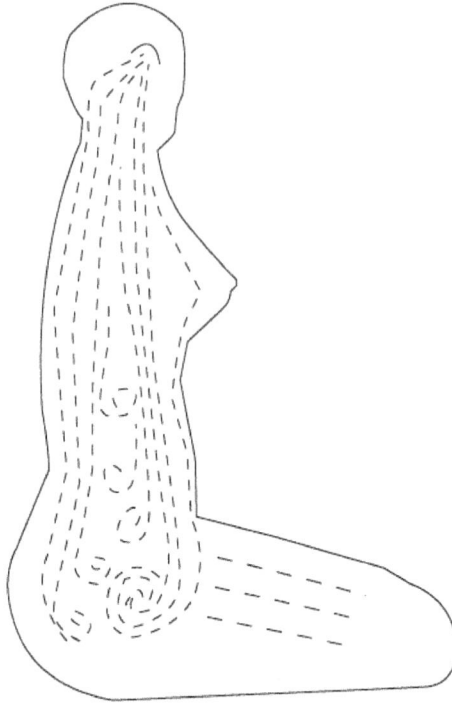

application in female psyche

It was about this time, that Srila Yogeshwarananda began to stay in my brahmrandra area. This greatly facilitated my practice and kept me constantly in touch with this great yogin.

February 22, 1999

Nutrition disc pull-up.

This is a celibacy practice.
Shiva gave this one.
This is for eliminating the sexual storage facility in the subtle body. That facility is a small bulb (kanda). After doing an intense session of breath-infusion, one does this while standing with hands on hips. One does a slower breath called the down-draw, where with a slow pulling force, in and out, in and out, the air is pulled to the bottom of the lungs until a subtle energy or sensation charge accumulates. As one pulls in breath, one pulls the subtle sexual energies up through the middle of the body.

One exhales whatever energy was not dissipated through an orifice that is under the nose. Even though the subtle sexual energy is in a bulb, when one pulls it up, one will feel as if one moves a flat disc. However as soon as the disc moves, its energy will vaporize in the subtle body. Some of this vapor energy will be exhaled through the orifice under the nose. It will feel as if heat flows through there on the exhale. By regularly doing this exercise, one eventually eliminates the kanda storage bulb, then the celibate practice becomes complete.

Shiva instructed that I add this notation:

A special technique may appear from Shiva's body and be inspired in the mind of a yogi. Shiva may not have sent that practice to the yogi. It is not necessary for Shiva to be concerned with a yogi. If one practices, techniques might emerge from Shiva's psyche and inspire the yogi.

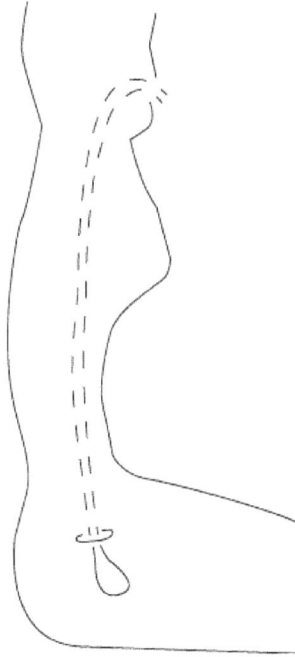

Brow chakra and kundalini compression.

In this practice one does breath-infusion while pressing down on the eyes gently with two fingers. As one presses, there will be lights in the brow area. These lights will convert into a circle of colorful light with a colorful, opaque or blank central space. One should take that central energy into the spine and compress it there with the other chakras. Then one should compress the total energy into one disc.

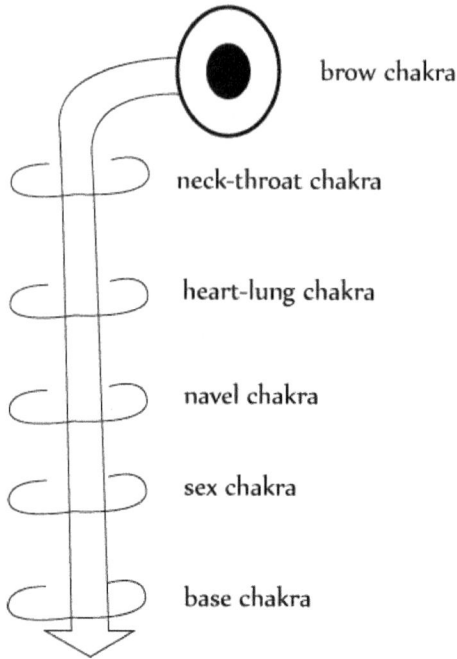

- brow chakra
- neck-throat chakra
- heart-lung chakra
- navel chakra
- sex chakra
- base chakra

February 23, 1999

Shiva

He showed a light in-suction procedure.

Remark:

This is retraction of a bright stream of light that emanates outward from the intellect organ

Murlidhara Krishna

He said, "Reduce the mass by increasing the quality."

Remark:

This is an instruction for increasing the food quality while decreasing the quantity. When doing kundalini yoga, one's appetite might increase. When this occurs one may increase the mass of food eaten. However after

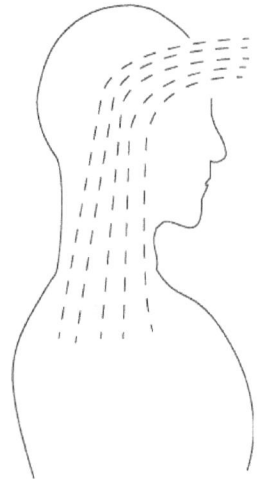

practicing for some time, the negative energy is mostly flushed out by the fresh energy infused during breath-infusion. One can reduce the mass of food by increasing its quality, eating a richer food in much less quantity. At first when kundalini yoga is done, the negative energy clogs the subtle channels, preventing free energy flow. The two energies remain in opposition. This creates a digestive heat which increases appetite. Later on by consistent practice, the body no longer holds so much negative energy and the digestive process decreases in a positive way so that one can eat a small quantity of richer food to curb the diet, This reduce the lifeforce's expenditure for digestion. It enhances celibacy yoga.

February 24, 1999

Vasishtha Muni Yogiraj

He said, "First pay attention to the light which falls like rain through that window. After having your fill of it, retreat within to the centralized position. Let the light rain down by itself. Let it come to you at the central position."

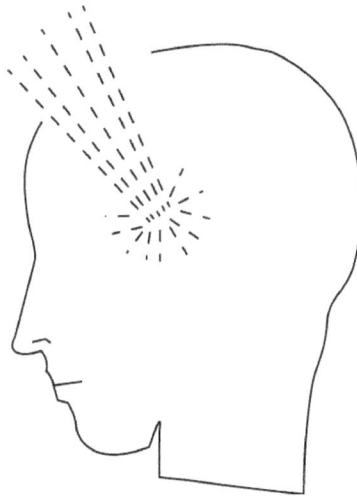

February 24, 1999

Shiva

He gave a method for handling mandatory social association.

In this procedure one meditates and pulls in the mandatory energy which was directed to oneself and which one cannot deflect. One pulls in the energy through the chakra which corresponds to the sender's strongest tendency. If for instance the energy comes from the sender's navel, then one should pull it to the corresponding area. One should pull it and then draw it in an upward direction out through the top of the head.

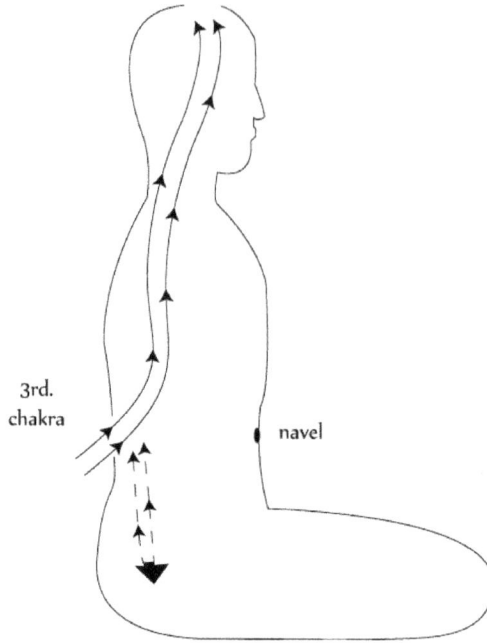

Shiva

The diagram below shows a flow of energy which He revealed to me.

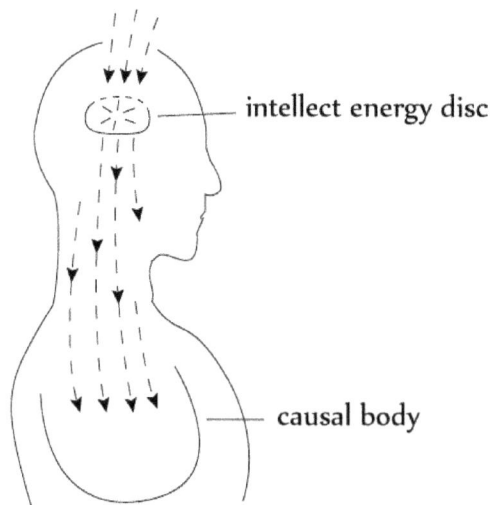

Part 5

Shiva

He said, "Eat here for a year. Then go to the diner."

Remark:

Shiva spoke of getting nutrients in the subtle world by sitting in the intellect organ and taking energy from the cosmic intellect. This runs through the forehead particularly on the right side. His reference of the next diner is the causal body and the possibility of taking energy from the cosmic causal reserve.

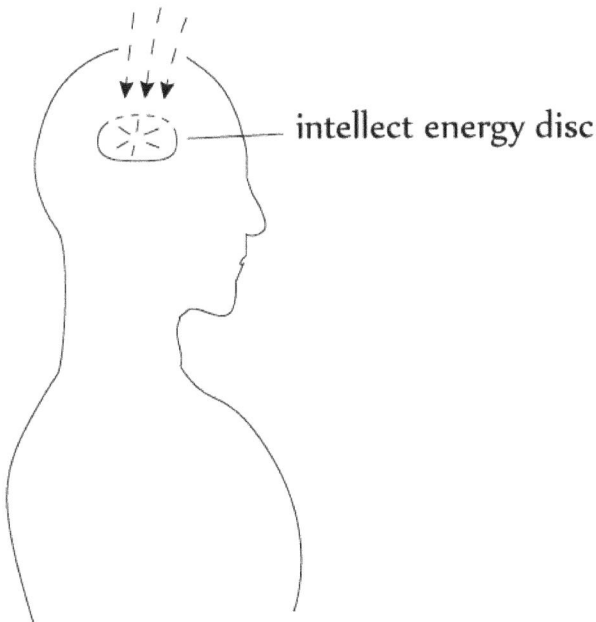

intellect energy disc

Shiva

He gave a practice for pulling hormones out of the lower trunk. This is done after intense breath-infusion. One should yirk up or pull under the stomach, while on sitting on the soles of the feet, with the soles as close together as possible and the knees apart. The hands should be on the thighs. When the stomach is drawn up it should be after an exhale. As one exhales, one should pull the stomach up and keep retracting it without inhaling again. This should be done until all parts in the stomach are drawn in near the spine under the rib cage.

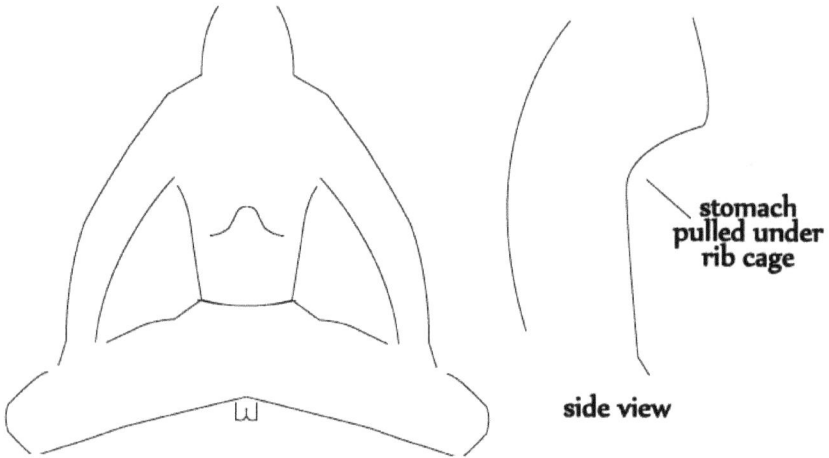

stomach pulled under rib cage

side view

March 5, 1999

Shiva

In-blast light pressure

eyes peer up into head

This is a practice for absorbing energy from the cosmic intellect. This cosmic intellect is the massive intellect from which the individual intellects were derived. By taking energy from it, one refreshes the intellect.

The pressure point shown as **X** is the place where the in-blast of light makes contact with the intellect. By that pressure, the eyes in the head of the physical form go upward.

Shiva

In-blast with an outlet

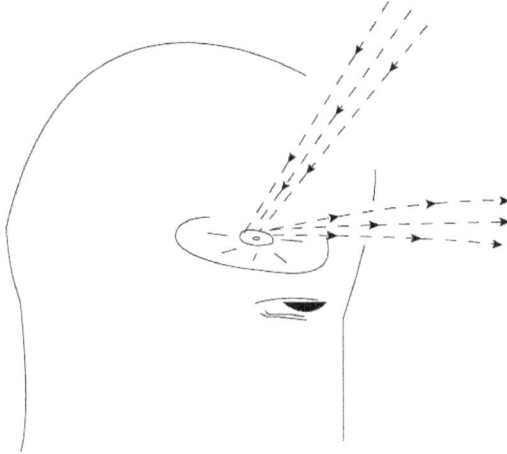

Shiva

Intellect moves down into the causal cove

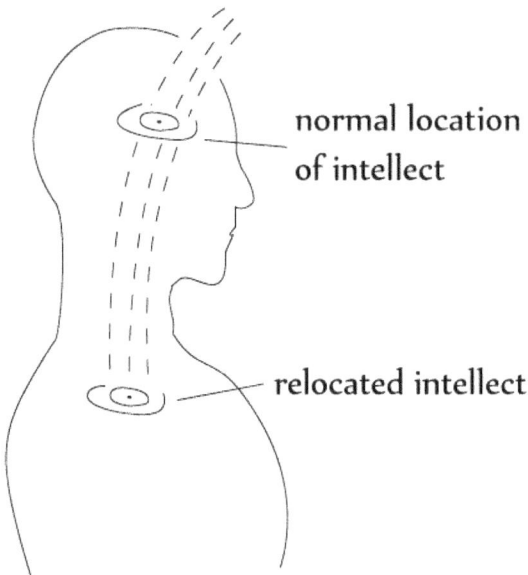

normal location
of intellect

relocated intellect

March 7, 1999

Murlidhara Krishna

In-blast.

In this diagram the eye force is pulled down to the intellect disc energy. This is caused by the in-blast of light energy. The sense of identity is in the center.

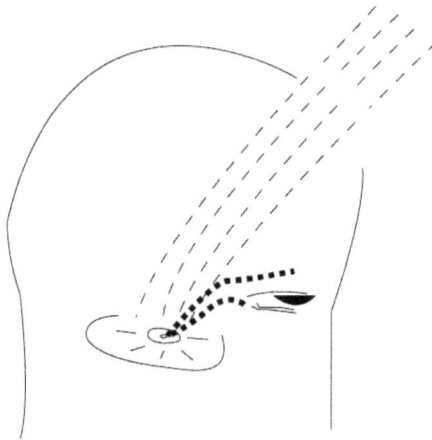

June 17, 1999

Agastya

He said, "Focus on short-duration transcendental states (samadhis). Later, long-duration states will be possible."

Many persons who want to do yoga begin with an idea that they should enter a transcendental state promptly. They feel that since they heard of an ascetic who by the blessings of a guru, went into samadhi, they too should have an immediate and lasting experience. When such beginners meet a practicing yogi they intimidate by suggesting that he should offer a glimpse of divine vision and realization. Actually no one can go into a transcendental state without having a suitable background in his past or present life. Thus if one does not have that history, one will be unable to enter higher levels even if one reaches a grace-bestowing teacher. It is a fact that even though a certain disciple sees light after being touched by a guru, other disciples of the same yogi may endeavor for years, without seeing anything but darkness or scattered hazy light. The difference is related to spirit category and intensity of practice. Whatever an ascetic could achieve is realized by consistent practice.

The anal tube illustrated below, was described by Yogeshwarananda some years ago. I could not see it, until I accumulated a certain quantity of practice.

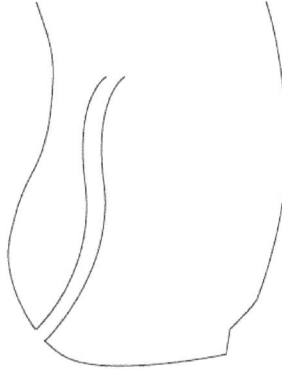

astral anal tube

June 16, 1998

Agastya

He said, "Study how it works. Why was Narad resistant to it?"

Remark:

I saw a lady in a dream. The circumstantial mood was for a sexual intercourse. Fortunately the dream ended before a relationship developed. Sometimes in the astral world, one cannot or does not carry the already-developed discrimination. One does many things which are inconsistent with spiritual progression. If this continues it feeds into the physical performance. This is why even sannyasis violate celibate vows.

Say what we will about it, sexual intercourse is always pushed or urged by ancestral pressure. That is the one sure motivator. Narad was resistant to ancestral influence but if one has a body which the ancestors can easily influence, one will be unable to resist sexual advances.

June 17, 1998

Agastya

Receiving subtle energy with eyes open.

Remark:

This is a mystic technique which is done with the eyelids open but without focus through the eyes. It is as if the eyelids remain open in a mindless focus-less way, as when a person daydreams, and does not see through the eyes though the eyelids remain open. This concerns allowing subtle energy to flow through the eyes in the way sunlight enters a room through a slot or window. Just as one might inhale through the nose, one would take in subtle energy through the eyes. The energy passes through the subtle eyes into the subtle body.

This practice is done when one encounters objects which seem to be irresistible but which are harmful to yoga practice. One allows the subtle energy which exudes from the object to pass through the eyes without allowing the eyes to focus on the object.

This is a sensual energy withdrawal practice. Later, in the year 2000, Yogeshwarananda showed me a more definite way of doing this. He claimed that it would not be possible to develop higher perception without first mastering sensual energy withdrawal. He feels that divine vision will not develop unless one exhibits a thorough disinterest in sensuality. This is called paravairagya.

Jesus Christ

He said, "Do not think of evading taxes. It is best to pay every cent required. If you do this, it will facilitate you. There will not be shortage."

Remark:

This falls under the practice of yama and niyama which are prohibitions and compliances. These are the first two steps of yoga. Though preliminary, these two stages remain with the yogi as he advances. In fact it was Jesus Christ and the Vedic deity Ganesh who showed me some of the advanced stages of honesty and non-stealing. Without proceeding through these advanced stages, one cannot be successful in higher yoga. The basic principles apply throughout all stages of yoga practice.

There are many religious groups which disregard the honesty stipulations and which become ruined as a result. Their idea is that since one serves a higher cause or since one serves the Supreme God, one does not have to pay heed to certain tenets. However if one is not careful, one may be ruined. One should do whatever is necessary for spiritual advancement but in the process one should avoid circumventing moral rules

June 19, 1999

Agastya

He said, "Track the subtle energy flow. Stay with it, even if it is not centered. This will train the intellect to stay with the lifeforce and make it become attached to short duration or mild transcendental states. This leads eventually to larger absorptions."

Remark:

When doing breath-infusion and even in meditations without that, one may find a flow of sensations somewhere in the body. It may be a small flow. It may be off-centered. Regardless, one should take the intellect organ to it. Usually the intellect organ and the subtle energy stay apart, like a separated husband and wife who are hostile to each other.

Sometimes such a husband and wife come to an agreement to have some pleasure. Sometimes the intellect organ and the lifeforce meets in the rush of sexual pleasure, when the intellect is overcome by the intense electrifying sensations of the aroused subtle energy. However in yoga, one tries to bring the intellect and lifeforce together, so that they remain together during experiences. Thus during disciplines such as doing breath-infusion, one should train the intellect to be attentive to any released subtle energy sensation.

June 20, 1999

Stretch-thigh, yirk-back technique.

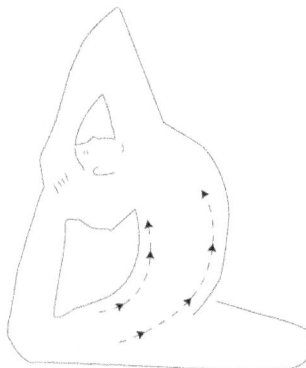

This posture is for the advanced levels of celibacy. This is effective after the pubic area is purified and the rest of the body needs to be made celibate. At that time, one finds any sexual hormones which linger or remain hidden in other parts of the body, especially in the thighs and back.

Actually the sexual energy is hidden in every part of the body but one does not know this until the pubic area no longer stores it. In the advanced stages of celibacy, one finds sexual energy which was stored in subtle areas.

June 20, 1999

Yogeshwarananda

He said, "Let me show this."

Remark:

In his subtle body, he showed this:

This posture concerns the control of air in the right arm. After a time, Yogeshwarananda produced large air bubbles in the arm. Later that day I did some small transcendental energy searches as I was advised by Agastya Brahmarishi Yogiraj

June 20, 1999

Shiva

He said, "The man wants to know how you will make out financially. He thinks that yoga is related to money. Why should a yogi of your caliber be concerned about social survival? To you what does it matter? These men over evaluate themselves while underestimating worthy yogis."

Remark:

Some persons feel that a yogi has insufficient influence to generate sufficient income. They become perplexed as to how a yogi makes a livelihood with a decent life in a decent house. To them, the life of a yogi in the forest, hut, or cave, is something of past legends.

June 20, 1999

Brahma deity

He said, "Agastya gave you much assistance. He is the most sincere among yogis. He is the very best in association."

Remark:

In yoga practice, Shiva is the supreme father. Agastya, kindness personified, is the uncle, Shiva's brother.

June 21st 1999

Agastya

He said, "They came off due to an excess charge. Return them. They will adhere to another victim."

Remark:

These were subtle sexual charges which jumped from a young woman's body into my subtle form. Such subtle energy may be returned to the donor, where it will adhere again, wait for a time, and then cling to another victim. It is like begetting children. In some cases, a woman or man has some ancestors lodged in the psyche, ready for rebirth, but waiting to become semen or embryo. As soon as the woman or man finds a partner, a pregnancy occurs. Sometimes however the partner does not engage in sexual intercourse or uses a contraceptive method, or has an infertile body. Then the ancestor loses a birth opportunity.

An ancestor may enter a woman's form. After doing so, he or she must be transferred into a male form by a romantic connection. Once transferred, he or she enters semen and then reenters the woman's form. If at first the ancestor enters a man's form, it simply waits, then enters a woman's womb during sexual intercourse. It comes out nine months later in a baby form.

At least for the first three months, the ancestor remains in a trance where his or her spirit stays so still that the subtle and gross materials used in the manufacture of a baby body, can accumulate and become formed according to the configuration of the subtle body. While this occurs, the spirit remains in a semi-sleepy, semi-meditative state. Usually it has little or no memory with short periods of incoherent visions. It stays in a state of involuntary concentration, with its subtle head bent over.

June 21, 1999

Yogeshwarananda

Funnel pull-in of eye powers and frontal intellect into causal cove.

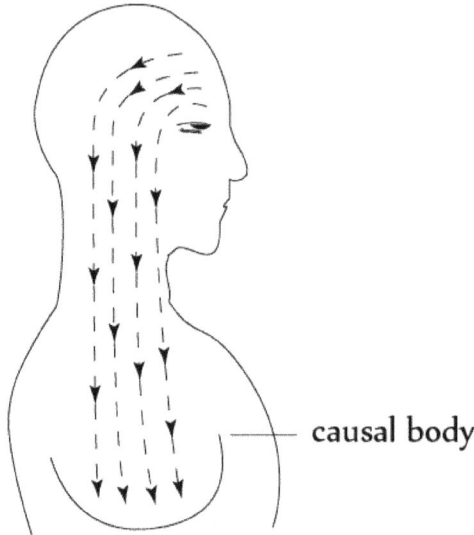

causal body

A small transcendence experience usually last for a short period of about 3 seconds or up to five 5 minutes. It has intense movement of energies to a certain point or area of the subtle form. In meditation, it happens spontaneously and vanishes just the same. It can occur after an intense session of breath-infusion. For an advanced yogis an experience may last for hours or days. Yogeshwarananda however, had strongly argued for higher experiences in terms of clearly seeing the inside of the subtle and causal forms, and identifying the primeval energies which make up this existence. Such investigations are done during a transcendental shift.

Sometimes one enters a short-duration experience suddenly without even doing yoga practice. However, I usually enter a short-duration experience, right after the early morning breath-infusion practice.

At night however even with more effort, I usually do not enter even a short-duration experience so easily. Sometimes however, in the afternoon, during the first part of my breath-infusion exercises, I enter a short-duration one. These occurs as the hormones are lifted from the various areas where they pool. As they flow upwards into the spine and brain, they cause small short-duration experiences, small concentrations of higher subtle energy which become shifted into transcendental planes of awareness.

June 22, 1999

Agastya

He stated, "Kumbhak breath retention without breath-infusion prior, is a waste of time for most yogis. In regular breathing the air does not penetrate deep enough. For beginners the alternate breathing practice fails to do so as well. The body should be healthy enough and have sufficient air compressed into the blood stream to tolerate kumbhak breath retention without strain. There should be movement of subtle energy at the navel. It should penetrate through the trunk of the body. It should feel like micro bubbles moving, being exchanged or as sparkling energy being packed tightly and transported at the navel or below or at the bottom of the lung cage."

Remark:

Kumbhak is a technique of restraining breathing. It is done most efficiently when the stomach and higher intestines are empty. To so this, one inhales or exhales, applies the various locks on the body and holds the body in a state of arrest without breathing for a time.

brow-chakra
centralisation lock

neck lock
chin drawn back
to compress throat

chest pull-under lock

lower abdomen
stomach-intestines lock

sex organs lock

anal muscles lock

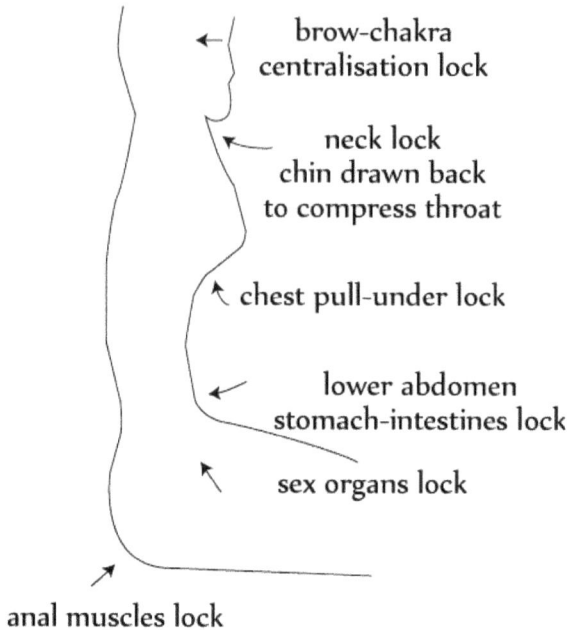

Prior to kumbhak breath retention, one should do an intense session breath-infusion. Then pushing all air out of the lungs and squeezing down the lungs to squeeze out all remaining air, or compressing the air in the lungs, one should hold the body in the state of compression, while focusing inside the psyche attentively to perceive the exchanges of energy and movements of subtle force. As soon as there is any feeling of discomfort; or as soon as there is a sense of needing air one should inhale and do intense breathing again. Soon after when one feels that the body is surcharged with air, one should do the breath retention again then apply the locks and study the arrested energy in the psyche. This should be done repeatedly until one feels that the gross and subtle bodies are saturated with fresh air and fresh subtle energy. Immediately after one should sit in lotus or in an easier posture to meditate. One should track the movement of subtle energy and experience the increased psychic sensitivity.

June 22, 1999

Agastya / Yogeshwarananda

In their presence I saw this pattern of energy.

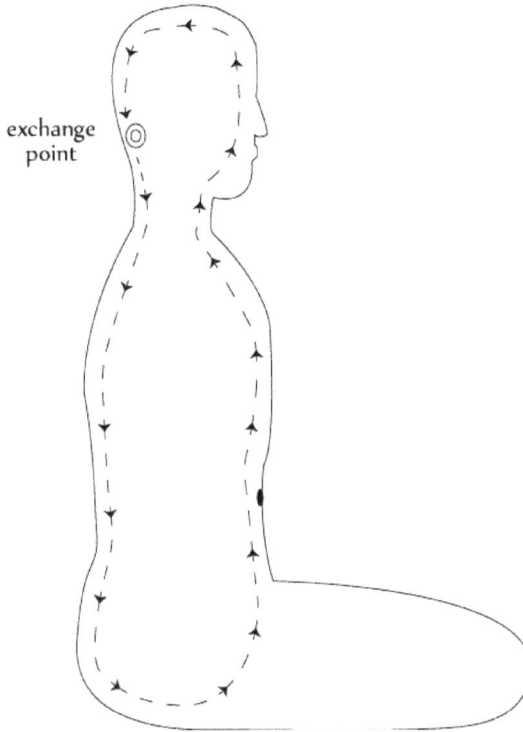

exchange
point

June 24, 1999

Agastya

These are some corresponding sex hormone areas which he identified. These are where sexual energy hides from a neophyte yogi. They are discovered in more advanced stages. Sometimes an ancestor hides in these places of the subtle body. When the yogi is not alert the hidden spirit comes out and goes to his pubic area.

Once the ancestral spirit stimulates that area sufficiently, the yogi might change his mind about celibacy and beget a baby form. In the advanced stages however, the yogi clears out these areas. Thus his psyche is not possessed by ancestors.

Such a possession occurs by virtue of the ancestor's beneficial social activities which were invested into the life of the yogi or into the life of a close relative or acquaintance of his.

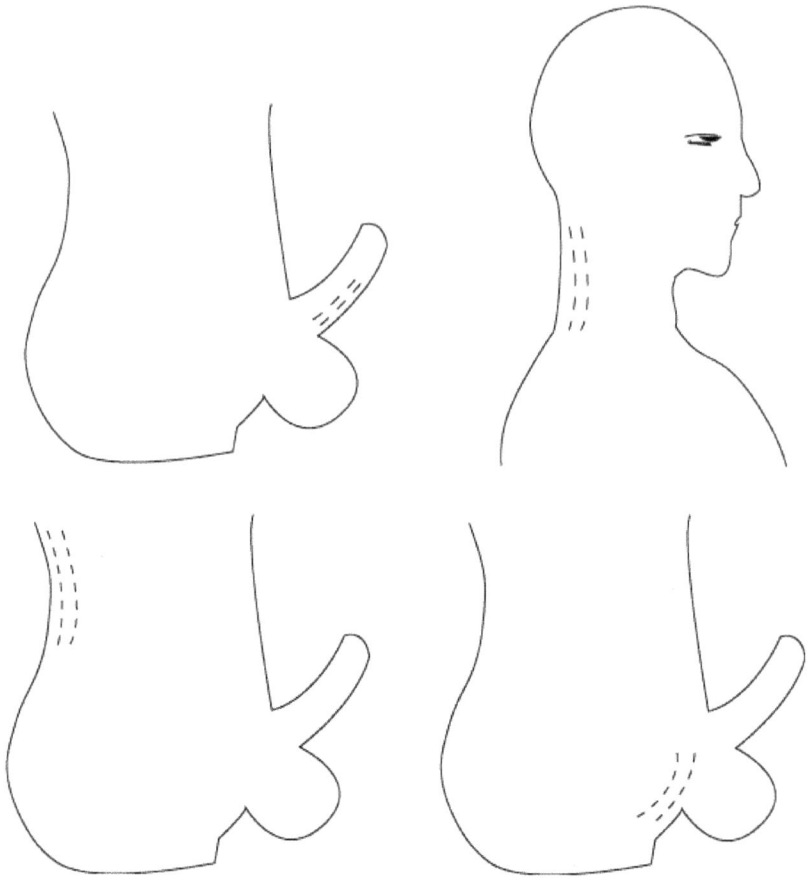

June 24, 1999

Karttikeya Kumara

He gave techniques concerning celibacy. His methods are generally unknown. He pioneered a unique procedure for celibacy. Usually I do not get his association. Here due to Agastya, I got a communication with him. To see Karttikeya on this occasion, I had to go in the southwest by west direction. I was at a location in Mississippi of the United States. At that time, the various deities were located around me is the directions shown below.

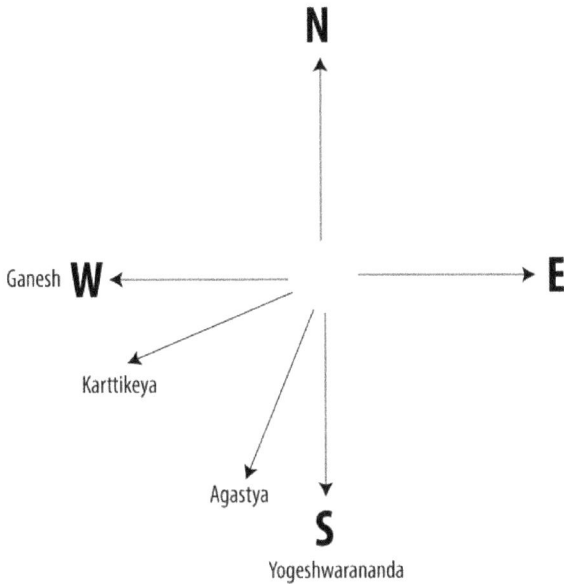

On that occasion, Karttikeya showed me how to check on a core-self or spirit, without having to disturb the spirit's mundane focus. This is done by going behind the coverings of psychic energy to see the crystalline spirit light. To do this, I had to shed my mundane designations.

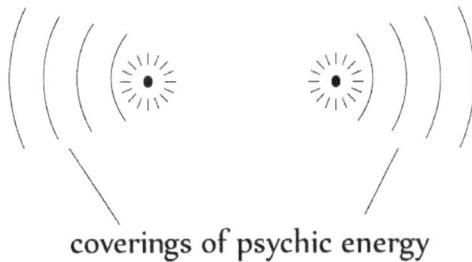

coverings of psychic energy

Soon after I had the communication with Karttikeya, I overheard Agastya Yogiraj discussing why Skanda became expert at a unique yogic process. Skanda is another name of Karttikeya.

Agastya explained that Narad influenced Skanda to go to the Krauncha Mountain. Narad trained Skanda on how to survive as a celibate youth in this creation. Devi is Goddess Durga, who is more or less, the Mistress of this dimension. Agastya said that initially it was important for one of Shiva's sons to be a celibate bachelor. Somehow Ganesh knew from before that it was not necessary to avoid the grhasta householder situation or to go on long pilgrimages. By intuition, Ganesh avoided that. Somehow Skanda took it seriously and went for pilgrimage. When he returned he was disappointed. With Shiva's approval many blessings for householder life were granted by Goddess Durga to Ganesh.

At that time Narad spoke to Skanda. Narad took Skanda for training

Skanda Kumara (Karttikeya)

He advised, "Be careful of transfer from subtle to gross. Protect the gross."

Remark:

This refers to sexual energy transfers. Even though the so called wet dreams are natural, one has to make an attempt to stop them. This is for the advanced stage. In the beginner's way, one should control the gross body and get it out of the sexual habit. In the advanced stages one works to reform the subtle force which is difficult to regulate.

The so-called wet or night dream refers to dreams in which a man or woman dreams that he or she has intercourse. That subtle sexual expression is sensed by the gross body. In response that form expresses sexual feelings, even to the point of emitting sexual secretions. Thus it is called a wet dream, since the gross body exudes the fluids it would normally emit during physical contact.

Interestingly, Skanda Kumar is such an expert at celibacy and has such an advanced body for it, that he advised me to reach a stage, where even if my subtle body was engaged in a sexual act, my gross body would not show it. There would be no wet dream. That would mean that I would restrict the emotions which transfer from the subtle to gross form. This would be a complete isolation of the subtle body from the sleeping or drowsy gross one.

Skanda Kumara

He said, "Do that for at least 6 months of transcendental meditation time to reach the kumara stage of the Four, myself and Narad. Then do this for 4 months. He showed the center of the bottom nerve of the sexual organ and the corresponding area in the throat.

June 26, 1999

Agastya

This technique concerns celibacy in so far as it is affected by food and air intake. This is done with breath-infusion or alternate breathing which is known as anuloma viloma.

As far as I heard from some ancient yogis, Agastya was the first person to do breath-infusion. Later he taught it to Skanda Kumara, who developed it even further. However, I heard that Bhava (Shiva) sometimes does breath-infusion but only to demonstrate it. For him it is not a necessity. He does not teach it, because he relies on others to demonstrate it. I learned breath-infusion from some students of Yogi Harbhajan Singh, who said that someone was merciful to him and showed him the technique. Yogi Bhajan's attitude is relevant. It shows that a master of kundalini yoga does not have the attitude of demanding worship and stipends from students.

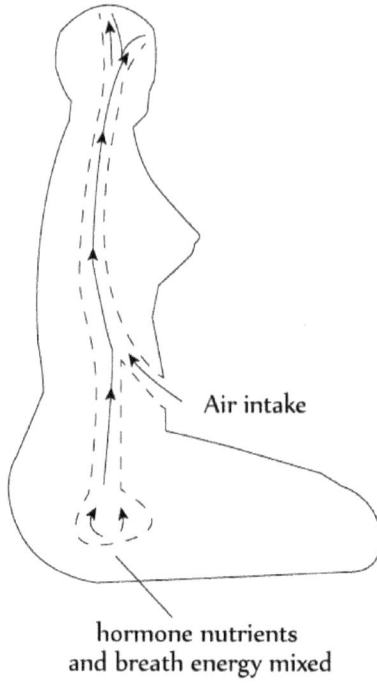

Air intake

hormone nutrients
and breath energy mixed

Agastya.

He showed me some corresponding areas.

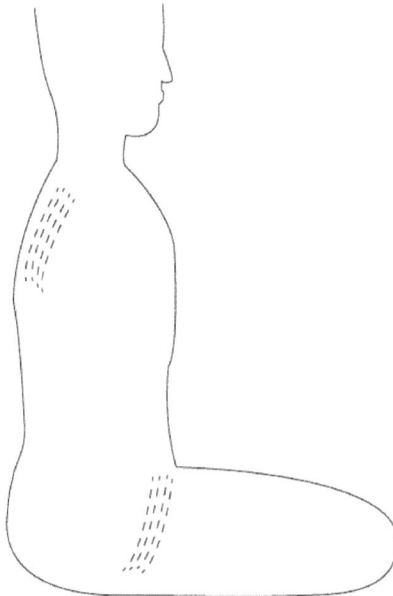

I remind readers that when shown this I was shown it in my subtle body. Usually these are shown to me immediately after or during an intense session of breath-infusion. That energizes the consciousness and gives insight about the subtle body. When I perceived this I saw by pranavision, subtle eye vision or intellect vision. On rare occasions, I see by spirit vision, without eyes or auxiliary mystic means. This is a form of direct inside perception. Even though I gave diagrams, a yogi who reads this and is inspired, should accept this an indication of what he may experience by sincere practice. He should not try to imagine this. This is not imagination. This is vision. By hearing of this, one may develop an interest and by that, one may strive harder to become worthy of the association of great yogi, in whose subtle presence, one will have similar experiences.

Skanda Kumara / Agastya

This was a small transcendence energy in the area shown in the diagram.

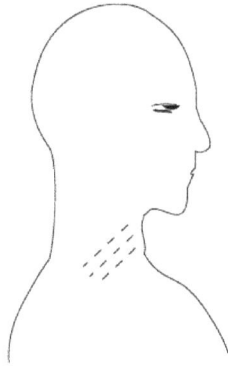

The subtle energy in the body moves nicely once the food in the body is the right type, taken at the right time, along with proper flexing, stretching and breath-infusion. When this occurs, the intellect keeps unified with the energizing energy. This causes focus into concentrations of elevated awareness.

Coincidentally, I typed this remark on December 31, 2000. On this morning Shiva said, "So long as the sensual energy disagrees, a yogi cannot practice consistently."

Remark:

He spoke of the practice of yoga. The point is that so long as the subtle energy (sensual energy) and the intellect organ (the deciding and planning faculty) view things differently, a person will ultimately satisfy the sensual energy. That means that he will not become a yogi of worth.

June 27, 1999

Agastya / Yogeshwarananda / Skanda Kumara

Under their combined influence, I had realizations. In yoga one may accept more than one guru. Each one has a particular credit according to how he assisted the student.

After a time, after consistent practice, the same powerful outgoing force goes inwards with as much impulsion and power as it used to go outward. As a neophyte helplessly watches his sensual energy pouring outward even though he really wants to restrain it, so an advanced yogi observes that same energy moving inwards as desired.

In conditioned life, the inward sensual energies moves outwards, towards attachment in the external world and the same energy then reverts inwards, reversing its flow. However in the interim stages, for a yogi who is neither neophyte nor advanced he notices that on occasion, the energy maintains itself with an inner interest and at other times, it pursues objects in the external world the way a hungry fox chases geese.

June 27, 1999

Digestion Technique

I did not make a notation of the yogi who shared this technique. However a good guess is Agastya. He specializes in techniques having to do with dietary control for celibacy and higher perception. In this one pulls nutrients from the chest, then one pulls that energy further to the back of the head

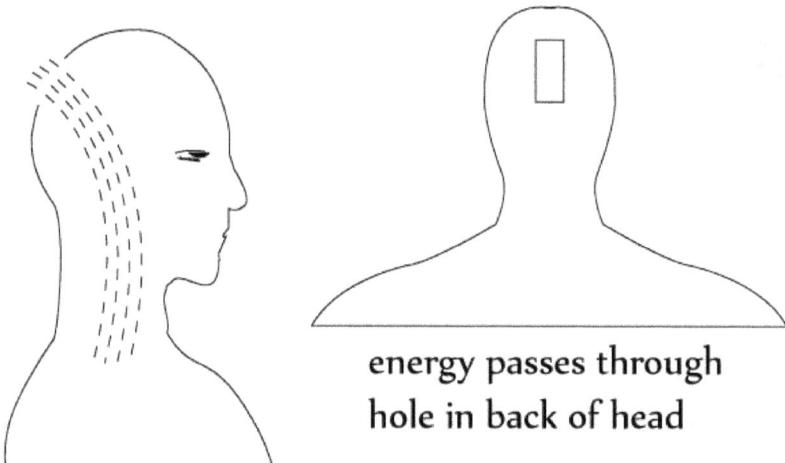

energy passes through
hole in back of head

June 28, 1999

On this day I took a notation about the importance of not taking water in the afternoon before doing the afternoon breath-infusion. If one becomes thirsty in the afternoon, one may take water and then do breath-infusion, but if one does this, one may nullified the effect of the breath-infusion and causes the lungs to take in much less air. One should instead, take only a sip of water, just enough to wet the palate. Then do breath-infusion, and then about 15 minutes later, take as much water as one desires. However in the late afternoon, one should not take much water since if one takes too much, the body will use the excess to make urine. This urine will continually trickle into the bladder while the body rests. That will reduce dream recall causing forgetfulness of astral experiences and descent into lower astral realms.

Early rest is important. I, for instance, usually take rest as soon as I am done the day's work, done afternoon breath-infusion and done meditation. This allows the earliest possible wake up on the next morning for doing breath-infusion and meditation before daybreak.

June 28, 1999

Shivananda

He was located in the southeasterly direction. Here is a diagram of where the authorities were located on that day.

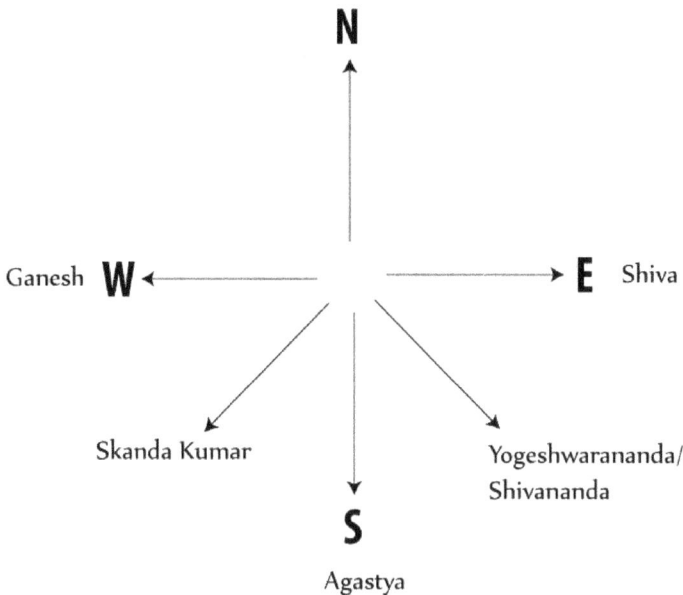

Readers should be alerted that these directions are not standard in all cases. For my location at that time, they were valid. The particular person or another yogi came to me from the particular direction but any authority may approach from anywhere. Even though the Puranas state that Shiva is located to the North at Kailash Mountain that does not mean that every person who goes to Kailash will locate him.

An astral location does not necessarily correspond with a physical one. Some astral locales are multi-dimensional. One will find the deity at the place where he is stationed when he communicates or inspires. Technique yoga is not stereotyped. I show directions in the diagram but a student should not think that these positions are valid for all times. What he may use is the method of recording the direction in which he feels a deity usually approaches him. It does not have to correspond with what I recorded.

Shivananda showed me something. He said, "Here are the visual subtle energies collected in a ball in the center. Collect these regularly to let the vision develop to see supernaturally with precision."

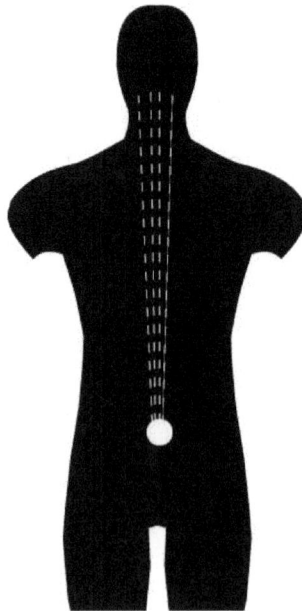

June 28, 1999

Agastya

On this day he directed a breath-infusion exercise. He said, "Squat. Do breath-infusion while pushing the fingers down. When the lungs are fully charged, stop on an exhale. Apply appropriate locks. Keep the eyelids closed. Monitor the energy movements in various parts of the body.

"When there is need for air, do breath-infusion again. When the lungs are saturated, stop on an inhale. Compare the perceptions after an inhale (kumbhak) and after an exhale (rechak).

Remark:

In this regard, Yogeshwarananda was one yogi who from within my head, would instructed while I practiced. He entered the head of the subtle body through the crown chakra, which is a small opening at the top of the subtle form. He was in an extremely small human form as a tiny as an ant. He would say, "Do this "or "Do that," according to what he wanted to show. Sometimes he would have me do exercises for his own practice. He would judge the effect of the exercises without informing me about it. On occasion it seemed to me that he was continuing his yoga practice using my body since his recently died in 1984.

Some deceased yogis who need physical practice may avoid rebirth by using the body of a student to complete the training. It is said that when he found out that he needed to know the details of sexual tantra, Shankaracharya who was a first class yogin, put his own body in a trance in a cave, and entered an almost dead body of a king. While executing physical duties, Shankaracharya lived with the king's wives in sexual engagements. Later he was alerted that he had left his physical form in the cave. Thus the great yogins can undoubtedly enter the body of others. I experienced this personally.

There is another example. Once some weeks ago, I sat in a house after being invited by some persons. They had a daughter, a young girl about sixteen years of age. While I spoke to the parents, Yogeshwarananda shined a light through my crown chakra. He was not in the crown chakra. He was above it in another dimension. He communicated from there. Suddenly this light, like a torch light, shun through my crown chakra and shone on the daughter of those persons. I was surprised by the light. I smiled within, not showing my reaction to her parents. In my subtle head I addressed Yogeshwarananda, "It is strange that a great yogin, who is liberated and already passed beyond the need for a physical form, desires to see a teenaged girl."

In any case, he did not answer. I may add here also that the reason for the yogi, not being in my crown chakra and being above it is this: On that day my crown chakra had a cloudy energy. If it had a clear energy, he would have entered. Since the subtle energy vibrated at a lower frequency, he did not enter.

June 28, 1999

Realization under the influence of Yogeshwarananda

The subtle body is hypocritical in terms of moral decisions made by the willpower in the physical world. Unless the subtle habits are altered, morality is cosmetic and superficial. Morality within the gross body is rarely observed by the subtle form. If one thinks that his moral condition is thorough, he fools himself. Unless a person curbs the subtle body, his moral condition is only applicable to his gross form. Hence the necessity for mystic disciplines.

Incidentally, in relation to the entry I made above, regarding Yogeshwarananda's shining the mystic light on the teenaged girl, he did answer me about it later on that day. He said, "I shun the light but I did not look at the object which it revealed. The purpose was to show you how a yogi can operate such lights through another's brahmrandra. The yogi does not have to use a physical body to see into the physical world. I did not see the object illuminated. The light itself by its sensitivity, followed the object as the object moved. In that way, he affirmed his astral celibacy.

June 29, 1999

Shiva

He said, "Some take energy from there. Others take from other parts of the sex organ. It is divided into parts."

Remark:

Here Shiva showed me where a lady took energy from my sex organ. This was an automatic mystic act carried out by her psyche. She did not deliberately do it. It just happened by the power of her subtle body. To her mind, she felt a sexual attraction and that was all. The subtle activities of the attraction were unknown to her. Shiva showed that the energy was drawn from my testes. In another

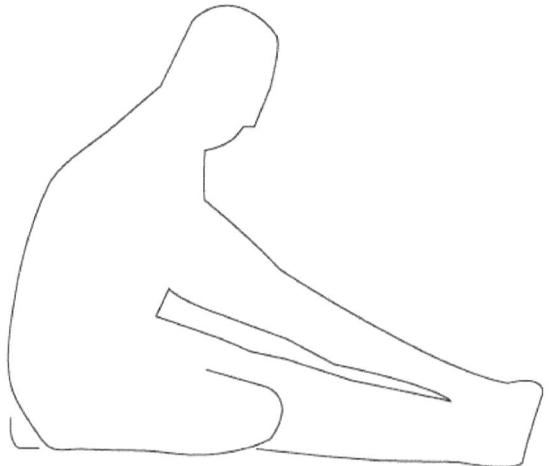

case with another woman the energy was drawn from the tubal flesh of the organ. These pulls of energies from either location occurred because of the different natures of the particular females. I was shown this while I did a celibacy exercise with breath-infusion.

While doing that posture, I pulled the energy back through the testes, doing the right, then the left, then the tubal organ on either side. Then I sat on both soles and pulled the sexual energy from the area under the abdomen. There is a pubic pad there, where the sexual energy is stored. Ultimately one has to eliminate those areas but that takes time with consistent practice.

I used to think that I could develop or produce a yoga siddha body before the deterioration of this material form, but at the rate of my practice now, I may be unable to do so. Previously I made a miscalculation about the rate of progress because I did not figure in the amount of mandatory cultural involvement, I would have to participate in. There is a verse in the Bhagavad Gita which explains this:

कायेन मनसा बुध्या
केवलैरिन्द्रियैरपि ।
योगिनः कर्म कुर्वन्ति
सङ्गं त्यक्त्वात्मशुद्धये ॥५.११॥

kāyena manasā buddhyā
kevalairindriyairapi
yoginaḥ karma kurvanti
saṅgaṁ tyaktvātmaśuddhaye (5.11)

kāyena — with the body; manasā — with the mind; buddhyā — with the intellect; kevalair = kevalaiḥ — alone; indriyair = indriyaiḥ — by the senses; api — even; yoginaḥ — yogis; karma — cultural activity; kurvanti — they perform; saṅgaṁ — attachment; tyaktvā — having discarded; 'tmaśuddhaye = ātmaśuddhaye = ātma — self + śuddhaye — towards purification

With the body, mind and intelligence, or even with the senses alone, the yogis, having discarded attachment, perform cultural acts for self-purification. (5.11)

Because of what is explained in that verse, I doubt if I would develop a yoga siddha form before I leave the body but at least after leaving I could stay in the astral world in association with great yogins to complete the practice. My earlier prediction about getting a yoga siddha form might fail. That would be due to mandatory cultural involvements which are being thrown on my path by destiny.

June 29, 1999

Here are diagrams showing the location of compressed transcendental energy, experienced during rapid breathing breath-infusion.

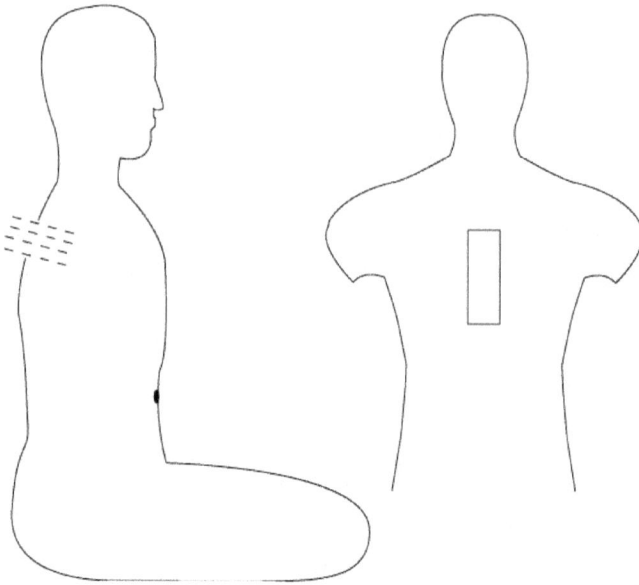

June 30, 1999

Agastya

He said, "These small isolated compressed higher energies occur in various parts, shifting from time to time. Due to being absorbed socially, you may not realize this."

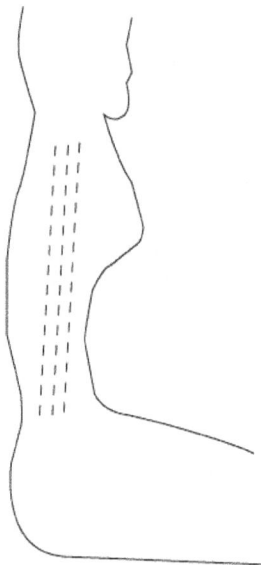

July 1, 1999

Babaji Mahasaya

On this day, he visited. This is the Babaji from the kriya yoga lineage, which was popularized by Paramhansa Yogananda. Actually if one sees Babaji with mystic perception, one has to admit that one is truly blessed. Usually he does not appear to anyone. He is isolated. I used to see him at Mount Kailash in a subtle body but once, when I approached he disappeared. I did not see him for a long time thereafter.

The idea is that one should not approach a great yogin. Instead one should simply practice and become more and more purified. Babaji does not relate to beginners until they reach a certain level of purity. In turn, even if they see him in the mystic landscape, they cannot approach him. There is no necessity for one to see a great yogin. At each stage one may be approached by yogis of lesser order who can introduce one to the disciplines required.

It is sheer nonsense when someone tells me that he needs the blessings of great yogi. It is not necessary. If someone practices, he (she) will become purified. As soon as one is fit for more advanced disciplines, those procedures will be shown, either by physical demonstration, astral instruction or inspiration directly into one's mind. Even if one is not conscious upon receiving the instruction, it will manifest in one's practice. One may feel that somehow one discovered an effective method. Therefore the idea that one must be touched by a great yogin is a fantasy.

I could state now on this day of January 1, 2001, I communicate with Babaji on a daily basis. He hardly gave special techniques. I get those from others. What he does is supervise what I eat. I now offer a morning citrus offering to him. Babaji hardly communicates with me. Usually he does not check my breath-infusion pranayama practice.

At the time when I wrote this remark on July of 1998, Babaji Mahasaya approached from the direction indicated:

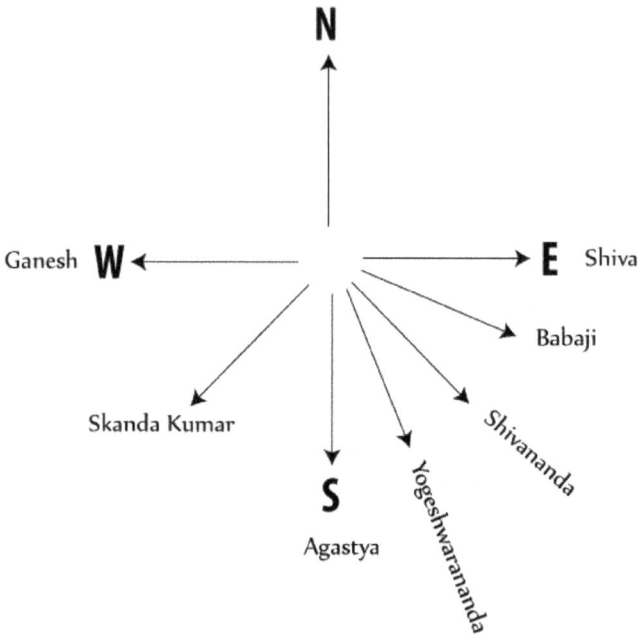

He gave me some techniques and said that I should use each focal-point as a pull-point, whenever the energy mixes and there is a star point, regardless of whether the energy is balanced or not. He said to pull it to develop the crown chakra and to straighten out the spinal energies.

In this respect I alert beginners. For most newbies the crown chakra at the top of the head is undeveloped. One should not assume that this chakra is operative. It has to be developed. One should push on with breath-infusion practice to manifest the crown chakra. After its development, the brahmrandra hole will manifest and the intellect organ will become clarified as crystalline clear light. This happens after much practice.

In the case where for instance Atmananda touched Yogeshwarananda and clarified Yogesh's brahmrandra, from then onwards, it was based on Yogesh's practice. If a man stands on the edge of a cliff and does not understand how to jump, he may be pushed. As soon as a student reaches the edge of perfection in the austerities, someone may touch him or without such a touch, spontaneously, he may have divine experiences.

For instance, we do not hear of anyone touching Shakyamuni Buddha. Without being touched he had divine experiences which yogis after him were unable to realize, even after being touched. In any case, in the astral world, I was touched by Yogeshwarananda and others. They touched my astral body and reveal certain things. Mostly, however it was through entry into my developed brahmrandra, that they were able to show me certain things. I can explain this in another way. Suppose you have never seen a banana. I saw one. I have a banana sprout. I gave you the small banana plant. You plant it. Later when the banana fruit is produced, I return. I show it, saying, "Here it is. This is a banana."

It is exactly like that. You practice. You develop. Then you are shown what was developed.

Here are diagrams of the pull-points shown by Babaji.

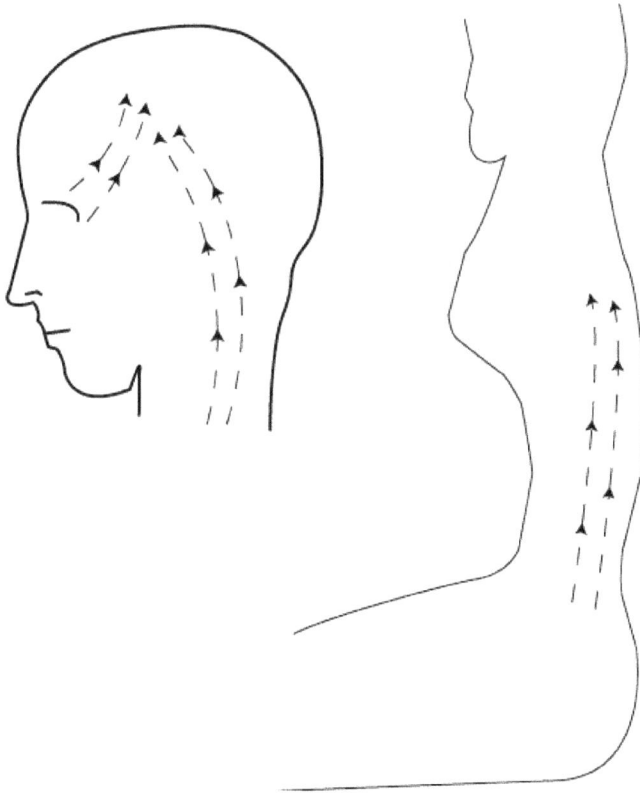

Part 6

Ganesh

He said, "Here is a technique he left for you. Until they are exhausted, I will give you one each day."

Remark:

Babaji Mahasaya visited the previous day. He left some techniques with Ganesh, who gave them to me. On that day, Ganesh showed this one. It was a sushumna clean-out kriya. In that practice energy from space enters the sushumna through the elevated brow chakra.

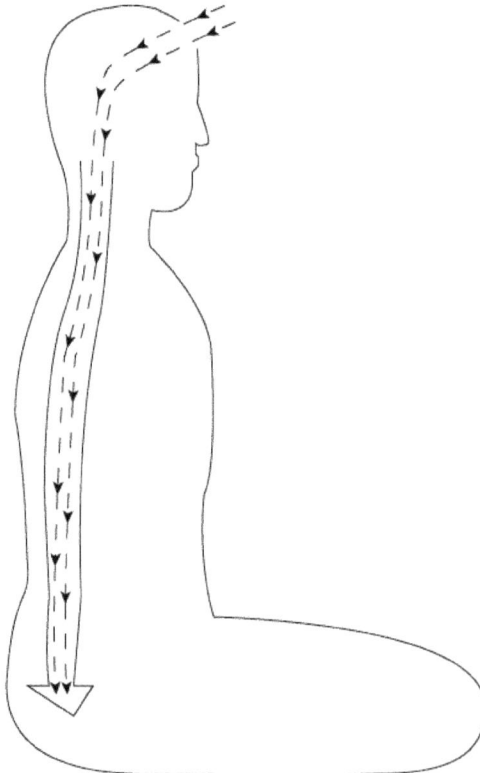

Moon deity with the Sun deity's energy

Remark:

Soma is the deity of the moon. Surya is the deity of the sun. At some times, the moon deity is infused with solar energy. Then the moon-ray energy is heat-producing. Otherwise the day energy may be warming but the night energy is cooling. Cooling subtle energy may slow yoga practice.

In breath-infusion one prefers to associate with the moon deity when he is infused with sun power. Since we do our main breath-infusion practice early in the morning before sunrise, we are dependent on the moon deity. If he is infused with sun energy, he gives more assistance to a yogi.

He gave this technique for clearing sushumna. It is similar to the one Ganesh showed. The deity said, "Try this Babaji method from the throat.

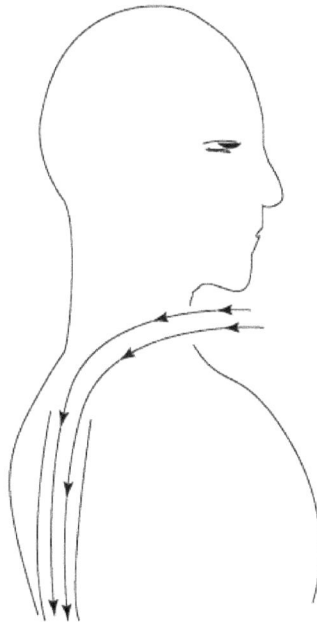

After doing that technique for some time, it changed into this:

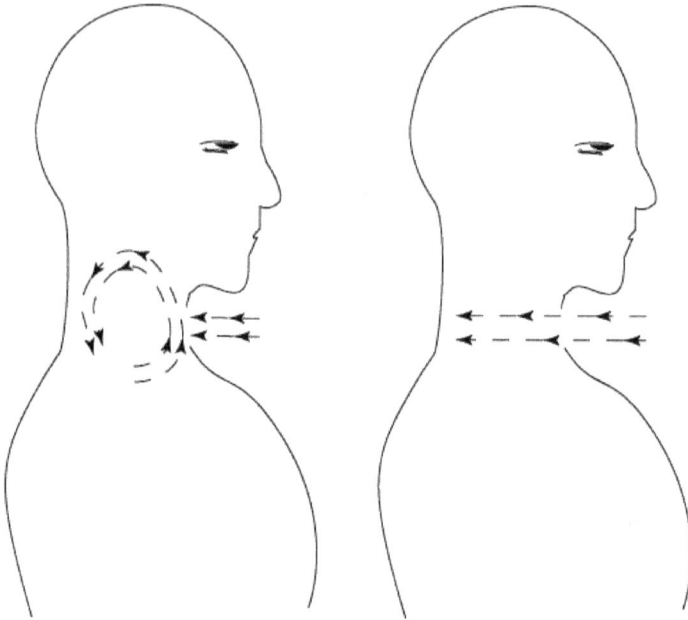

July 4, 1999

Ganesh

He said, "Keep the chest in this state in the morning. Gradually learn the gravity feel and go to the causal cove for transcendence."

Remark:

At the time of getting this instruction, I stopped eating solid food during the day. Instead, I took milk cream especially if I did strenuous work. However, since I did not take the milk cream on this day, the hormones in the body were exhausted. The bones felt dry.

The subtle body began to lose its configuration. The chest of the subtle body caved in. With this I had some experience which yogis have when they stop eating for days before entering trance states. I felt the causal cove as a pulling force.

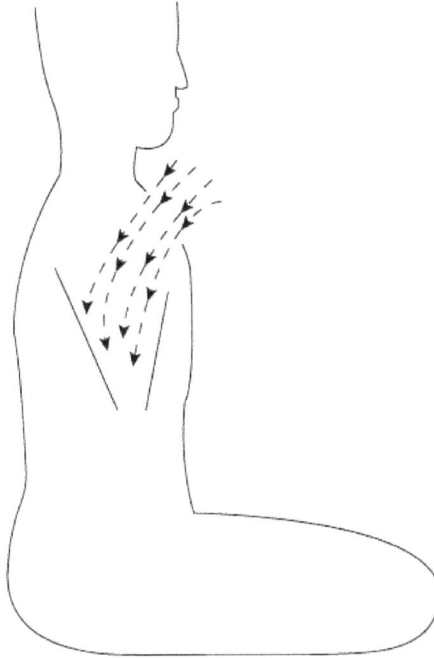

Ganesh advised that I starve the body in order to develop longer-duration transcendental states. When I wrote this comment at the beginning of the year 2001, I was still working to bring the body to the stage where it would naturally subsist on one early morning meal taken about 5 am.

There are many people who rake and scrape their brains for easy methods for going into samadhi higher states and for experiencing spiritually what great yogis of the past described. Most of these persons will continue their brain work until they develop a valid practice. From time to time, such people ask me about an easy method but I report here that I found none.

July 5, 1999

On this day I had the realization that breath-infusion also removes heat from the body. It removes carbon dioxide which produces laziness and discomfort in the body. It removes blood heat and lung heat. Some persons feel that since breath-infusion is a vigorous method, it is dangerous. Some feel that it should not be done in tropical climates. However I report here that in tropical climates, bhastrika, though vigorous, removes heat from the body Thus it is not dangerous. After doing a good session, on a hot day, in the shade in a tropical place, one feels the body cool off. The body sweats profusely and cools down immediately. But one should drink water after the body cooled.

That prevents dehydration, which may result in constipation, drying out of body waste.

July 5, 1999

Babaji Mahasaya.

He said, "Always review the last two lessons. That will create a memory habit in the intellect."

Remark:

By doing that one brings the intellect to the infused subtle energy. This reinforces practice. Babaji gave this technique:

release sushumna
central passage hot-air

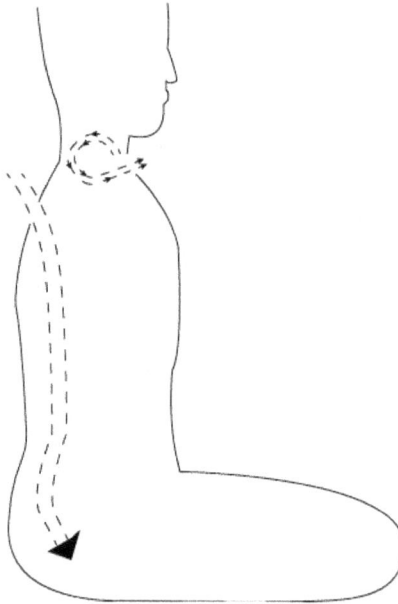

Since I describe many techniques, a student might wonder if there is an end to this. The main point is that technique yoga is progressive. It is not stagnant. It changes daily.

July 6, 1999

Krishna said, "Loosen here. Release the rest. Put the serpent in this position to shine at the muladhar base chakra."ts.s?ppp 10snblszssz

Krishna-Balarama Deities

Krishna said, "Loosen here. Release the rest. Put the serpent in this position to shine at the muladhar base chakra."

Krishna is a teacher of technique yoga, which he explained to Uddhava who was the last person instructed before Krishna left the earthly form, which was the son of Devaki.

In the course of technique yoga, I got little instruction from Krishna. His first instruction to me was to be close to Balarama. When I tried to comply, Balarama referred me to Shiva. It was Shiva who established me in the association of some great yogins, who are masters of the practice.

I published Krishna's instruction to Uddhava which includes the instruction about how to perform technique yoga. Even kundalini yoga and chakra configuration is in that important discussion.

Agastya

A throat to brow-chakra, drawn-down to the causal form.

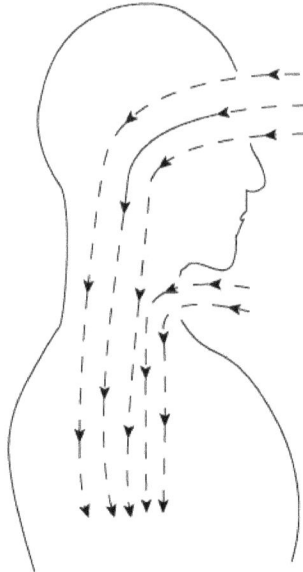

　　　　Procedures like this are part of pratyahar sensual energy withdrawal. Although pratyahar is listed as the 5th stage in the 8th staged yoga process, it functions through the higher stages. It is listed as the 5th stage because after one gained some mastery of pranayama breath-infusion, one shifts the focus to reservation of sensual powers. Initially this consist of trying to avoid sense objects which demand unwanted sensual responses. For instance if one craves sweets, one may avoid eating. If one craves sexual indulgence one may avoid meeting attractive persons. Though it minimizes this, avoidance does not remove the craving. It merely reduces the impulsions at the time of the restraint

　　　　To completely stop cravings, one has to retract the sensual powers and restrain them in such a way as to cause their transformation into totally different urges.

　　　　Since the sensual energies are prone to seeking outside matches for gratification, it is an ongoing task to keep them restrained. The effort to change their nature is a continuous one. Ultimately, one has to evacuate the energies of the psyche by replacing the outward-going forces with energy which naturally remains stabilize in the psyche and satisfied with the quest for something higher.

Some yogis admit that their sober self is boring and uninteresting. Many give up yoga practice. They go away from advanced yogins who are settled in the psyche. Ultimately however, one should realize that subtle and gross sensuality leads to suffering. All sorts of excitement in the subtle and gross material world, leads to a greater dullness than that which is experienced in the sober self. Thus eventually a living being, if he or she is able, must learn to be satisfied with sober energy.

The spirit itself does not crave sensuality but when it is unified with the sensation energies of the psychic material nature, it certifies the needs of those sensations. Those needs operate to acquire excitement. To gain this, one has to indulge sensually, even though sensuality turns into sorrow. This is the way of material existence

July 7, 1999

Babaji Mahasaya

He said, "Do the same as yesterday. Notice this. Those desires and requests are based on survival. They will expand when their forms hit the intellect.

"Go down. Swallow them."

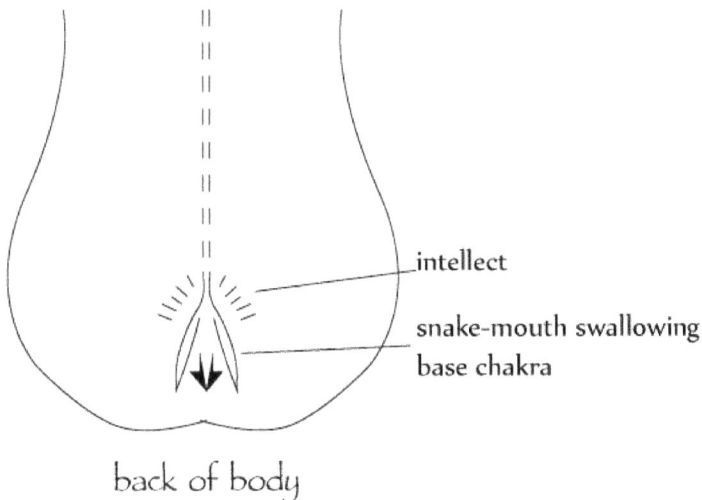

intellect

snake-mouth swallowing base chakra

back of body

The desires and requests of others entered my psyche at the base chakra. Babaji showed a way of eliminating these motivations before they would target my intellect in the subtle head. If they hit the intellect, they expand into thoughts and pictures. Once visualized, one may be compelled to fulfill the urges. Even if one successfully evades the compulsions, that involves time that might otherwise be more constructively used for yoga practice and fruitful meditation or divine association.

Babaji's procedure makes the intellect take the form of a serpent. One takes it down the spine, and swallows the minute desires which float up the spine like tiny bubbles.

July 7, 1999

Shiva

He said, "Even with me, these Chandikas are resistant to advice. They rate me as a mahayogin, a mere mystic."

Remark:

As one advances, one will pass through certain astral realms even while the gross body still lives. This is one of the key points of technique yoga. The student can assess progress while his physical body lives. He does not have to wait until death to rate success. At the time of making this notation in 1999, I passed through the zone of Goddess Chandika. I was just about to pass through that place, when Shiva told of their estimation of Him. This is a realm where only females reside.

Progression through their zone is also an important aspect of developing celibate practice. Once the ascetic seals off celibacy, he easily transits across their territory.

Until then, no matter who he is, he will have to encounter them. If his celibacy is incomplete, he will not be allowed transit. He will remain in lower worlds, regardless of whether he has a physical form or not.

July 8, 1999

Shiva

He showed some matching points within the subtle body. If they are brought together in meditation these points give each other satisfaction. Their psychic unification calms the psyche and makes it self-satisfied.

anus

nose

July 8, 1999

Shiva

He said, "Kumbhak in-breath retention is the best position from which to observe how subtle energy moves in the lungs and body. During kumbhak since there is no out breathing, and since the psyche has sufficiently stored energy from an intense breath-infusion, the lifeforce can penetrate the nadi subtle passages. Kumbhak cannot be done properly if there is insufficient reserve of energy."

Remark:

Kumbhak is the condition of the subtle body when it has a reserve of fresh subtle energy and when its air pollutions were expelled from it for the most part. During kumbhak in-breath retention one may exhale and hold the breath out of the physical and subtle bodies. Then one should observe how the energy moves in the subtle form.

First one should surcharge the gross and subtle forms with physical and subtle air energy. One should expelled all lingering polluted gas and stale energy from the psyche. Then one should inhale and hold the locks. That is kumbhak in-breath retention. It relies on a complete expulsion of stale energy with complete surcharged fresh subtle energy all over the body.

Shiva

He said, "Take up resentments and complaints as raw energy, not as personalized force."

Remark:

This is a procedural attitude for dealing with resentments and complaints. At the time I tried to reduce incidences of resentment but they still came.

July 9, 1999

Shiva

He said, "Use the small samadhi. Try double beam focus and single focus. The small samadhis are the natural way to develop into larger spans of time for samadhi."

Remark:

To put this into practice, I had to observe the way the mind focuses externally. Even though the mind focuses one may hardly notice how it achieves this. In yoga, one should stop and observe operations in the psyche. We are so caught up consuming this world that we do not notice the operations in the psyche.

Recently in the year 2000, Yogesh taught me how to observe how the intellect focuses within itself and within the slightly wider region of the mind. This is usually ignored by a human being. Humans are naturally absorbed in consuming the world. They have no time to observe how their mental and emotional mechanisms operate.

Another aspect taught to me by Shiva is that one should do these practices without thinking of any result to be derived. Even though there will be results, and even though one acts to gain the result of spiritual advancement and self-realization in association with divine beings, still, if one does not forget the result desired, one will make very little progress. An active memory of the results desired, keeps one from realizing the very objective. Frequently, one desires an incorrect result because of unavoidable misconceptions. Thus if one adheres to the way of technique yoga, which is to practice and not to be alarmed about results, one will become successful and will realize the rewards of the process.

Shiva told me that one should be like an embryo. For the most part, the embryo remains still, with full absorption on drawing nutrients from the mother's form. Merely by that the infant develops. If one practices with full absorption, on just being in the association of great yogins, one will of necessity, develop spiritually.

Agastya

He said, "Learn how to focus outside. Then employ that inside. Study the embryo's development. How do their eyes develop? How is vision for this dimension developed?

Remark:

This concerns pranavision. To develop that, one has to curtail the external vision which flows down the optic nerves. These nerves are in the gross and subtle bodies. When this external vision is curtailed, one can turn the seeing impulse within and develop pranavision, and other types of psychic and spiritual ways of perception.

Babaji Mahasaya

He guided me to experience some local intense transcendence areas.

These are of short duration. It may extend throughout the whole psyche or be limited to a tiny part of it.

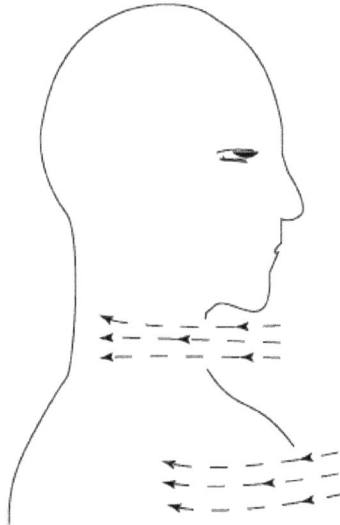

Shiva

He gave this technique.

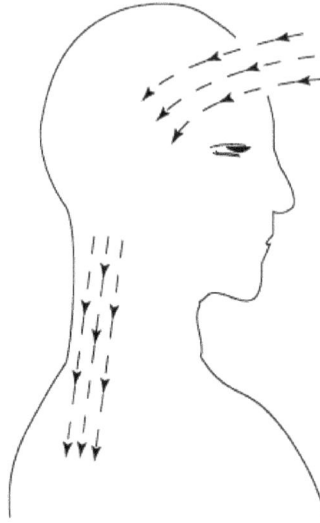

In relation to the above technique there is a realization that a light diet contributes to kundalini sensitivity. A heavy diet with much food and irregular eating, especially eating in the later afternoon and at night, contributes to desensitization of the kundalini energy. It makes the kundalini energy dull. Agastya made a comment explaining that commerce, business and the related activities are part of passion. He said that I should do the least of it and keep those dealings prompt and exact.

He instructed that in terms of the business world and my income, I should do only what is necessary and nothing else. Otherwise, my spiritual life will be adversely affected.

July 12, 1999

Babaji Mahasaya

He said, "Stay away. Keep a safe distance. Immediately continue your inner work."

Remark:

This was advice from Babaji on how to deal with thought energy which comes from others, especially from persons, whom I may be employed by. For Shiva, Babaji supervises a group of kriya yogins. These technique yogins are called kriyabans. Once a person embarks on the process of kriya yoga, he gains the protection of Babaji or one of the other masters of the process. However, rarely, can a student cannot suddenly drop cultural activities. He is advised on how to do so gradually.

Particularly, if one is a parent to minor children, he is given advice on how to practice and still maintain family responsibilities. The idea is that after a time, one will be detached from the responsibly, but in the meantime, one should maintain it.

Eventually when the yogi curtails family involvement, it is expected that his inner need for it will decrease to nil. On some other paths, a person quits his parental status and becomes a sannyasi or a vanaprasthi suddenly. In technique yoga, one has to work on the inner nature to be sure that whatever one shows externally is a reflection of what one already developed internally.

Here is a diagram of how I steered clear of the thought patterns.

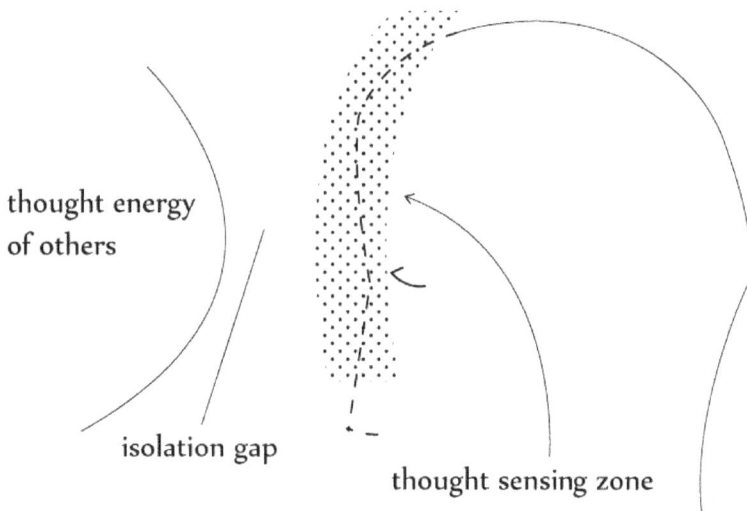

thought energy of others

isolation gap

thought sensing zone

July 12, 1999

Babaji Mahasaya

He said, "Always have a meditation project. The tendency of having a purpose and a directive must be used. It is persistent. If it is not engaged, stray ideas will engage the psyche. Keep an ongoing meditative purpose that the psyche can achieve. You may focus on a new directive from a teacher or the last one given to you."

Remark:

This above is self-explanatory. Babaji, even though rated as a mahayogin, and even though he has many mahayogins disciples, still he does not picture himself as anyone's only guru. His disciples are free to take instructions from other yogis. This is a feature of genuine kriya master.

July 13, 1999

Agastya

He said, "How did they see? How did you see what they perceived?"

Remark:

There were some hereafter people in the astral world, who, using some crystal rays, peered into my testes. I saw them by looking backwards through the same rays they projected. When they looked they saw no semen. Yet, they continued peering because a lady told them that I could beget bodies.

Actually I had no recent karmic connection with these ancestors. There was a connection from the long lost past. Based on the lady's advice, they tried to activate that. The lady was their scout in this world, who located what she considered to be fine young men, to be fathers for them.

When they looked into my testes, they could not believe that there was no semen. They could not understand the effects of kriya yoga practice to remove sexual energy from the pubic area. They continued looking through those crystal rays thinking that they would find the required energies for a rebirth through my body.

In cases like this if semen is found, the ancestors focus on it. By supernatural focus, they inhabit it. The man then feels an urge for sexual intercourse. As soon as a female is available he ejaculates semen into her body. An ancestor comes out nine months later as a crying baby.

July 13, 1999

Shiva

He said, "Each must apply himself separately. No one can do that for another."

Remark:

This is a comment about creating a yoga siddha body. Such a form is created by the practicing yogi through his practice. It is not by blessings, except by blessings for the persistence of proper practice. The places where the yoga siddhas reside in the astral world are created by supernatural persons, who have the power to create such astral zones. However to attain such places one has to accelerate one's individual practice.

Some years ago, I felt I could create a yoga siddha form while using this gross body. During 2001, seeing my situation as it was, I gage that I may not achieve that. Currently (2017), I am hopeful to reach a place in the astral world, where I could continue the practice and then develop the siddha form.

I will avoid assuming another material body. If I can create a yoga siddha form in the astral world, after leaving this body or even prior to that, which is hardly likely, then I would not take another material body in the near future.

On January 8, 2001, concerning my assuming an embryo, Yogeshwarananda questioned me about my preference of country and parent. I told him that I did not desire to take birth in a developed county nor in any country in which video media was prominent. I do not want that my infant body would be subjected to electronic screen culture. As the occupant, one cannot control the senses of an infant form. Thus I would desire that my infant body not be exposed to video media. Otherwise, if it were, it would mean that my yoga practice for that life would be ruined from the very start. By the time, I would begin the practice in earnest, my mind would be filled with the images received impulsively from the media. I would not want to be subjected to computer technology during infancy.

I prefer to take birth in a more primitive less-developed culture where my mind is only subjected to nature's scenes. This is what I discussed with Yogesh. He also asked about taking birth in a modern American or European family which practices yoga. I told him that I did not desire that since the vast majority of modern yoga families, have video media and are greatly addicted to computers and music.

July 14, 1999

Lahiri Mahasaya

He said, "Take the intellect to find where subtle energy is active in the spine.

"In any living body, there will be some activity somewhere. Locate it. If you cannot find it, the activity is subtler than your perception. Keep searching nevertheless. There is also a corresponding area in the brain. For instance:"

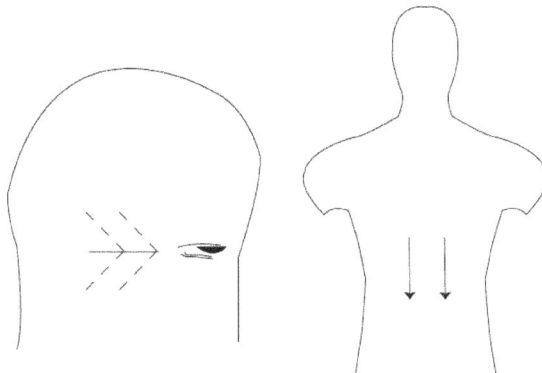

He continued, "Do not focus on the brain, even though it is easier for the intellect to do so. When the intellect meets freshly-charged subtle energy, it merges. It is like air passing through or staying in the spaces of a loosely woven straw mat. That is a type of transcendence. If there are bothersome thoughts some may be put in the line of focus between intellect and subtle energy or behind intellect as it focuses all depending on which is the best way to handle that energy to decrease its negative effects.

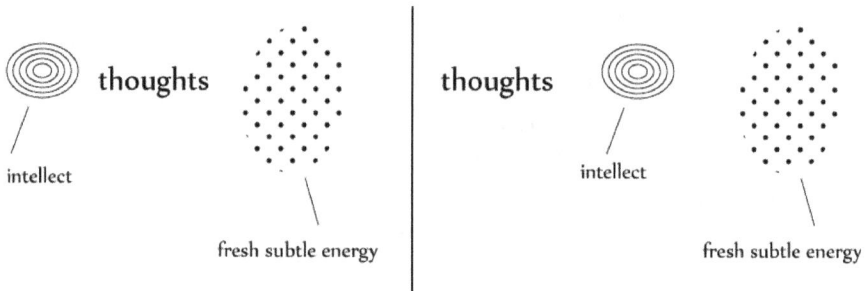

thoughts | thoughts

intellect | intellect

fresh subtle energy | fresh subtle energy

Remark:

Lahiri Mahasaya is one person whom I do not see regularly. He is a mainstay in the kriya yoga lineage. He pioneered certain techniques which were shown to him by Babaji Mahasaya. The succession from Lahiri Mahasaya is still extant. Some of his family members still practice consistently and teach others.

July 16, 1999

Shiva

Ahamkara separation.

Shiva showed me the sense-of-identity (ahamkara) as an object, a little dot, like a speck of dirt, like a brown-colored crystal of sand. The sense of identity is the first reflection of the core-self in psychic material nature. The individual soul, when it first becomes aware of itself in the subtle material energy, reflects in that energy as a dot with rays of power emanating from it.

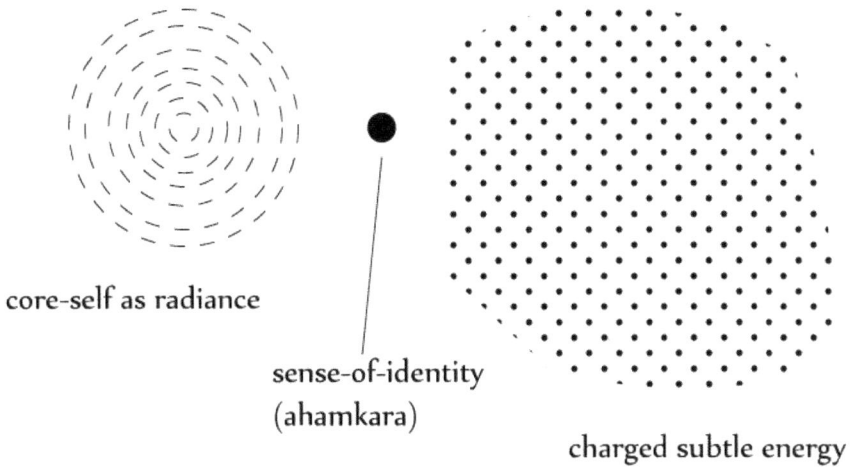

core-self as radiance

sense-of-identity
(ahamkara)

charged subtle energy

July 16, 1999

Babaji Mahasaya

Neck samadhi

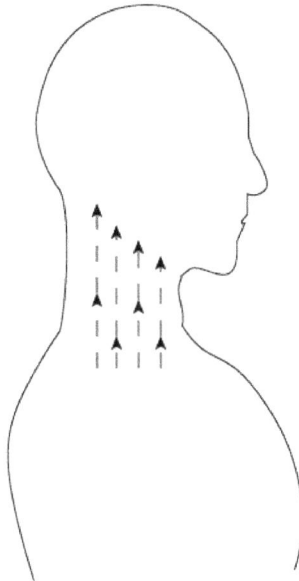

Remark:

This felt like a flow of energy gushing through the neck.

It flowed to the intellect organ in the head. The energy lit up the intellect. In the advanced stage, the intellect stays lit continuously. In the lower stage, it is lit some of the time only. Otherwise, it remains dull like a low glow bulb which does not receive sufficient voltage.

July 16, 1999

Babaji Mahasaya

Localized transcendental energy saturation in the forehead.

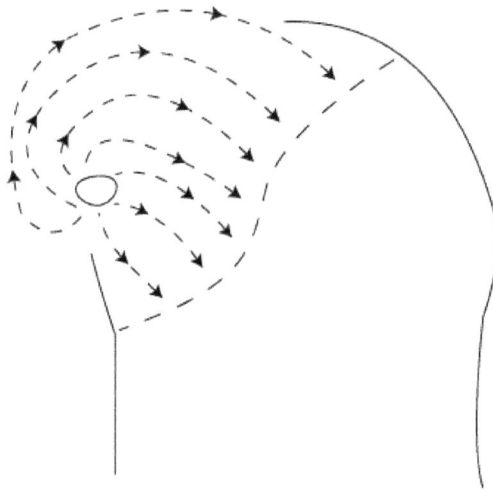

When doing breath-infusion one must be constantly on the alert for localized bliss energy concentrations. When these occur, one should suspend breathing to facilitate the focus of these small concentrations of energy. This habit will develop into longer-duration and larger spreads of such energy.

One should not feel that one will enter long periods of transcendence for hours, days or months. That may happen later after many years of practice. Initially, one should appreciate the small sessions or compressions of high energy. Failure to appreciate this, leads to lack of motivation to continue doing breath-infusion, concentration, meditation and related disciplines.

As a poor man must save pennies and should not waste his mental energy fantasizing about saving millions, so a beginner must become absorbed in the small but cumulative progressions.

July 16, 1999

Shiva

On this day he showed me the sense-of-identity which is the reflected presence of a spirit. This reflection adopts designations in the subtle material energy. Through it the spirit is encouraged to make a claim in the causal energies. As citizens are permitted to stake claims on land, so at a certain phase of this creation, the spirits spontaneously make claims for sensation energies. They do this with the sense-of-identity. Shiva showed this identity located to the right side of the core-self. Previously, Yogeshwarananda shown the intellect organ in the subtle head. During the year 2000, he showed me the sense-of-identity as a tiny dot like a speck of dirt.

July 16, 1999

Shiva

Sex energy moving into the pubic area from the thighs.

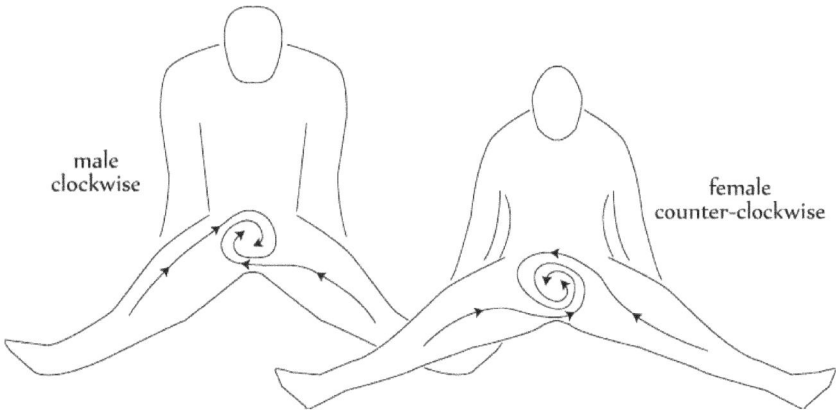

male
clockwise

female
counter-clockwise

July 12, 1999

Combined chakras

The following diagram is the subtle body as seen in the astral world. It is of the sushumna nadi passage and brow chakra. There is also another configuration of the sushumna nadi passage and the lower part of the back of the brain. This looks greenish, because of the composite purity and impurity.

Yogeshwarananda informed me that in the advanced stages, this looks crystal-clear, with no coloration. That is with full purity.

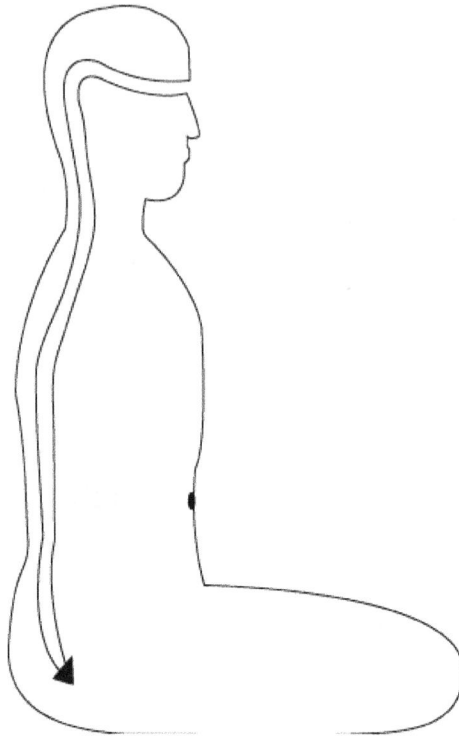

July 18, 1999

Shiva

Losing concept of the chakras

In this technique one sees all the chakras as one energy. This is visual but it can be seen by pranavision. In reality, the chakras in the spine are expanded from subtle fiery air energy. Yogeshwarananda feels that kundalini energy is not that important. In his view it is not even part of the essential subtle body. His idea is that it is part of the gross system of expansion of subtle force. To his view, kundalini is not part of the essential subtle form, which he says consists of mind and intellect. He says that the causal body consists of chitta sensation-producing energy and the sense-of-identity. However for those who are not advanced, the kundalini is considered a part of the subtle body. On their level of consciousness it is.

July 19, 1999

Sushumna nadi disc.

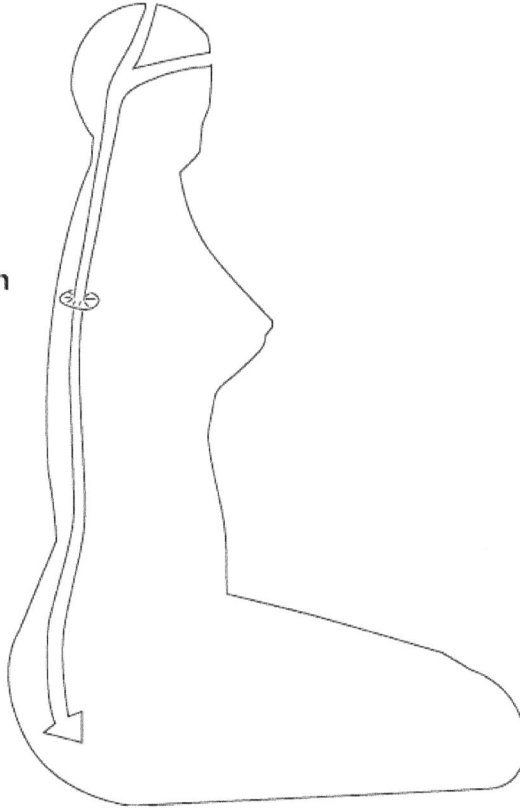

disc moves
up and down
sushumna
passage

July 19, 1999

Shiva

He instructed, "Face Krishna and Balarama in a northwest direction."

Remark:

This is a meditation for finding Krishna and Balarama. However, the directions given may not be valid from another place or at another time.

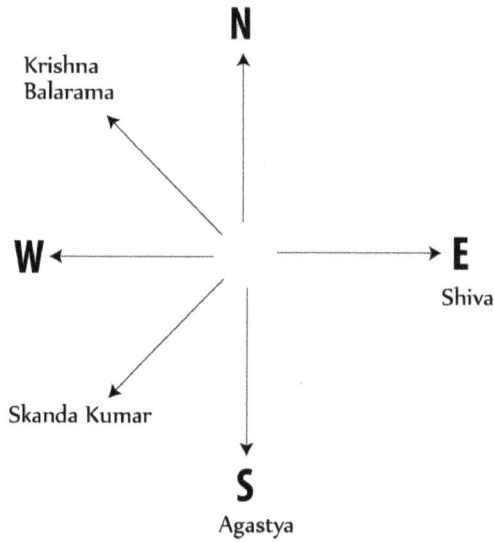

Usually Shiva is found in the north but here he was located east. Within the human body there are also stations for the deities. These can be realized if the yogi's body is purified. When the material form is polluted, lower deities take stations within it.

On this day, Shiva gave techniques which accelerate purity

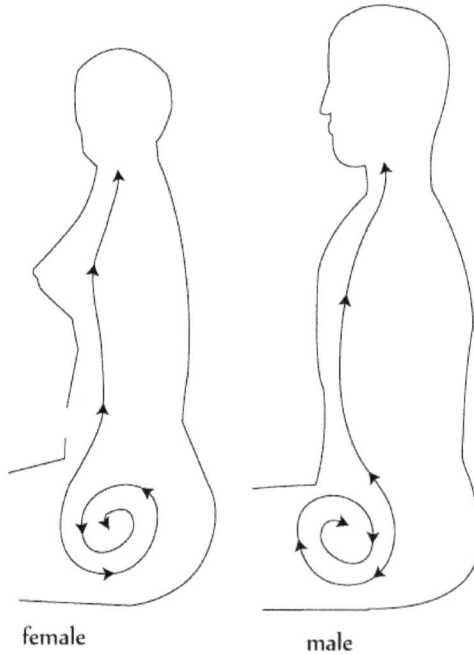

female   male

July 19, 1999

Shiva

He said, "Eating causes the excess. Keep the body lean. Train it to be satisfied with just enough."

Remark:

Eating causes the buildup of passionate energy. As it is in this creation, passionate energy serves for expansion. Socially speaking that means that sexual intercourse becomes an absolute necessity. By such a law of providence, one who overeats will have to engage in sexual affairs sooner or later, in this life or the next, in proportion to how much he over-ate.

To utilize or work off this energy, one has to perform karma yoga in socio-political affairs, either on a large scale as a servant of a government or on a small scale as a servant of a set of departed ancestors who promote a family clan. Of course that is not yoga, but it must be done if one over eats.

July 20, 1999

Shivananda

Small bliss-energy compression in the neck.

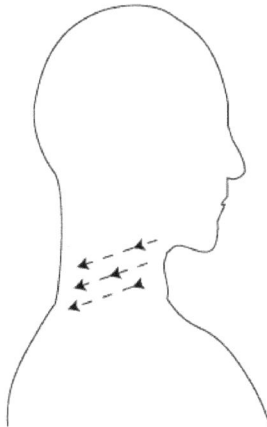

July 12, 1999

Ganesh

This technique was shown by Ganesh. Interestingly usually he specializes in the musical and martial arts. It is said in the Devi Purana and also in the

Shiva Purana that initially Ganesh fought courageously with Shiva. He has no prior training but he gave Shiva a challenge. When Durga Devi and her expansions would have a religious functions, which were powerful ritual acts, Ganesh would be like a humble son to any of them. He would play devotional music and serve appropriately. He was expert in all such matters without formal training. On the other hand, Skanda Kumar, another son of Shiva was adept in yogic renunciation, isolation, simplicity and indifference to women, from the very beginning. However, Ganesh too, is a mahayogin.

Agastya explained that even though Ganesh is hardly seen practicing he knows the important yoga techniques. In the one Ganesh gave me, the subtle energy which is stirred up and generated by breath-infusion rapid breathing, is pushed down the right side mostly, down to the base chakra. One uses the slow-draw breath from the standing position. After fully compressing the subtle energy into the body, one inhales and pushes down the subtle energy by exerting a downward lock on the lower abdomen and inner lower back.

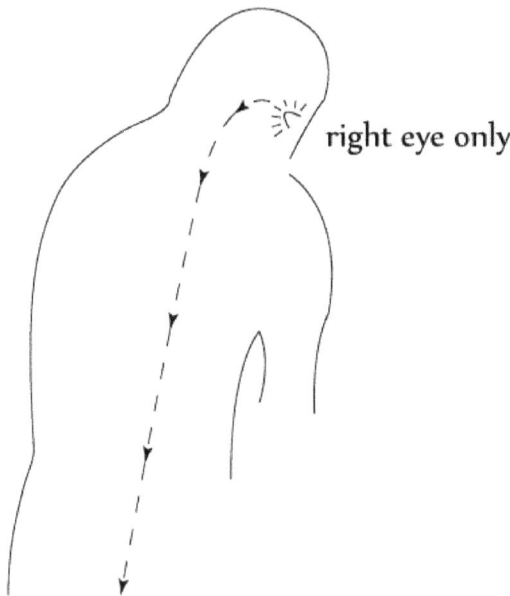

right eye only

July 22, 1999

Agastya

A throat pull-down technique.

These techniques which pertain to specific areas of the body are necessary in the course of purification. One cannot at first service the whole body. To an impure yogin, a beginner, the whole body is too much to purify and curb in one effort. One has to take a part of the body, work on it, as advised by senior yogis, and then take another part, until one redesigns the entire psyche. Even in the process of pratyahar sensual restraint and withdrawal from attractive objects, one has to work with one sense or one part of a sense, and gradually bring the psyche under control. Those who want rapid success are unrealistic. They waste time, trying to curb the whole psyche in one sweep.

Some beginners look for a guru who can give them a once-and-for-all instant control over the psyche. They go from one teacher to another, trying this, trying that, in the quest for instant success. Most of this endeavor is a sheer waste of time. One cannot reform the psyche instantly. It must be done bit by bit over a period of time.

Here is the throat pull-down procedure.

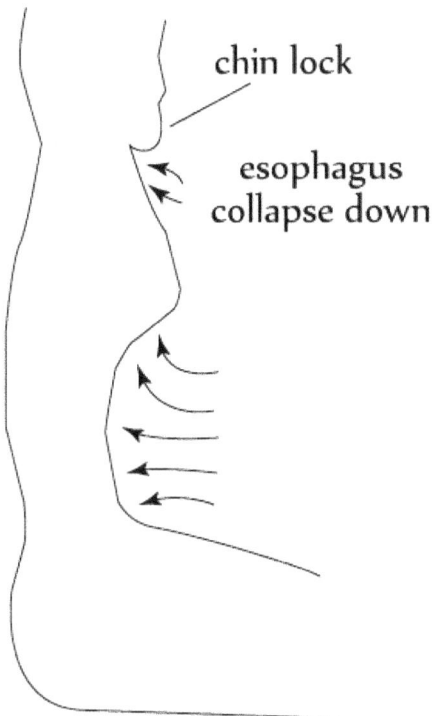

chin lock

esophagus
collapse down

Early in the morning, one should do an intense breath-infusion before doing this technique. Stomach and throat related techniques do not work efficiently if one has not curbed the diet by eating early in the day and not eating in the afternoon or at night. In this technique, the esophagus is pulled down towards the abdomen. The abdomen is pulled up and back into the body as indicated.

Agastya

He said, "Hanuman is here. See him as desired."

Remark:

Hanuman, that mahayogin, gave a sex-releasing technique, one which throws out of the body any sexually-charged sensations which might force the yogi to desire sexual involvement. Hanuman said that the bottom sensations create the sex urge. If these are thrown out, the sexual tendency is curtailed. To take help from certain deities, I did this technique in the various directions shown below.

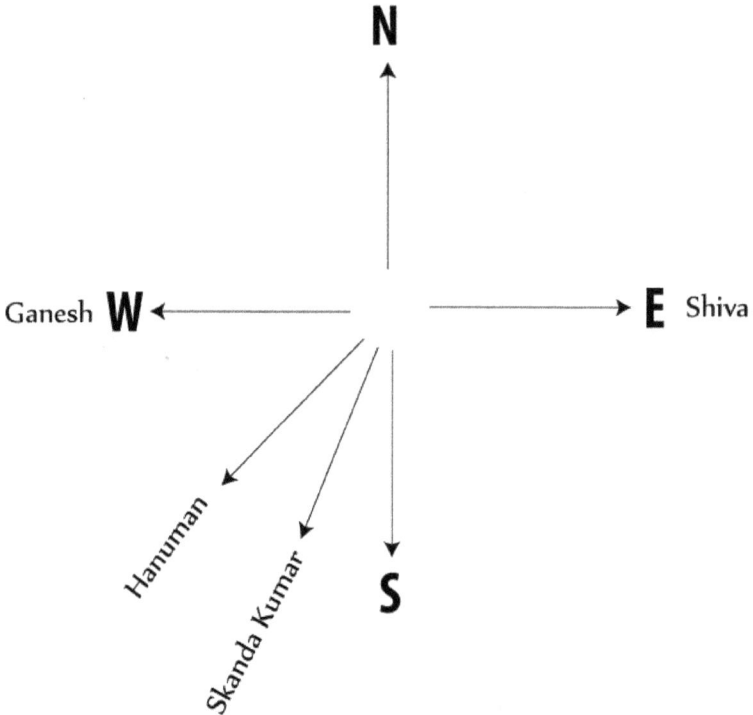

Agastya told me that Hanuman, a favorite deity of millions of Hindus, studied pranayama from him in the Pampa forest, the place where Rama met Hanuman nearby in Kishkindhya forest. Hanuman mastered the removal of passion from his body, even when it was in a youthful condition. Usually yogis are unable to achieve that during the youthful days. Valmiki Yogiraj, also studied from the disciples of Agastya. He too is a master of breath-infusion. Patanjali, though he hails from modern times, is a mahayogin. By a careful study of his Yoga Sutras, and by careful practice one can form the correct estimate of a yogi.

Hanuman gave a standard meditation for arousing kundalini. However, unless one's body is sufficiently energized by breath-infusion, one cannot raise kundalini. Simply by imagining, one cannot do so because kundalini is unresponsive to conceptualization and willpower. When the subtle body is surcharged with fresh subtle energy by breath-infusion, it becomes responsive to the yogi's will power. He can then track sensations accurately.

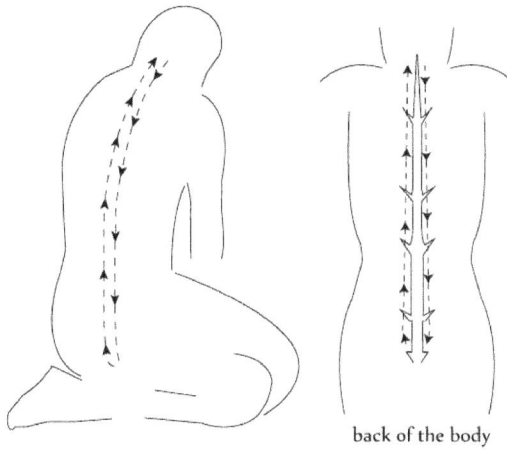

back of the body

July 23, 1999

Hanuman

He said, "It cannot be achieved without flushing the polluted subtle energy. The sex eyes, the color-seeking vision, comes from that energy. Its quality determines the type of activities. Desire, righteous aspirations and moral acts do not remove the polluted sensations."

Remark:

He gave a technique to eliminate the sex and color seeking vision. In this meditation, one finds the knob points and compresses those into the eyes. Then one reverses this action by compressing the eyes into the knob points. I can report that I compressed this vision somewhat. It is not as dominant as it was previously.

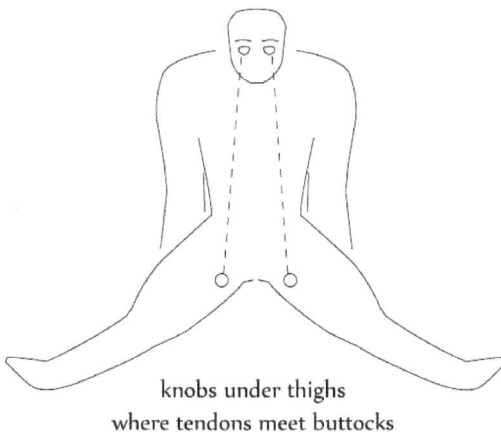

knobs under thighs
where tendons meet buttocks

The sex vision is part of the optic power which instinctively seeks out sexual indulgence. Modern people are mostly expanding and encouraging this power. Video media aids in the exploitation of this power. However for success in celibacy the sex vision will have to be decreased to nil.

A person who embarks on the celibate course may not understand exactly what that process entails. As soon as this ignorance is removed he sees what celibacy involves and what it will deprive him of.

The color seeking vision is the one through which one pursues bright objects outside the psyche in the gross and subtle worlds. This vision is slightly different to the sex-seeking vision but they are related. They usually expand together. The modern civilization has made great advances under the direction of the color seeking vision. Thus we have television, internet and other means of viewing.

Some religious teachers branded kriya yoga as being impersonal. Their idea is that the colors are positive if they are used in the service of God. They present the deity of God, particularly a colorfully designed painted or dressed sculpture or painting, as the proper focus of the color vision.

Some teachers believe that if we focus on such color in such forms, then because the forms are sanctified and because these forms are designed as the transcendent deity, as they advocate and believe, our color vision will be purified. But for all that is and all that it is promised to be, it is not kriya yoga. This yoga is concerned more with purification of the personal energies, as defined in Bhagavad Gita.

तत्रैकाग्रं मनः कृत्वा
यतचित्तेन्द्रियक्रियः ।
उपविश्यासने युञ्ज्याद्
योगमात्मविशुद्धये ॥ ६.१२ ॥

tatraikāgraṁ manaḥ kṛtvā
yatacittendriyakriyaḥ
upaviśyāsane yuñjyād
yogamātmaviśuddhaye (6.12)

tatraikāgraṁ = tatra — there + ekāgram — single-focused; manaḥ — mind; kṛtvā — having made; yatacittendriyakriyaḥ = yata - controlled + citta — thought + indriyakriyaḥ — sense energy; upaviśyāsane = upaviśya — seating himself + āsane — in a posture; yuñjād = yuñjāt — should practice; yogamātmaviśuddhaye = yogam — to yoga discipline + ātma — self + viśuddhaye — to purification

...being there, seated in a posture, having the mind focused, the person who controls his thinking and sensual energy, should practice the yoga discipline for self-purification. (6.12)

July 23, 1999

Hanuman

He said, "Be sure you regulate the breath, even in exercises when there is no breath-infusion. An example is, the head stand. Carefully regulate breath to facilitate concentration. Steady the body."

Remark:

On this day I was inspired in this exercise and the related muscular movements.

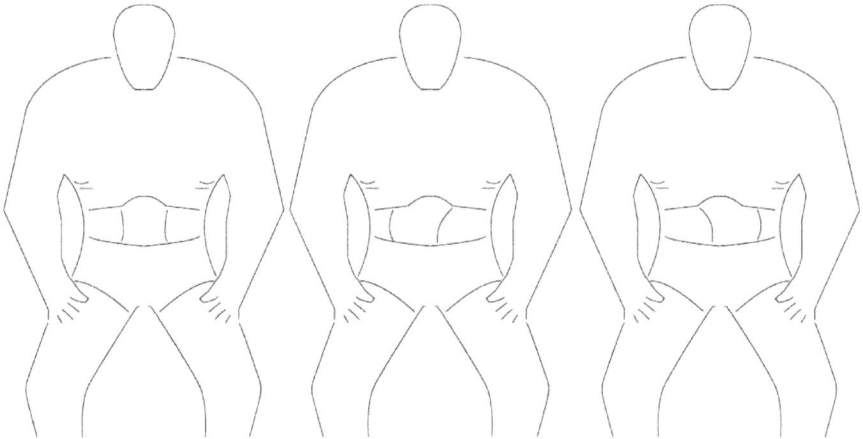

Part 7

Hanuman

He said, "Do not be seen where you were yesterday. Be progressive always."

Remark:

This is standard advice. The process is progressive. A yogi should not be lazy. Even if there are impediments, the one thing on a yogi's mind, is the practice. It is important that he not tell most people what he is about in terms of the techniques. Some people who know that he is a mystic, may plan to use him to work supernatural wonders in their lives.

A yogi sometimes moves from one village, town or country to another, just to get away from people who pester for the use of mystic skills. The yogi moves on since if he becomes absorbed in social affairs, his progress decreases. The rule is that a yogi should be isolated. Sometimes however an isolated yogi, is observed by others. They visit him with the idea of providing basic amenities. They influence him and his practice is ruined. As such it might be better for a yogi to be in the public and to be isolated only in the sense of not being known as an ascetic. This is a technique which is promoted by Babaji Mahasaya. He is said to have trained many great yogins in how to live in public and not be known as ascetics or mystics.

There are many people who after becoming attached to a yogi, and being fascinated with ideas of what yoga practice can do, begin to think of how they could benefit a yogi by putting him in an opulent setting where he will not have to worry about money. All such people are complete idiots. It is best, therefore, to avoid such persons. If at all possible one should be so sensitive to protect the practice that if one discovers such a person one should never let him know that one is a yogi.

There are some others who are the most dangerous persons for obstructing yoga. They feel that perhaps a yogi might save many souls if he were known or if the masses were to learn the easier parts of yoga from him. Such people are completely out of their minds. If a yogi becomes known to such people his progress is finished. Thus if a yogi senses such people, he should never let them know of the practice. He should always present himself to human society as a dunk-head, a mere nobody, who is only useful in menial tasks but he should not allow people to use him nevertheless. Thus he should be known as a person who avoids striving for material things, and who somehow is not smart enough to understand the value of ambitions and their resultant accomplishments. A person who becomes known as a dunk-head, a non-ambitious nobody, and who simultaneously practices, makes rapid progress.

I knew a man who lived on the island of Trinidad. Somehow by a stroke of providence, I had, during the year of 1974, a few students in Trinidad. They were mostly teenaged boys but a few women who were of the age of my mother, also become interested in breath-infusion. I used to teach them rapid breathing with postures. One day, I saw a man sitting on a street in Port of Spain, the capital city. I immediately understood that he was an advanced soul but I knew he was hiding from human society, while secretly making spiritual progress.

I had a discussion with him. His body was caked with dirt because he had not taken a bath for at least two or more years. He had a cloth on his body which was dirt ridden. Understanding that he was hiding out from human hassles, I did not challenge him. I asked him a few questions and from that I could gage where he was in yoga in his past life and where he was at present. I could gage the rate of his progression. In order to ward off social pressures and to advance secretly he gave up prestige. He was very educated but he left all that for the sake of advancing spiritually.

All the same, for myself, fool that I am, I became a little known here and there. Subsequently, I run from place to place, trying to escape the people who know that I am a yogin. On the other hand, I have a few people who see me as a somebody. Some pester me for help in yoga, meditation and religion. The problem is that some hardly understand a word of what I say.

Hanuman gave this technique on this day.

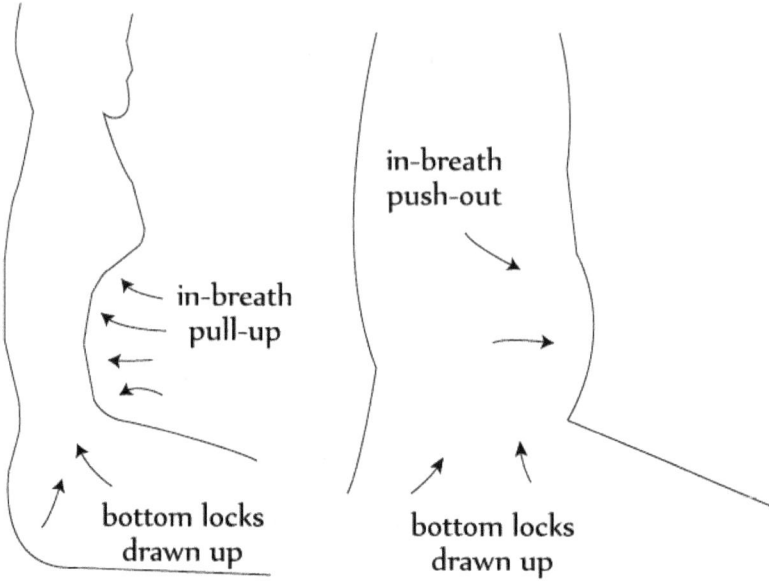

in-breath
pull-up

in-breath
push-out

bottom locks
drawn up

bottom locks
drawn up

This is a stomach pull-in with air out of the lungs. This can be done properly if negative food habits are curbed. This is done by squeezing the same area with breath in the body. It is important that food be curbed. I have told many about this but few heed it. I must stress that those who eat late in the afternoon or at night are phonies. It may be that you will get the food habit under control in the future. That is approved. In the meantime however, try to understand that your problem is the wrong psychic association.

Someone wants to do kriya yoga but he eats late at night as a routine. He thinks that what I said about late eating is not important; that it can be avoided in his case. He is incorrect. I am correct. I say emphatically that he will not be successful because of the laws of nature which govern the lifeforce. There is a verse: in the Bhagavad Gita.

अपरे नियताहाराः
प्राणान्प्राणेषु जुह्वति ।
सर्वेऽप्येते यज्ञविदो
यज्ञक्षपितकल्मषाः ॥ ४.३० ॥

apare niyatāhārāḥ
prāṇānprāṇeṣu juhvati
sarve'pyete yajñavido
yajñakṣapitakalmaṣāḥ (4.30)

apare — others; niyatāhārāḥ — persons restrained in diet; prāṇān — fresh air; prāṇeṣu — into the previous inhalations; juhvati — impel; sarve — all; 'pyete (apyete) = apy (api) — also + ete — these; yajñavido = yajñavidaḥ — those who know the value of an act of sacrifice; yajñakṣapitakalmaṣāḥ = yajña — austerity and religious ceremony + kṣapita — destroyed, removed + kalmaṣāḥ — impurities

Others who were restrained in diet, impel fresh air into the previously inhaled air. All these ascetics whose impurities were removed by austerity and religious ceremony understand the value of an act of sacrifice. (4.30)

Try to let Krishna explain directly in a vision, or through inspiration precisely what He taught in this verse.

When doing breath-infusion one should pay close attention to how the energies move in the psyche. Understand that what is usually called the self is not the self. It is a composite of various energies, subtle organs and the core-self. The English word for the composite is psyche. In breath-infusion, one should be attentive to the energies in the psyche. When one does intense breath-infusion and then stops breathing on an exhale. That is called rechak.

Rechak is not a magic Sanskrit world. It is simply holding the body in a posture with no air in the lung. Of course if there is no air held in the lung, the lifeforce from within the body, will be putting air in the lung cells because that is the way it operates, but this air will be polluted energy or carbon dioxide, which is to be breathe out of the body. However immediately after an intense rapid breathing, there will be such a charge of oxygen (prana) in the body, that the lifeforce will be busy distributing that extra charge. That distribution should be tracked. By tracking it, one gets an idea of where the nadis are located.

When after intense breath-infusion, one stops with an inhale, with fresh air drawn into the lung that is called kumbhak. That means that you hold the body in a posture after fresh air is drawn into the body. If the body is supercharged with oxygen, the last pull of oxygen into the lungs will not be distributed rapidly. The lifeforce will be busy putting away the already stored charge. Thus one will observe that the lifeforce is slow to absorb the last draw of air which entered the lung. It will be hastily distributing the excess charge which is already in the blood stream and in the subtle nadi channels. Here are two other techniques from Hanuman.

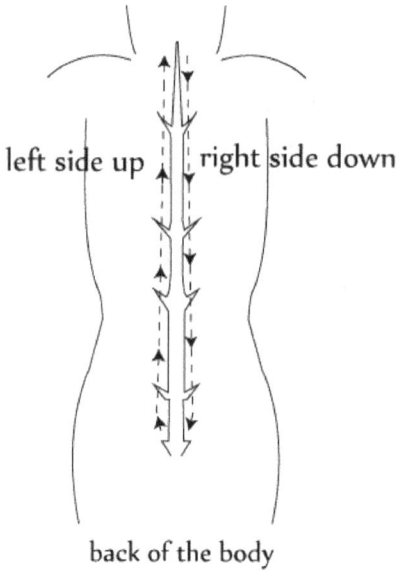

left side up ¦ right side down

back of the body

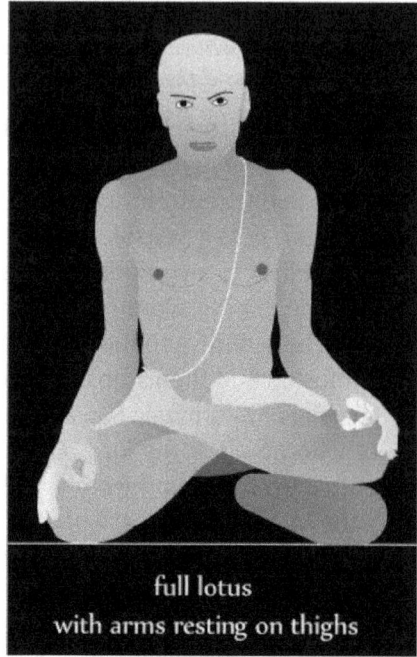

full lotus
with arms resting on thighs

July 26, 1999

Hanuman

He stressed the overstretching of certain parts of the body to find various tendons which are tensed and which need to be relaxed. This overstretching is done slowly and with great care not to harm the tendons. Most of this is done with breath-infusion (rapid breathing).

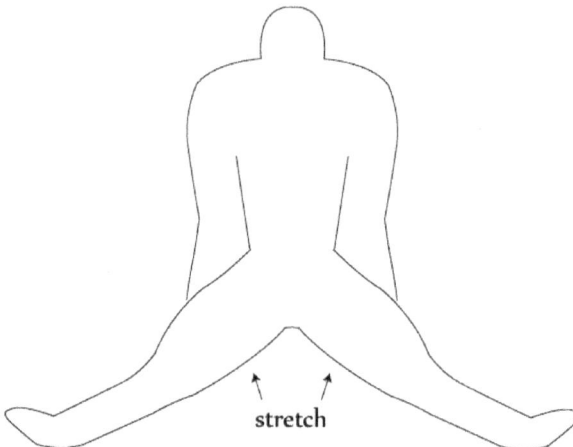

stretch

While doing breath-infusion, one may relax the neck or slacken it backwards if that increases the rate of air compression into the lungs. However, if one relaxes the neck in any way, one must be sure to track the energy moving in the psyche. One should apply whatever pressure is needed to cause it to rise in a centered way. One should always be attentive to the rise of energy and the movements and expansion or contraction of consciousness. If one finds that the kundalini rose quickly and moves to penetrate the brain, one should immediately apply the neck lock so as to influence the energy to penetrate the brain from a central position, through the spinal column.

July 27, 1999

Satyeshwarananda Giri

This ascetic is a disciple of Babaji. He wrote some books on Babaji of the kriya lineage. I have not seen this Swami physically but I associated with him astrally. Usually he does not reveal techniques unless one accepts initiation from him. That seems to be his attitude. However he does stress that the issue of kriya yoga has to do with self-development, and that other methods used for spirituality are ultimately useless.

Self-purity, self-development and self-realization is the pivot point of any type of asceticism.

On this day, Satyeshwarananda said that I should internalize the criticism since, I need to critique myself. This issue may be explained as follows.

In kriya yoga, on cannot afford to criticize others because the critical energy is very important for progression. Without using it on oneself or investing it in one's development, one cannot reach the culmination of practice.

What happened was this: A lady who has a reputation as a religious person met me in the astral world to discuss religion. I noticed that her abdomen was wrapped in a girdle to confine it to a smaller shape, to hide its actual size. At that point, my intellect took a critical view of the woman. Somehow Satyeshwarananda happened to be in that astral vicinity. He chastised me by saying that I should self-direct the criticism.

As a master of kriya yoga, he has a right to criticize any student or to offer suggestions for improvement. I took his criticism as a kind act.

After that occurred, Hanuman showed me something that Yogeshwarananda spoke of previously. It was the fact that the brilliant shining of the intellect is directly related to the conservation of sexual energy with the practice of breath-infusion. It is not the same if you conserve sexual energy without breath-infusion because stagnant non-passionate sexual energy does not produce celibate energy.

The expression of sexual energy in the natural way of sexual intercourse causes the dulling of the intellect. Hanuman showed my intellect shinning with a golden hue. I took it down to the throat and chest area. He also showed that when a seductive woman was observed by the organ, it became duller and duller.

On the other hand Satyeshwarananda in a rare act of compassion, even though I am not his disciple, gave advice. He said, "Just as you would not open a letter, which you suspect as having information, which if read would ruin your life, do not read the intellect's ideas. The intellect takes energy automatically whenever there is a deliberate or undeliberate interest in its ideas. This taking of energy can be curtailed by detachment or lack of interest in its presentations, done with the motivation of accelerating yoga success. Ultimately, regardless of the guru or gurus, the aim of elementary kriya is internalization."

After this conversation. Hanuman showed a compressed bliss force.

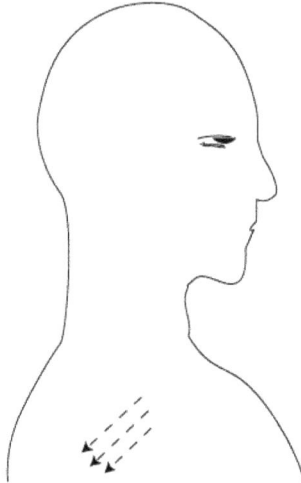

July 28, 1999

Hanuman

He said, "Stay in any location which facilitates practice. After getting sufficient air, you may move to try another, but do not move until you have absorbed as much air as the system will take.

"Watch the breath suspension period carefully. See where the absorption occurs. Perceive the direction in which the spiral moves.

"The intellect is adjusted by change of subtle energy, not by thinking, nor by decision-making. As soon as a higher quality of subtle energy is taken, the mood changes.

"Always use the critical analysis of the intellect to criticize yourself for reform."

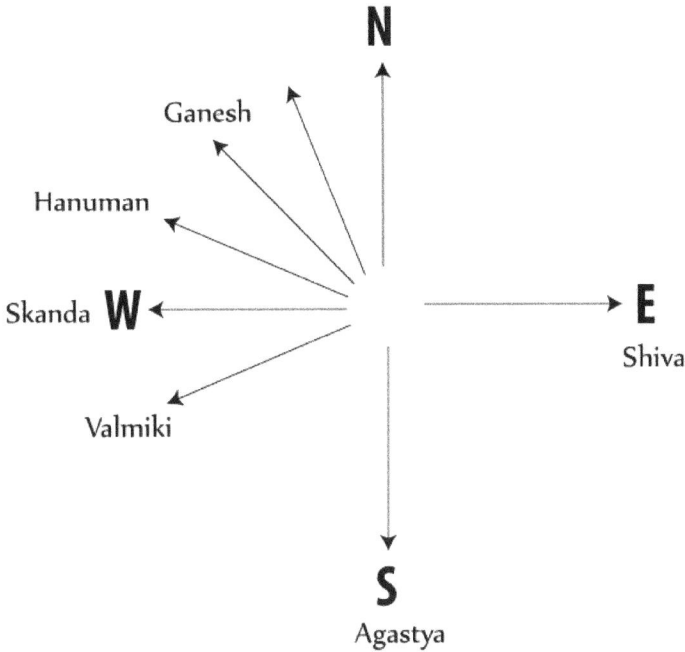

Concerning Valmiki's attitude, Shiva told me this, "Valmiki of Ramayana fame does yoga practice differently. He stays to himself. He is the perfection of isolation.

July 29, 1999

Hanuman

He gave me this pull-down of center-gully technique This Is done standing after doing rapid breath-infusion and down-draw breath.

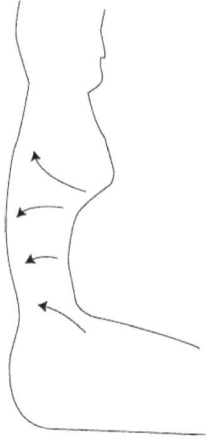

When doing this one realizes that the so-called person is actually a composite of the core-self and the subtle sensations, being mostly sensations. Chastisement or deprivation is put on by the whole energy as a disciplinary act for the good of the individual limited spirit. It is for that matter, a form of loving care in so far as the whole energy can afford to be concerned.

July 29, 1999

Valmiki:

He hailed from the direction indicated in the diagram.

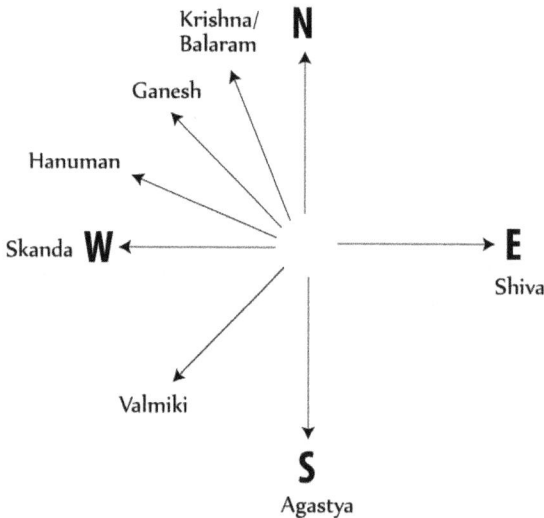

He said, "First use Hanuman's arm posture. Do a subtle check by ignoring obvious currents. Move intellect around from right to left. Go down right. Come up left."

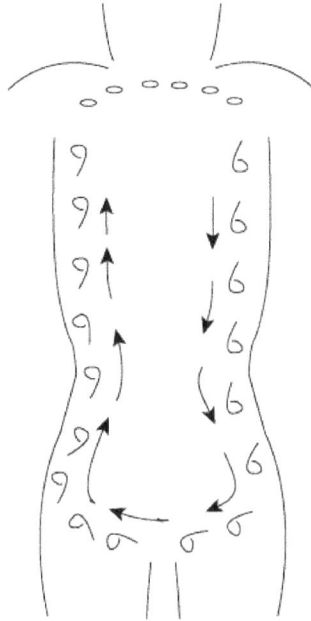

July 31, 1999

Agastya

He said, "Use Hanuman's hand posture. With lotus, pull the subtle energy firmly to compress sushumna into the intellect in the head. Compression should be upwards only.

August 1, 1999

Valmiki

He instructed, "You should see Hanuman. He knows to mix activity and yoga for success."

On this day Hanuman gave this technique.

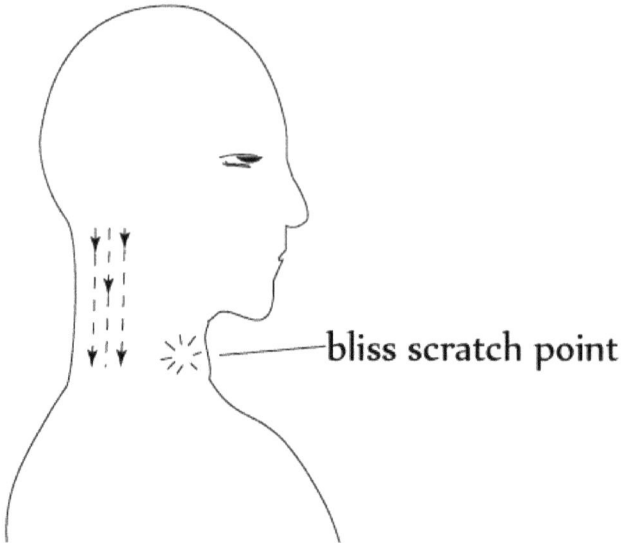

bliss scratch point

August 2, 1999

Valmiki

He stated, "Samadhi cannot be achieved when there is association which causes a series of itches or a numbing of consciousness. Eventually that association should be eliminated."

Remark:

I met a lady and an Indian man. Their association affected my practice negatively. Valmiki Mahamuni Yogiraj advised that I should see Hanuman who is an expert at working in the material world, and still secretly but surely maintaining yoga practice.

August 3, 1999

Agastya

He asked, "What of the quality and mode of different types of sleep?"

Remark:

I observed the difference between morning drowsiness and sleep which comes on in the late afternoon. The late afternoon sleep leads more to a trance state especially if it is done after a session of breath-infusion. The morning drowsiness if there is any, can be warded off or converted positively if breath-infusion is done when it is felt or before it is anticipated.

Hanuman

He said, "That type of association is troublesome for a yogi."

Remark:

This was an association contacted in the astral world. To avoid this, one has to do three things. First one has to maintain two daily sessions of breath-infusion; one early in the morning soon after rising and another, just before resting in the late afternoon or early evening. Secondly one should rest in a well ventilated area. The ventilation must not be by fan or air conditioning, but merely by open windows or doors. Thirdly one should rise early any time after midnight but before sunrise, to do breath-infusion. These are the requirements to avoid bad astral association.

In addition, for efficient breath-infusion there should be no late eating.

On this day, I met a dakini supernatural person. She is the patron deity of sex. In my subtle body, she taught how not to be attached nor expecting, of a final sexual release. This is important. Unless one detaches from the need for a final sexual release, one cannot attain sexual neutrality. Sooner or later flirtations will be concluded in a final release. Thus one should shed attachment to that energy. This is of interest in reference to an incidence which occurred a week ago. I worked for a lady who had a sexual attraction for me. I had not seen the lady for some months. Suddenly I received a phone call from her husband requesting me to do some work at their home. When I got there, the lady took the opportunity to unload her sexual energy in the atmosphere. It was pervasive. Since it was directed to me, I could not avoid it. However due to my progress, when the energy entered my psyche, it first entered into my sexual chakra and then, all by itself it move up in a gush to my throat.

Formerly I applied techniques to move sexual energy up through the body. Now after much practice that movement occurs without the effort, without the application of locks or mystic action. This yoga process is wonderful!

The dakini I saw, advised that if an ascetic must have an astral sexual connection, he should decrease the sensations to make them as mild as possible. He should decrease the excitation. She showed several holes in her sexual pad in a sort of sponge like tissue.

To see this I assumed a miniature subtle form, just like that of the dakini.

Hanuman gave me a small samadhi practice on this day.

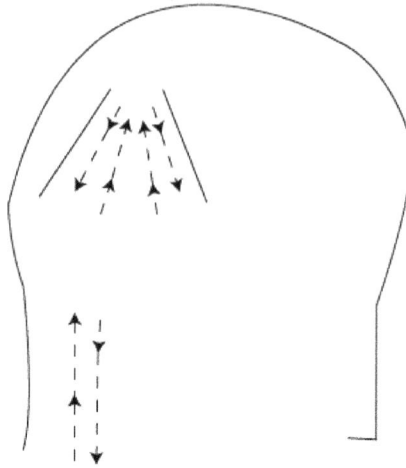

August 4, 1999

Ganesh

He said, "Take a mouse out of a trap. The likelihood is that it will foolishly re-enter the mechanism again. Its nature is to be bound. No one can free it permanently because it is not the trap that captures it. It is its need to be confined.

Remark:

This is a general explanation of human tendencies. By this our history is repeated frequently. It is more than our proneness. It is not just our nature but the external nature and the interactions with it. From a careful study of the self and the interactions we can begin to understand how our lives repeatedly occur with similar patterns.

As the existence is constructed, we find however, that it is easy to observe physical manifestation but we hardly perceive that which is subtle. Without that, we can make no subtle adjustments. Thus our history continues just as if we were incapable of removing the impurities.

If a mouse enters a trap, it is hardly likely that the creature will escape. Sometimes however, it does enter and then leave without getting harmed. If the trap is not triggered upon entry or exit, the mouse develops no fear. Instead the creature becomes confident and returns. It will repeatedly return until it is killed.

In other cases, the mouse enters the trap then the device triggers in such a way, as to harm the mouse a little. The mouse then escapes with some fear.

It thinks, "Someone tried to kill me. By the grace of God, the killer could not harm me. In the future, I will take care in this vicinity. There is no telling if this grace of God would service me again."

Thus the mouse leaves with some satisfaction that life operated in its favor. However such a mouse will return to the trap and be killed. On the other hand, some mice enter a trap and are killed instantly. These leave their physical bodies and scamper away in great trauma and fear in their astral forms, thinking, "What happened? O what happened? Such a frightening noise. I heard it. I scampered away. I feel that something hit me. Someone was hidden there. He tried to kill me, the cruel person."

In that way, the mouse does not immediately realize that it lost its material body. Sometimes a mouse escapes from a trap after being harmed. Then he is told by another mouse, "It is better not to go there. Even if there appears to be an easy meal, still do not go. As it is in this world, we mice are meant to scour the forest for meals. We should not expose ourselves, since the birds may devour us. Other creatures like cats consider us to be palatable. We should be humble to our fate and not take chances. Let us stay in our allotment as nobodies, remaining hidden and living a long life, with the precautions that are necessary."

The escaped mouse however, being daring and not cowardly to destiny, may reply, "Your advice makes sense but it is not practical for me. I do not accept this cowardly destiny. It is unnatural to accept one's position in this creation. I will return to the area, where the trap was set for the likes of me, but I will not be caught. I studied the way it operates. I can outsmart the trapper. It is not likely that he will catch me. I understand that his intentions are to kill me. Nonetheless, I feel that it is my life's purpose to get the food in the trap. It is tasty."

At that point, the advisor mouse said, "You may return but it is a risk. I cannot go. Go alone. If you survive, you will eat. If you are killed, you may reflect on the incidence in your ghost body."

Ganesh made the remark that the mouse's nature is to be bound. Thus the mouse is attracted to conditions which will defeat it. It feels that its nature is to be victorious.

August 4, 1999

Valmiki

He said, "Rising early is a special award given by Shiva. Thank him for it."

On this day, Valmiki Yogiraj, gave me this local area bliss compression experience.

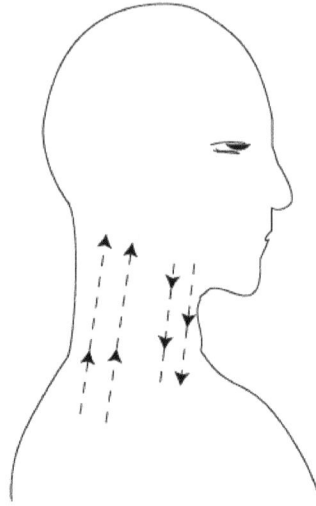

Aug: 5 1999

Skanda Kumara

A sunk-in eyes pratyahar

This is sensual energy withdrawal to bring the optic power under control. The uncontrolled optic focus is a great impediment for a yogi. This controlling procedure is done while doing breath-infusion in a squatting position or with the buttocks sitting between the heels.

I may do an exercise for many years but then later the same posture may be recommended for another purpose. At such time, I do not think the instruction is pointless. In the new stages, the practice of an old technique gives entirely different results.

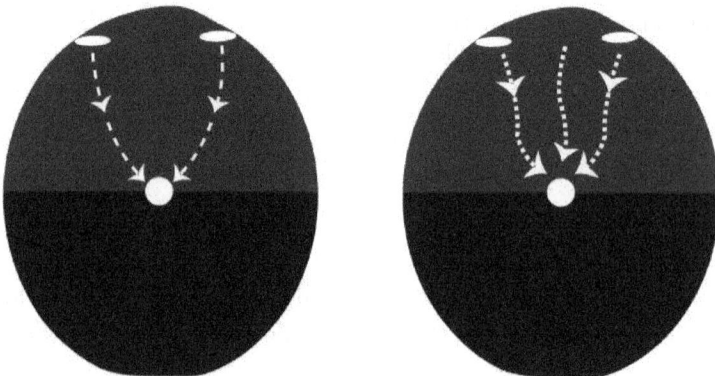

As one endeavors to leave the lower zone, one faces a pulling force from the lower level and one from the higher plane. The pull from the lower one, endeavors to keep one in its association while that from the higher one endeavors to attract in its direction. It is up to the yogi to go to the higher level. He must strengthen himself and continually advance. Otherwise he will remain with the lower influence.

In terms of sexual indulgence, one cannot get out of it without working very hard to complete obligations. Just as a sexual flirtation or affair is consummated and temporarily ended by a sexual intercourse, so by working hard in social connections, one may neutralize sexual attraction. The attraction is an introduction to the discipline and seriousness of responsibility. It is like the golden sheen on the bridle of a rich man's horse. The animal appreciates the brilliance of it but the creature regrets the significance of being harnessed. Without the sweet introduction of sexual contact, an insightful yogi faces the music. He voluntarily serves his time by completing obligations. This falls under karma yoga. Instead of getting sexual contact as prepayment or inducement for obligatory work the yogi just fulfills social obligations without deriving sexual pleasure. He remains satisfied without sexual excitation and romantic overtones.

Skanda Kumar is a leader in this science of fulfilling social obligations without requiring pleasure payments. He explained that the sexual apparatus is heavy and should be removed. For yoga siddhas the genital weight must be removed.

The hint given by Skanda Kumar is that the sexual apparatus has to be removed from the subtle form before the yogi can assume a yoga siddha form. One has to retract the genital part. A hint of this was given by Yogeshwarananda when he said that in some astral locations, there is no sexual intercourse. The organ is only used for urination of subtle fluids.

August 2, 1999

Ganesa

He gave some techniques which involve having the gross body in one posture while putting the subtle body in another. In one such posture the gross body is in lotus while the subtle hands are in the back so that the subtle hand is behind the neck with the fingers together pointing to the left, behind the middle of the back, the gross hands would remain with palms up on the knee in the lotus posture

Physical Body

Subtle Body

A technique

This is done after an intense session of breath-infusion. While squatting, one releases the force from two tubes under the buttock at the end of the thigh. Each tube begins at an eye.

direction of energy
from either eye

side view

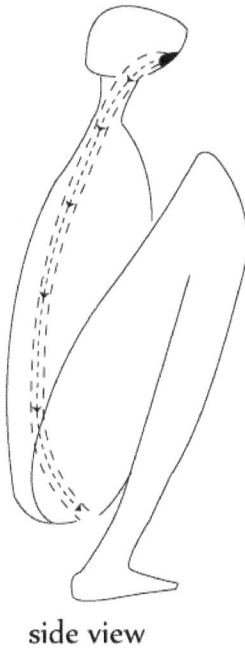

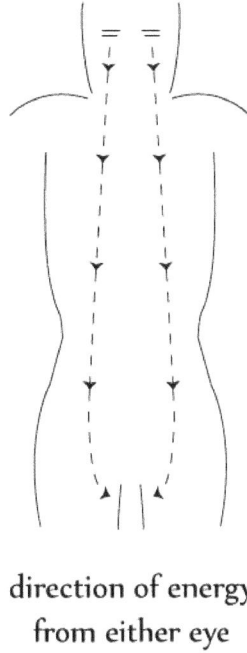

In this procedure, by the grace of the Brahma deity, I had an important realization which I must practice. Many realizations come but that does not mean that they are automatically integrated. With some, one must apply a practice for a time for integration. The realization is this:

Misfortune and dishonesty are conducted by the cosmic force. That is subtle cosmic energy which we realize as sensations in our psyches. The sensation-responsive subtle energy called chitta is the cause of misfortune and dishonesty. That energy does not victimize anyone in particular.

It is not concerned about personal actions or reactions. It discharges energies to keep a balance of power. When a yogi comes to understand this, he becomes freed from resentments. He can become liberated from material existence. Since he is not important to the universal situation, he does not have to remain in the gross or subtle material manifestations for any particular reason. His presence is not required for solving social equations, not even for ones which are formed from his involvement in past lives. Nature will be used by the subtle energy, to solve even those equations which were produced by the liberated entities. It is not a fact that a yogi must be there to solve out reactions which developed due to a part he played previously. Someone else can be made to absorb the reactions. The yogi can abandon the idea of being indispensable. He can focus fully on the effort for liberation.

Brahma

Another technique

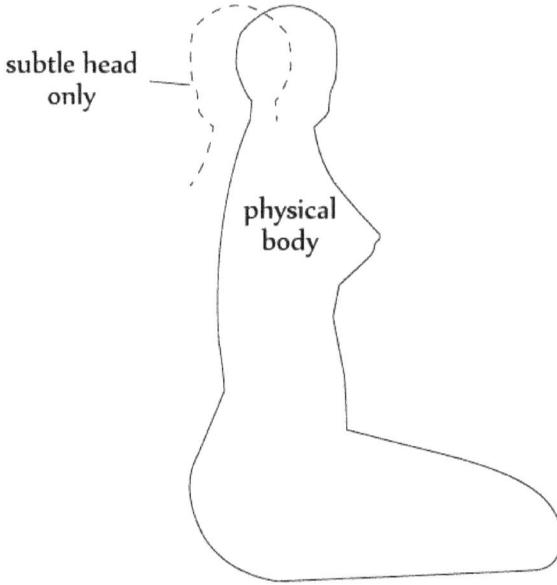

subtle head
only

physical
body

Rama of Rama-Sita-Lakshmana-Hanuman Deities.

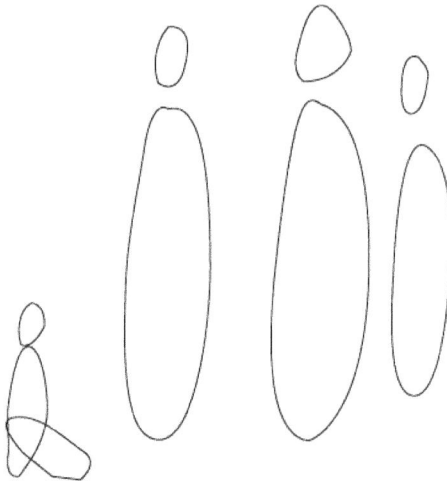

Hanuman, Lakshman, Rama, Sita

Sri Rama said, "Yoga practice should not be displayed. Hanuman is the example of a great yogin. He is accomplished with the siddhi perfectional powers but hardly anyone knows he practices yoga."

Hanuman said, "So long as you are aware of the problems of others, you will never be a great yogi. The ideal devotee is he who is one-pointedly concentrated on the assignments of his yoga-guru."

Remark:

Hanuman is both a yogi and a devotee. Some are not aware of his yogic accomplishments. In him we see a harmony of yoga and devotion. It appears that some persons become atheistic as soon as they assume yoga practice, and for that reason yoga is suspect as a practice which leads to a disbelief in a Person God. Many devotees shun yoga and yogis.

Once I was sent away from a Vaishnava society because I was seen meditating. A prominent disciple of the founder of the society chastised me, He emphatically said, "You cannot meditate here. Our guru prohibited it. It is impersonal. Go away. It is not devotional."

Thus meditation and yoga are considered to be contrary to devotion but in Hanuman, these were in a harmony.

August 9, 1999

Shiva

He said, "A leakage occurs when after a session of exercises, the mind becomes hypnotized by communication with non-yogis. During sessions cease non-yogic contact."

Remark:

This was explained during the year 2000 by Yogeshwarananda. He gave some mystic techniques for banishing non-yogic communication. It can be done but one must build mystic strength to refuse the association by becoming disinterested in just about everything and everyone in the material world. That takes tremendous sincerity of purpose and continuous psychic association with ascetics who are advanced.

August 9, 1999

Valmiki

Compression technique:

This is done in the lotus posture, after the body is surcharged with fresh subtle energy. In this usage, body means the physical and subtle forms. All subtle energy in the psyche is compressed into the sushumna canal. This is not imagination. This is a mystic act that actually occurs, where by mystic and subtle pressure and by yogic locks in the physical and subtle bodies, the aroused sensations are forced into the sushumna.

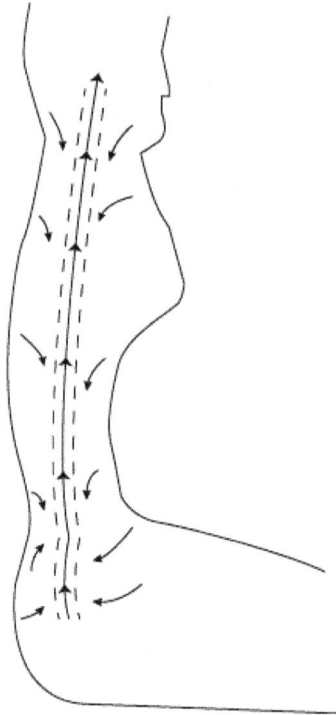

August 10, 1999

Ganesh

He said, "A good student reviews yesterday's lessons."

Remark:

From this advice I applied the compression technique again. This is what happened:

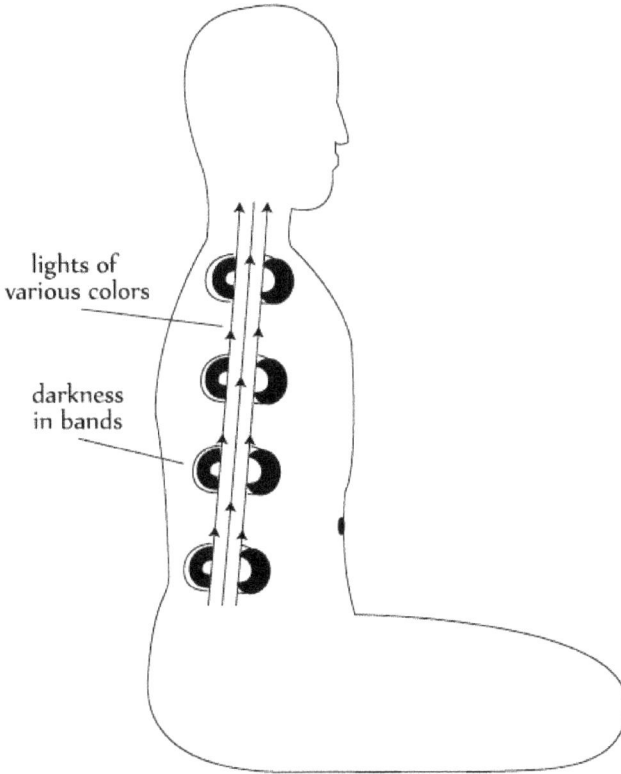

August 11, 1999

Skanda Kumara

He said, "Remember the subtle energy conversion. Forget the personalities. Do not allow the old pattern to remain."

Remark:

This is a technique to always remember to use pranavision. By that one does not see a personality but rather a core-self and a conglomeration of energies which seems to be one personality. Through pranavision one sees that most of the operations are carried out by subtle energy and not by the core-self. It is as if the core was harnessed to the subtle energies for being used by them as a perpetual energy-interaction reference point. It is not that the subtle energy takes power from the spirit directly. The subtle energy cannot convert core-self radiance but it performs its motions around the core, just as a wheel rotates on a stationary axle. The axle does not provide the energy for the rotation even though in a casual observation, one may think so.

Sometimes, it is said that the core moves the energy for these operations but in actuality it does not. The pranas or subtle energies themselves cause the motion.

On this day, Skanda gave me this technique.

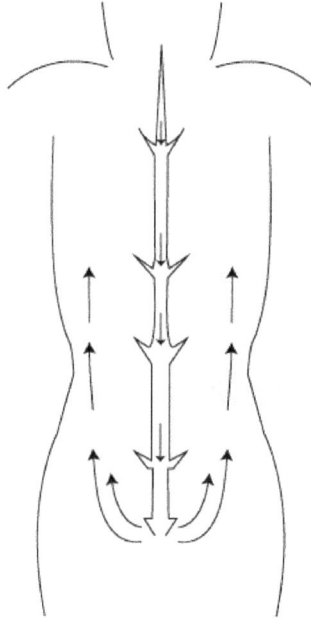

August 12, 1999

Valmiki Muni

He gave me a push-down-the-center technique. This is for doing an intense breath-infusion session, then pushing down in the center of the energy. The center may be in the central spine, central trunk and central chest. In some experiences, the center is found to be off-center, not centralized geometrically. Wherever it is found, it is pushed down by applying locks which force the sensations downwards. To make keen observation of the turmoil of energies one keeps the eyelids closed.

After being pushed sufficiently, the energy will stabilize either at the bottom of the trunk or halfway by the navel area. One should stay very still, and one may detect rotating or gyrating light. This will be pranavision or inner visual sight through sensation perception. Any lights perceived should be pushed downwards. Lights occur as scintillating twirling masses of multicolored, twisting, inter-moving spheres of color energy. During the experience one may become aware of colorful energy in the subtle head. That would be the intellect organ with sensuous feelers injected into it.

August 13, 1999

Shiva

He said, "Work on that side alone."

Remark:

This means that if the right side is clogged, I should work on the left side of the subtle body. In some yoga practice, as given by some teachers, the student works on the clogged side until he clears it. If he succeeds, he shifts to the center. Here however, Shiva instructed that I should forget about the clogged right side and only work on the open easily-facilitated left side. Here are diagrams.

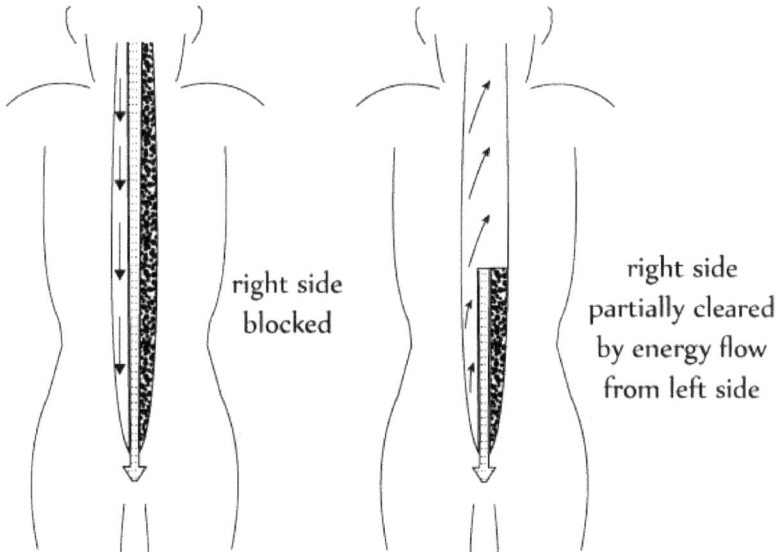

right side blocked

right side partially cleared by energy flow from left side

Back of Body

Later on this day, a strange thing occurred, where a yogini wanted to enter my psyche. When she first attempted, she was unable to. She returned with her teacher, who was a mahayogin. When he came to enter, I told him to go around to the back. He did so by entering my psyche through the sushumna passage. In the meantime, the yogini stood out front by my brow chakra with a baffled look on her face. Apparently she could not go around the back or she did not understand what that meant, and she could not penetrate the passage through the brow chakra.

When her teacher entered my psyche, I took a miniature form as yogis frequently do. I began talking to him. He wanted to know if I could help the yogini, his disciple. I told him that I could not because the lady had no confidence in me. Without confidence, one cannot take assistance from another. He left, commenting that even though he felt some obligation to her he was not her teacher. He did not agree with her tactics. When he departed the yogini followed him.

August 18, 1999

Vasishtha

He gave me a neck bliss energy accumulation technique.

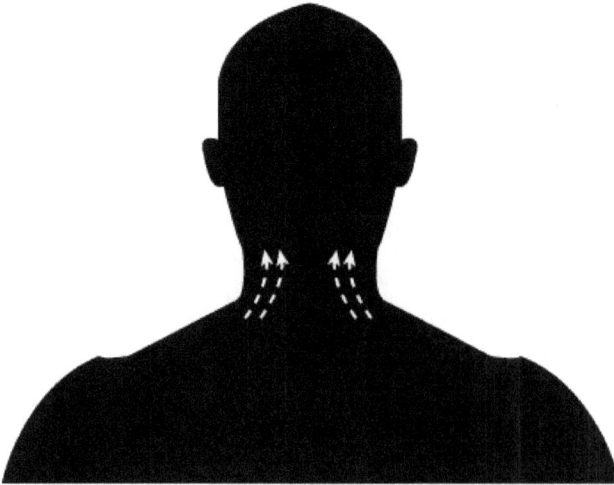

August 19, 1999

Yogeshwarananda

He gave an intellect focus procedure.

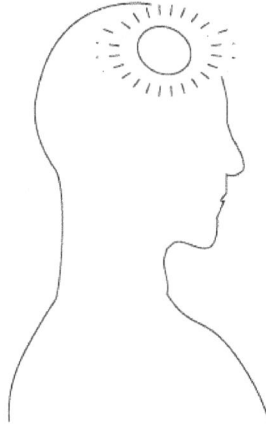

Hanuman

During the same session for meditation, Hanuman gave advice. He said, "Pull it from the front circuit to the back. Feel that back spot. Feel the front one. These are entering positions."

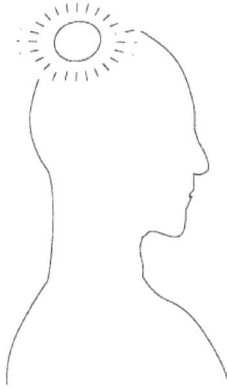

August 19, 1999

Paramhansa Yogananda

He showed me a technique on this day. Usually I neither see him nor get methods from him. This is a rare visit by this world famous yogi. He directed me to move a ball of fire light. First I moved it down the left with the breath coming up the right. Then I let the breath go and followed the subtle body rhythm under the influence of the ball. It moved down the left and up the right side.

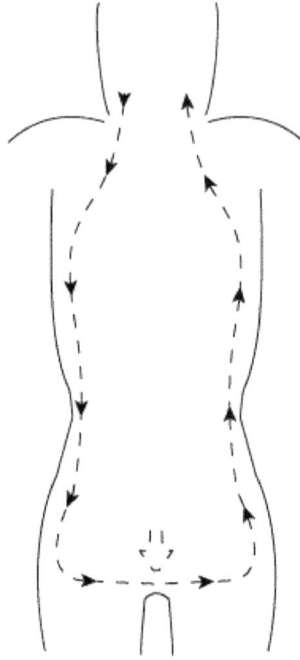

August 21, 1999

Yogeshwarananda

He asked, "What did the Paramhansa say?"
I replied, "He instructed that I take the ball in this direction."
Yogeshwarananda instructed, "Now take it in the opposite direction."

August 22, 1999

Shivananda

He instructed that I sense the continuous beaded current that is broken though sexual intercourse. That beaded current should be reformed to prevent it from being used in sexual sightseeing and thinking. Here is the technique.

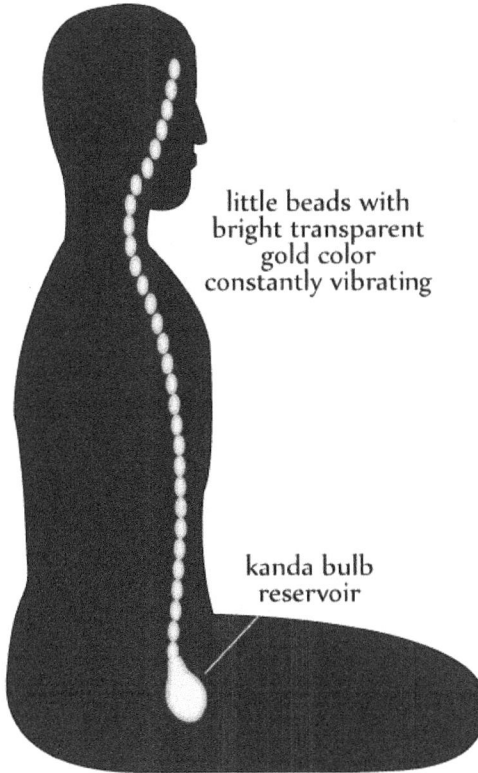

little beads with
bright transparent
gold color
constantly vibrating

kanda bulb
reservoir

   The beaded energy is a combination force. According to Yogeshwarananda there is a misunderstanding about kundalini chakra. People feel that it is the primordial primal power. It may be that this misunderstanding was promoted by Woodroffe, Avalon and others who as Westerners, went to India and then translated some tantras which describe kundalini chakra in a glorious way. Yogeshwarananda proposed that people stop seeing kundalini as anything other than a driving force for the gross body, being composed of prana, apana and bhasvara fire.

   This energy also comprises sexual energy in the gross body and to an extent in the subtle form. In sexual intercourse this energy is aroused and it expends itself. Thus the line of continuous beads of sensations, as shown in the diagram, is broken

   Basically speaking, kundalini means that when the sexual force, is caused to move upwards, the yogi experiences the orgasmic release of energy in the spine, brain and elsewhere but not in the genitals. Conversely when it is used for sexual release, a person experiences it in the genital only as sensed there by nerves which are connected to the brain through the spinal column.

After a long time, as a celibate practicing yogi, the beaded energy becomes fixed. After this is achieved, one may enter into transcendental mental states for long periods.

Shiva

Lung and causal body connection technique

In this technique one pushes down subtle energy into the lungs, just as if the lungs were one container instead of two sacks as they are in the physical form. After long practice this technique causes one to perceive the causal body.

Even though this technique cannot be done properly nor consistently in the lower stages, one can do it when one advances. It comes about naturally or by inspiration from great yogis at an advanced stage.

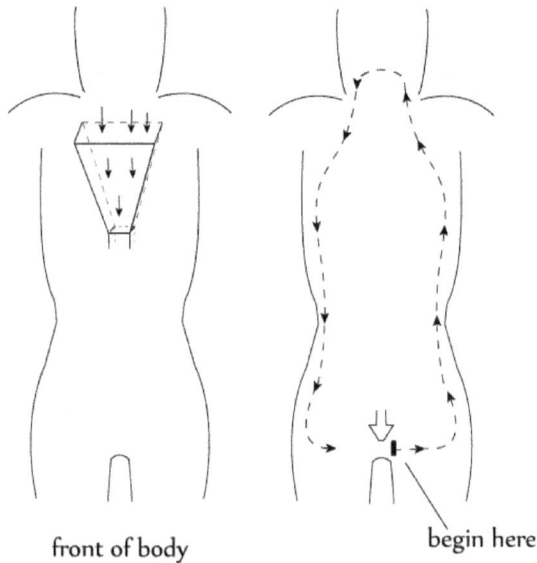

front of body   begin here

Ganesh

He said, "Work on the causal cove. The bottom distribution is proportionate to the top outlet energy. Blast out the old energy. Bring in fresh subtle energy."

He gave this technique.

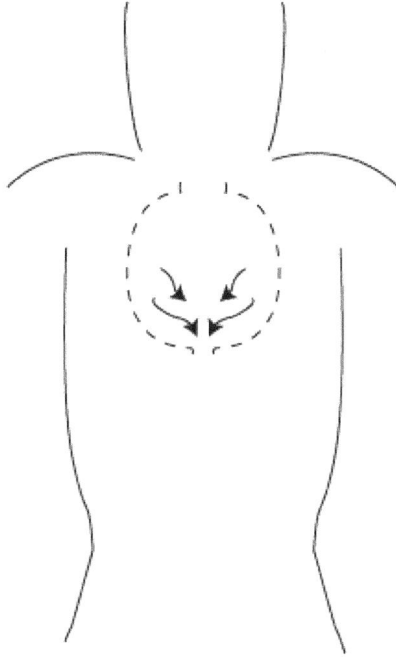

August 24, 1999

Yogeshwarananda

This entry was listed without a teacher's name. At the time I received this vision I could not identify the instructor. However I know for certain that this was done by Yogeshwarananda. He showed me either directly or it was revealed in his association.

The stools are formulated and pushed out of the body by certain lights or energizing powers. When the power shines downward, it is of a dark blue green color but when it shines upward, it is of a light green color. It ascends to the throat once stools are released.

When the stools are being formulated the light shines downward but as soon as they are excreted, it gradually turns upwards and shines on the throat. This shining is interpreted by the mind as an eating urge. If one checks carefully, after passing stools, he will feel as if an energy has moved up to the throat. This is the movement of that light.

Part 8

Chaitanya-Nityananda

Nityananda said, "If working hard does not impede, but facilitates advancement, then why do some sannyasis sit on high seats enjoying the hard work of others."

Remark:

This is a rare entry. Usually I do not get communication in yoga tapasya from Nityananda. He came with Chaitanya. Their main idea was to engage persons in chanting the holy names of Krishna and Balarama, and engage people in devotional service without yoga practice.

The point He raised is that if I made advancement even while doing manual labor, then why are the sannyasis spiritual leaders merely sitting on high seats receiving adoration from others who are industrious. Why do the sannyasis not work strenuously? If labor intensive word does not bar advancement, then perhaps everyone should get a good dose of it.

In my experience, hard work springs from sexual involvement. So long as there is any type of slight or intense sexual interplay in any way of thinking, feeling or touching, there will be hard work as a consequence. Sooner or later sexual involvement is converted into manual labor.

The earthly plane is basically a place which consists of passionate energy, at least for the human beings. This situation is surcharged with passionate urge which converts into working power. Men are here for the purpose of working in order to support women who rear children, and who exhibit the nurturing energy, which is a dire necessity for human survival.

It may be that the sannyasis know this intuitively. All the same, they fail to understand that their current involvement of taking services from others will lead them to another womb and will cause their repeat of the feared sexual life. Most sannyasis are phonies. Originally a sannyasis was not supposed to be involved with the public. Most institutional renunciants are administrative agents who pose as renunciants. They take formal renunciation in order to derive the status of a spiritual leader who is honored by the public. It is a very neat trick but it is wholly dishonest and dishonorable.

August 25, 1999

Yogeshwarananda

Under his association, I realized that when the intellect is sharp, it is critical, due to its increased accuracy of perception. It has to be trained to disregard what it sees. It should instead focus on the internal critique and self-rectification. In this way, it is trained to assist the core-self which it is aligned to.

In the year 2001, Yogeshwarananda trained me in another way of dealing with the intellect whereby it did not focus on external factors, nor on internal critique but rather on the causal body. This has to do with tratak focus. Tratak focus is a process of staring either into nowhere or upon a specific object, using the optic energy which streams out of the eyes. In the advanced version of this practice, one uses the stream of energy which exudes from the intellect. One steers it to the causal body. This is not a pin-point or squeezed focus. It is a focus of a stream of power which is like a continuous broad beam of light.

August 25, 1999

Hanuman

He advised that I blow through the passionate energy, use it and work industriously to expend it. I was to rise early as usual to do yoga practice, making sure that my body stayed trim and fit with the proper diet. He showed a technique which involved compression of the subtle body from the purpose of perceiving the causal form.

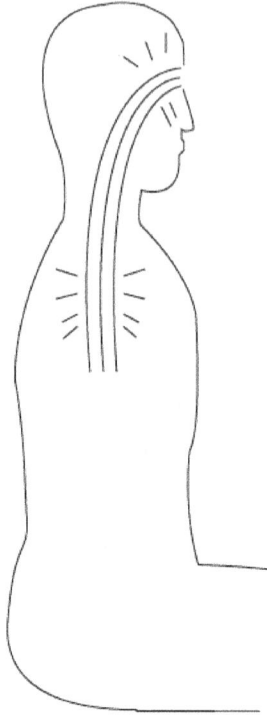

August 26, 1999

Yogeshwarananda

He gave a technique for moving the intellect into the neck-chest connecting area.

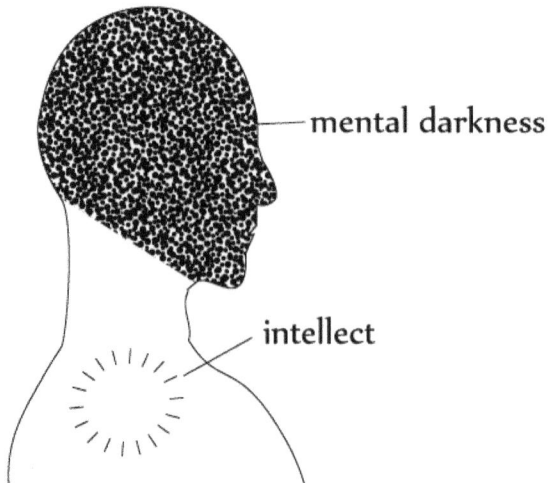

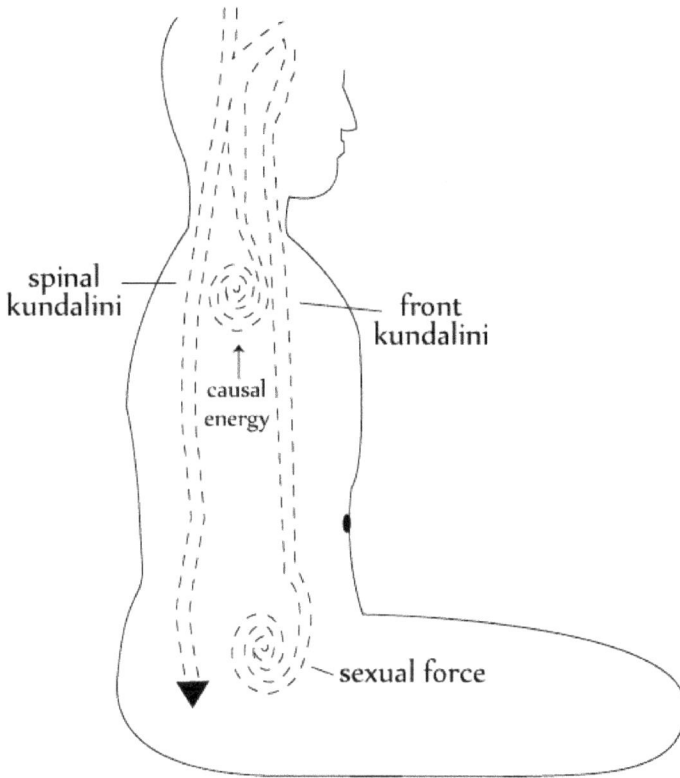

spinal kundalini

front kundalini

causal energy

sexual force

August 27, 1999

Matanga Rishi Yogiraj

Here is a diagram of where he sat with other authorities.

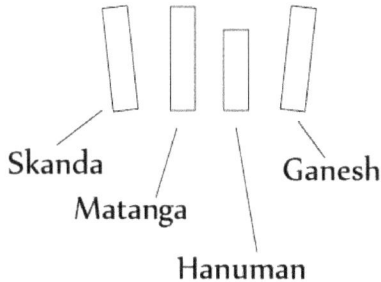

Skanda

Matanga

Ganesh

Hanuman

Matanga Rishi said, "By retracting the brow chakra, you may enter the causal space.

He quoted a verse from the Bhagavad Gita, having to do with withdrawing the sensual energies of the subtle body, the way a tortoise pulls its limbs under the shell of its body.

He said, "The prohibition for using siddhis is realized after one retracts the subtle form. The siddhis are functions of that form. The inappropriate identification is removed when breath-infusion is done properly."

Matanga Rishi Yogiraj explained that since some students conceive of the subtle form as the person, they fear a complete withdrawal of the subtle apparatus. He said that such fears are ungrounded. Any form which was developed over the course of time, may be produced again. One need not fear retraction practices, because the psychic material nature may recreate a demolished form in the nick of time.

August 28, 1999

Matanga Rishi Yogiraj

He gave an intellect light withdrawal-out-of-the-head technique.

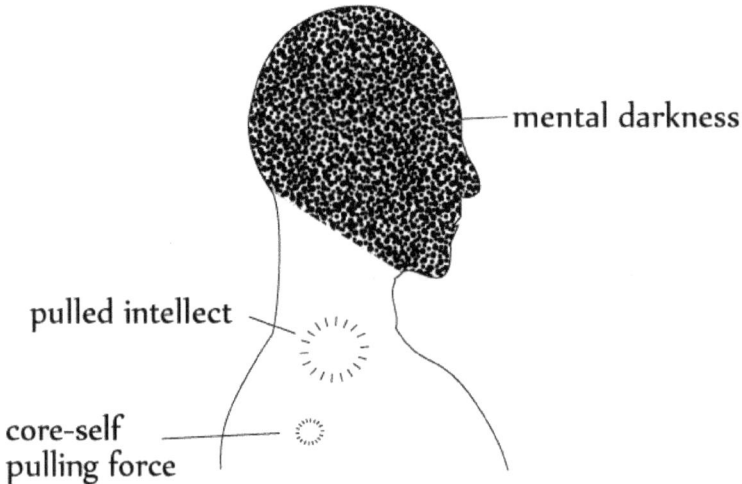

mental darkness

pulled intellect

core-self
pulling force

August 28, 1999

Yogeshwarananda

He showed me something about stool retraction. This, though a very mundane topic, is of prime importance to a yogi who desires to upgrade the pollutants in the subtle form.

Yogeshwarananda showed that the body may retract stools which linger in the anal pouch. Once the stools move into the anal pouch, the nerves of that region signal to the brain to operate the muscles which expel the waste. A human being may stop that operation if he is not in a place where he feels he may privately evacuate. If he impedes the process the absorbing nerves which line the pouch may absorb nutrients from the waste. This absorbing is negative towards yoga advancement but positive towards mundane cultural life. Such stools may release gases which in turn cause the waste to harden in the anal pouch.

Shiva

He said, "First, do the exercises and the prayers for contacting the influence of the mahayogins."

Remark:

On this day I wanted to house-clean. I planned to make that the first activity after rising but Shiva stopped me. He said I should stick to the routine of doing the exercises first.

Yogeshwarananda

A down-draw technique

Remark:

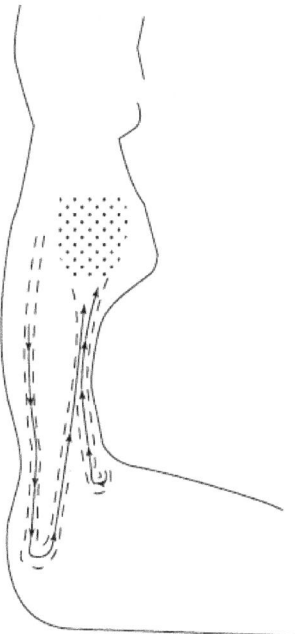

Down-draw is a breathing exercise done in a standing, squatting or cross legged position. Mostly it is done from the standing position, but the yogi may be humped over or he may have his back straight being supported by his hands on the hips or his hands in the back on the torso.

Down-draw is usually done after doing a session of breath-infusion, in which the body is surcharged with fresh air energy. The yogi draws down the air at a slower rate with one, two or even three in-breaths in succession, packing the air into the lower part of the body.

In the specific technique, Yogeshwarananda showed how a part of the subtle form is pulled up from underneath the causal zone.

August 30, 1999

Shiva

He said, "Carefully study the capacity of others. Then act accordingly. Many are incapable. Get the best result after subtracting their deficiencies and cultural limitations."

Remark:

This instruction is related to yoga practice. It has to do with the reform of compassionate energy. If such energy is not reformed it prevents advancement. In assisting others one has to understand their ideal level of functioning, as well as their practical life which is limited by deficiencies and cultural limitations. If this is understood it saves one time and energy by not investing in persons who cry out for help but who cannot advance because their deficiencies and cultural hang-ups bar them from progression.

Unless the yogi can counteract such negative energies in the lives of those who seek his assistance, he cannot assist them. Thus he should estimate this and not waste time. He should never bar anyone from progression, nor assume a superiority complex over others, but he should perceive material nature's power over a particular individual and properly judge if the teaching will be nullified.

August. 31, 1999

Shiva/ Yogeshwarananda

Under their association, I realized that the dualities of material existence end when the subtle body is withdrawn and the dual current which comes out of the causal form is retracted. There are many definitions for duality. Here I describe the duality of higher and lower energies, which form the intellect organ and the kundalini energy. The energy that comes from the top of the causal body forms into the intellect organ. The energy that exudes from the bottom of it, which is a slower moving sensation force, forms into the kundalini chakra, which is in the lower subtle trunk.

Yogeshwarananda is of the opinion that the kundalini chakra is the lifeforce of the gross body. The intellect is the primal power in the subtle form.

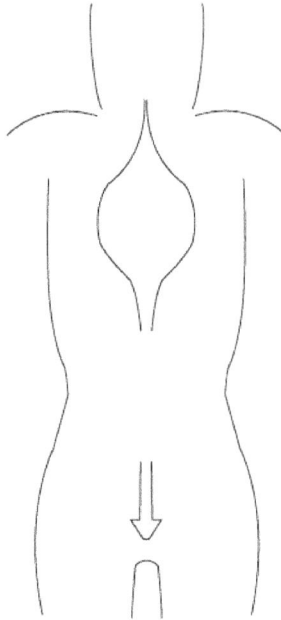

September. 2, 1999

Shiva

He said, "Use the sexual references as a trigger to do techniques such as the intellect pull-down in the top the causal form. Use the sexual calls as a positive force to reinforce appropriate techniques. If there is a sexual attraction or diversion it is beneficial if it causes you to do additional techniques. The sexual advances will then become impetus which accelerates the practice.

September. 3, 1999

Shiva

He gave an in-and-out exercise for converging and diverging the top entry of the causal body.

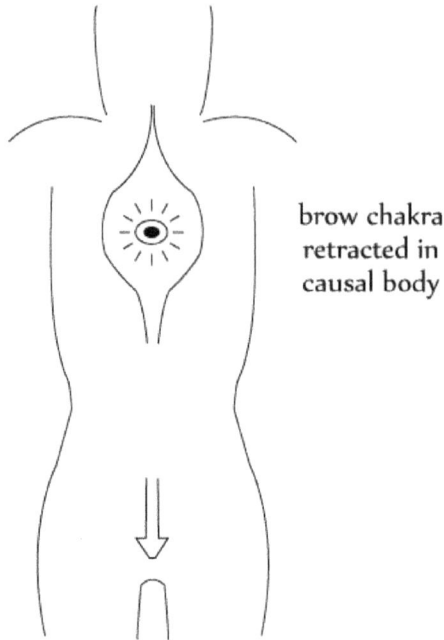

brow chakra
retracted in
causal body

Vasishtha Yogiraj

I was directed to him by Ganesh. Vasishtha pointed to my lower abdomen. He said, "That has to be drawn up for voluntary controlled transcendence states."

This meant that the top abdomen has to be empty and have clean pranic energy, if one is to enter into clarifying transcendental states.

September 3, 1999

Shiva

He said, "You are the same. It is another core-self. The difference is the sensation-energy. When the subtle energy facilitate it works."

Remark:

This was a comment about relationship with persons who desire either to understand or to practice yoga. Their receptivity depends not on willpower decisions but on the type of subtle energy in the psyche. Even if someone was a promising yoga student in his or her past life, in this life, the same person might reject the practice merely on the basis of having hostile psychic energies in the subtle form. A yoga teacher should be perceptive and not waste time with persons whose subtle forms have hostile energy.

Yogeshwarananda

He gave a subtle body pull-in technique.

In this procedure I saw the intellect organ in the subtle head. It was like a 60 watt bulb, shining down. At first I regarded it as a bulb. Due to mental instability it disappeared upwards.

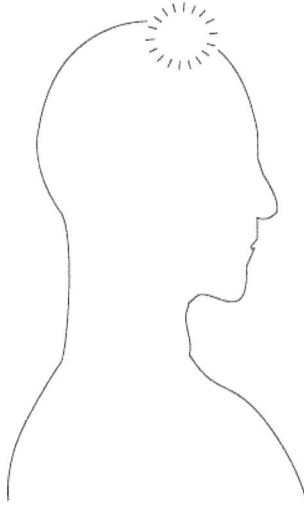

Later, in the year 2001, Yogeshwarananda showed me that the intellect can be controlled by the mental stability which comes from not using it for mundane pursuits and not allowing it to use itself in such causes. It is used by the core-self and by itself, as well. Mostly it uses itself, since it has an automatic functioning ability which causes it to focus on gross and subtle mundane objects according to the sensing functions of the various gross and subtle senses.

When a yogi can stop the automatic sensing operations, and stop the intellect from interacting with them, he gains more control of the organ. He can then move it here and there at will. Under the power of a great yogi, with his help, one may achieve this.

Ganesh

He said, "Use this inner sketch."

He gave some locations to find three deities in the causal form.

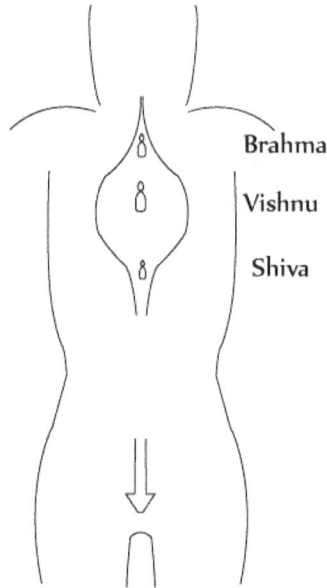

Brahma

Vishnu

Shiva

September 8, 1999

Intellect fallback-in technique

This is a practice to be used if one plans to retract his subtle body into the causal one in the process of eliminating his mundane existence. Ultimately whether we like it or not, whether we desire it or not, our mundane existence will be retracted. Then it will be put into manifestation again, according to the repeated process of manifestation and disintegration. This is something that a limited: spirit cannot control. However one may practice some of this retraction of one form into another and be prepared for universal collapse, or one may advance the collapse of the subtle form for the time being, according to the allowance of power one is naturally endowed with as a certain type of spirit

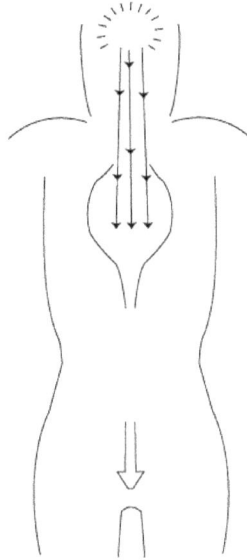

Sept. 9, 1999

Vasishtha Muni Yogiraj

He said, "Only when you are in, can you make real progress."

Remark:

He spoke of the causal body, which is a non-dual system. It has a neutral polarity. The subtle body is divided into higher and lower sensations. However, the causal form is the source of the duality in the subtle body. Only when one studies the causal form can one understand how the subtle and gross forms emerged.

Index

teaching, resentments, 75
technology, 167
television, 84
tenets, 128
terminal sex connections, 64
testes, entry, 11
thighs, 100
thought creation, 106
thread-to-base chakra, 77
thrusting force, 58, 62
Tibet, 88
touch points, 22
transit, astral details, 73
tratak, 213
Trinidad, 182
tubal fish, 147

U

Uddhava, 157
uddhiyana bandha, 21
uncertainty, useful, 12
under-brain cove, 81
Urdhvaretacharya, 68
urination, function, 62
US Air Force, 32

V

vaginal pranavision, 42
Vaikuntha, 84
Valmiki, 109, 178
vanaprasthi, 165
video, 167
Vishnu, 84
Vishnudevananda, 48
vision,
    energy retraction, 89
    orb, 99
    types, 91
visual apprehension, 25
visual subtle energies, 144
visual vision, 18

W

wait-and-see, 84
wet dreams 138
window, eyes, 128
woman alluring, 49

womb return, 50
Woodroffe, 209
working hard, 212

X, Y, Z

yama, 128
yirk-back, 129
yoga,
    atheistic, 201
    deity, 107
    masters, 81
    siddha body, 166
    tantra, 64
Yoga Ma, 107
Yogananda, 49
Yogeshwarananda,
    ant-size, 145
    spiritual master, 88
Yogi Bhajan, 13
yogi,
    association, 182
    atheistic, 201
    money, 131
    not required, 199
    rebirth process, 49
yogini,
    astral, 64
    failed entry, 205-206
yoni, 59
Yudhishthira, 75

About the Author

Michael Beloved (Yogi *Madhvāchārya*) took his current body in 1951 in Guyana. In 1965, while living in Trinidad, he instinctively began doing yoga postures and tried to make sense of the supernatural side of life.

Later in 1970, in the Philippines, he approached a Martial Arts Master named Arthur Beverford. He explained to the teacher that he was seeking a yoga instructor. Mr. Beverford identified himself as an advanced disciple of *Śrī* Rishi Singh Gherwal, an Ashtanga Yoga master.

Beverford taught the traditional Ashtanga Yoga with stress on postures, attentive breathing and brow chakra centering meditation.   In 1972, Michael entered the Denver, Colorado Ashram of *kundalini* yoga Master *Śrī* Harbhajan Singh. There he took instruction in bhastrika pranayama and its application to yoga postures. He was supervised mostly by Yogi Bhajan's disciple named Prem Kaur.

In 1979 Michael formally entered the disciplic succession of the Brahmā - Madhava-Gaudiya Sampradaya through *Swāmī* Kirtanananda, who was a prominent sannyasi disciple of the Great Vaishnava Authority *Śrī Swāmī* Bhaktivedanta Prabhupada, the exponent of devotion to Sri Krishna.

However, yoga has a mystic side to it, thus Michael took training and teaching empowerment from several spiritual masters of different aspects of spiritual development. This is consistent with *Śrī* Krishna's advice to Arjuna in the *Bhagavad Gītā*:

Most of the instructions Michael received were given in the astral world. On that side of existence, his most prominent teachers were *Śrī Swāmī* Shivananda of Rishikesh, Yogiraj *Swāmī* Vishnudevananda, *Śrī Bābāji Mahasaya* - the master of the masters of *Kriyā* Yoga, *Śrīla* Yogeshwarananda of Gangotri - the master of the masters of *Rāj* Yoga (spiritual clarity), and Siddha *Swāmī* Nityananda the Brahmā Yoga authority.

The course for kundalini yoga using pranayama breath-infusion was detailed by Michael in the book *Kundalini Hatha Yoga Pradipika*. This current book was composed from meditation and breath-infusion notes which were originally shared in staple bound booklets as Yoga Journals.

Michael's preliminary books relating to this topic are *Meditation Pictorial*, *Meditation Expertise*, and *Meditation ~ Sense Faculty* (co-author). Every technique (kriya) mentioned was tested by him during pranayama breath-infusion and samyama deep meditation practice.

This is a result of over forty years of meditation practice with astute subtle observations intending to share the methods and experiences. The information is published freely with no intention of forming an institution or hogtying anyone as a disciple.

Publications

English Series

Bhagavad Gita English

Anu Gita English

Markandeya Samasya English

Yoga Sutras English

Hatha Yoga Pradipika English

Uddhava Gita English

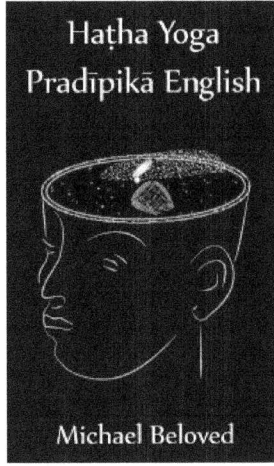

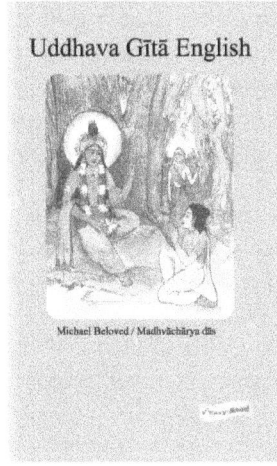

These are in 21ˢᵗ Century English, very precise and exacting. Many Sanskrit words which were considered untranslatable into a Western language are rendered in precise, expressive and modern English.

*Three of these books are instructions from Krishna. **In Bhagavad Gita English** and **Anu Gita English**, the instructions were for Arjuna. In the **Uddhava Gita English,** it was for Uddhava. Bhagavad Gita and Anu Gita are extracted from the Mahabharata. Uddhava Gita was extracted from the 11ᵗʰ Canto of the Srimad Bhagavatam (Bhagavata Purana). One of these books, the **Markandeya Samasya English** is about Krishna, as described by Yogi Markandeya, who survived the cosmic collapse and reached a divine child in whose transcendental body, the collapsed world was existing.*

Two of this series are the syllabus about yoga practice. The Yoga Sutras of Patanjali is elaboration about ashtanga yoga. Hatha Yoga Pradipika English, is the detailed information about asana postures, pranayama breath- infusion, energy compression, naad sound resonance and advanced meditation. The Sanskrit author is Swatmarama Mahayogin.

*My suggestion is that you read **Bhagavad Gita English**, the **Anu Gita English, the Markandeya Samasya English,** the **Yoga Sutras English,** the **Hatha Yoga Pradipika** and lastly the **Uddhava Gita English**, which is complicated and detailed.*

For each of these books we have at least one commentary, which is published separately. Thus your particular interest can be researched further in the commentaries.

The smallest of these commentaries and perhaps the simplest is the one for the Anu Gita. We published its commentary as the <u>Anu Gita Explained</u>. The

Bhagavad Gita explanations were published in three distinct targeted commentaries. The first is Bhagavad Gita Explained, which sheds lights on how people in the time of Krishna and Arjuna regarded the information and applied it. Bhagavad Gita is an exposition of the application of yoga practice to cultural activities, which is known in the Sanskrit language as karma yoga.

Interestingly, Bhagavad Gita was spoken on a battlefield just before one of the greatest battles in the ancient world. A warrior, Arjuna, lost his wits and had no idea that he could apply his training in yoga to political dealings. Krishna, his charioteer, lectured on the spur of the moment to give Arjuna the skill of using yoga proficiency in cultural dealings including how to deal with corrupt officials on a battlefield.

The second Gita commentary is the Kriya Yoga Bhagavad Gita. This clears the air about Krishna's information on the science of kriya yoga, showing that its techniques are clearly described for anyone who takes the time to read Bhagavad Gita. Kriya yoga concerns the battlefield which is the psyche of the living being. The internal war and the mental and emotional forces which are hostile to self-realization are dealt with in the kriya yoga practice.

The third commentary is the Brahma Yoga Bhagavad Gita. This shows what Krishna had to say outright and what he hinted about which concerns the brahma yoga practice, a mystic process for those who mastered kriya yoga.

*There is one commentary for the **Markandeya Samasya English**. The title of that publication is Krishna Cosmic Body.*

There are two commentaries to the Yoga Sutras. One is the Yoga Sutras of Patanjali and the other is the Meditation Expertise. These give detailed explanations of ashtanga Yoga.

The commentary of Hatha Yoga Pradipika is titled Kundalini Hatha Yoga Pradipika.

For the Uddhava Gita, we published the Uddhava Gita Explained. This is a large book and requires concentration and study for integration of the information. Of the books which deal with transcendental topics, my opinion is that the discourse between Krishna and Uddhava has the complete information about the realities in existence. This book is the one which removes massive existential ignorance.

Meditation Series

Meditation Pictorial

Meditation Expertise

Core-Self Discovery

Meditation Sense Faculty

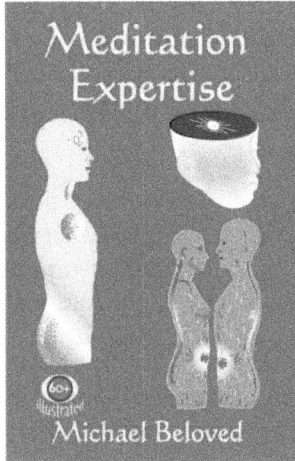

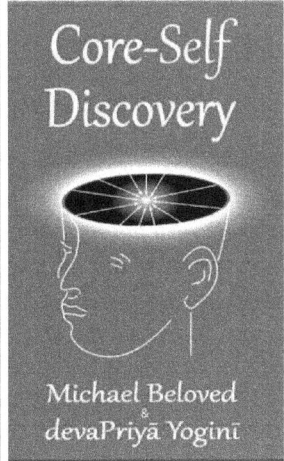

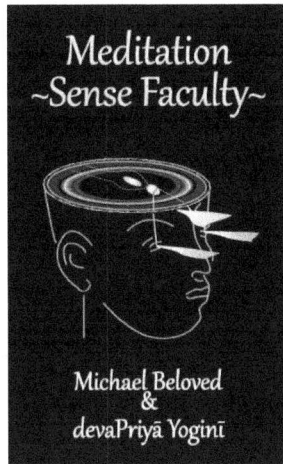

The specialty of these books is the mind diagrams which profusely illustrate what is written. This shows exactly what one has to do mentally to develop and then sustain a meditation practice.

*In the **Meditation Pictorial**, one is shown how to develop psychic insight, a feature without which meditation is imagination and visualization, without any mystic experience per se.*

*In the **Meditation Expertise**, one is shown how to corral one's practice to bring it in line with the classic syllabus of yoga which Patanjali lays out as the ashtanga yoga eight-staged practice.*

*In **Core-Self Discovery**, (co-authored with* devaPriya Yogini*) one is taken though the course of pratyahar sensual energy withdrawal which is the 5th stage of yoga in the Patanjali ashtanga eight-process complete system of yoga practice. These events lead to the discovery of a core-self which is surrounded by psychic organs in the head of the subtle body. This product has a DVD component.*

***Meditation ~ Sense Faculty** (co-authored with* devaPriya Yogini*) is a detailed tutorial with profuse diagrams showing what actions to take in the subtle body to investigate the senses faculties. The meditator must first establish the location and function of the observing self. That self must be screened from the thoughts and ideas which usually hypnotize it.*

These books are profusely illustrated with mind diagrams showing the components of psychic consciousness and the inner design of the subtle body.

Explained Series

Bhagavad Gita Explained

Uddhava Gita Explained

Anu Gita Explained

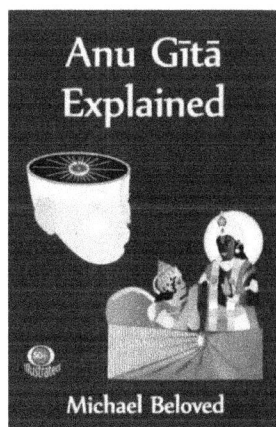

The specialty of these books is that they are free of missionary intentions, cult tactics and philosophical distortion. Instead of using these books to add credence to a philosophy, meditation process, belief or plea for followers, I spread the information out so that a reader can look through this literature and freely take or leave anything as desired.

When Krishna stressed himself as God, I stated that. When Krishna laid no claims for supremacy, I showed that. The reader is left to form an independent opinion about the validity of the information and the credibility of Krishna.

There is a difference in the discourse with Arjuna in the Bhagavad Gita and the one with Uddhava in the Uddhava Gita. In fact these two books may appear to contradict each other. In the Bhagavad Gita, Krishna pressured Arjuna to complete social duties. In the Uddhava Gita, Krishna insisted that Uddhava should abandon the same.

The Anu Gita is not as popular as the Bhagavad Gita but it is the conclusion of that text. Anu means what is to follow, what proceeds. In this discourse, an anxious Arjuna request that Krishna should repeat the Bhagavad Gita and again show His supernatural and divine forms.

However Krishna refuses to do so and chastises Arjuna for being a disappointment in forgetting what was revealed. Krishna then cited a celestial yogi, a near-perfected being, who explained the process of transmigration in vivid detail.

Commentaries

Yoga Sutras of Patanjali

Meditation Expertise

Krishna Cosmic Body

Anu Gita Explained

Bhagavad Gita Explained

Kriya Yoga Bhagavad Gita

Brahma Yoga Bhagavad Gita

Uddhava Gita Explained

Kundalini Hatha Yoga Pradipika

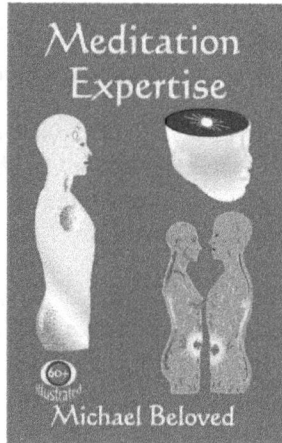

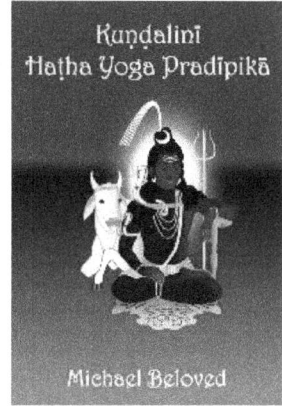

Yoga Sutras of Patanjali *is the globally acclaimed text book of yoga. This has detailed expositions of yoga techniques. Many kriya techniques are vividly described in the commentary.*

Meditation Expertise *is an analysis and application of the Yoga Sutras. This book is loaded with illustrations and has detailed explanations of secretive advanced meditation techniques which are called kriyas in the Sanskrit language.*

Krishna Cosmic Body *is a narrative commentary on the Markandeya Samasya portion of the Aranyaka Parva of the Mahabharata. This is the detailed description of the dissolution of the world, as experienced by the great yogin Markandeya who transcended the cosmic deity, Brahma, and reached Brahma's source who is the divine infant, Krishna.*

Anu Gita Explained *is a detailed explanation of how we endure many material bodies in the course of transmigrating through various life-forms. This is a discourse between Krishna and Arjuna. Arjuna requested of Krishna a display* of the Universal Form and a repeat narration of the Bhagavad Gita but Krishna declined and explained what a siddha perfected being told the Yadu family about the sequence of existences one endures and the systematic flow of those lives at the convenience of material nature.

Bhagavad Gita Explained shows what was said in the Gita without religious overtones and sectarian biases.

Kriya Yoga Bhagavad Gita shows the instructions for those who are doing kriya yoga.

Brahma Yoga Bhagavad Gita shows the instructions for those who are doing brahma yoga.

Uddhava Gita Explained shows the instructions to Uddhava which are more advanced than the ones given to Arjuna.

Bhagavad Gita is an instruction for applying the expertise of yoga in the cultural field. This is why the process taught to Arjuna is called karma yoga which means karma + yoga or cultural activities done with yogic insight.

Uddhava Gita is an instruction for apply the expertise of yoga to attaining spiritual status. This is why it is explains jnana yoga and bhakti yoga in detail. Jnana yoga is using mystic skill for knowing the spiritual part of existence. Bhakti yoga is for developing affectionate relationships with divine beings.

Karma yoga is for negotiating the social concerns in the material world. It is inferior to bhakti yoga which concerns negotiating the social concerns in the spiritual world.

This world has a social environment. The spiritual world has one too.

Currently, Uddhava Gita is the most advanced and informative spiritual book on the planet. There is nothing anywhere which is superior to it or which goes into so much detail as it. It verified that historically Krishna is the most advanced human being to ever have left literary instructions on this planet. Even Patanjali Yoga Sutras which I translated and gave an application for in my book, **Meditation Expertise**, does not go as far as the Uddhava Gita.

Some of the information of these two books is identical but while the Yoga Sutras are concerned with the personal spiritual emancipation (kaivalyam) of the individual spirits, the Uddhava Gita explains that and also explains the situations in the spiritual universes.

Bhagavad Gita is from the Mahabharata *which is the history of the Pandavas. Arjuna, the student of the Gita, is one of the Pandavas brothers. He was in a social hassle and did not know how to apply yoga expertise to solve it. On the battlefield, Krishna gave him a crash-course on yogic social interactions.*

Uddhava Gita is from the Srimad Bhagavatam (Bhagavata Purana), *which is a history of the incarnations of Krishna. Uddhava was a relative of Krishna. He was concerned about the situation of the deaths of many of his relatives but Krishna diverted Uddhava's attention to the practice of yoga for the purpose of successfully migrating to the spiritual environment.*

Kundalini Hatha Yoga Pradipika *is the commentary for the Hatha Yoga Pradipika of Swatmarama Mahayogin. This is the detailed process about asana posture, pranayama breath-infusion, complex compressions of energy, naad sound resonance intonement and advanced meditation practice.*

This is the singular book with all the techniques of how to reform and redesign the subtle body so that it does not have the tendency for physical life forms and for it to attain the status of a siddha.

These books are based on the author's experiences in meditation, yoga practice and participation in spiritual groups:

Specialty

Spiritual Master

sex you!

Sleep Paralysis

Astral Projection

Masturbation Psychic Details

Spiritual Master

sex you!

Sleep Paralysis

Michael Beloved

michael beloved

Michael Beloved

Astral Projection

Masturbation Psychic Details

Michael Beloved

Michael Beloved

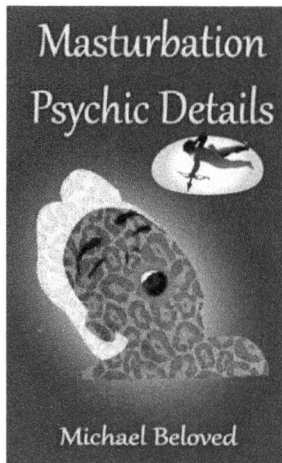

In **Spiritual Master**, Michael draws from experience with gurus or with their senior students. His contact with astral gurus is rated. He walks you through the avenue of gurus showing what you should do and what you should not do, so as to gain proficiency in whatever area of spirituality the guru has proficiency.

sex you! is a masterpiece about the adventures of an individual spirit's passage through the parents' psyches. The conversion of a departed soul into a sexual urge is described. The transit from the afterlife to residency in the emotions of the parents is detailed. This is about sex and you. Learn about how much of you comprises the romantic energy of your would-be parents!

Sleep Paralysis clears misconceptions so that one can see what sleep paralysis is and what frightening astral experience occurs while the paralysis is being *experienced. This disempowerment has great value in giving you confidence that you can and do exist even if you are unable to operate the physical body. The implication is that one can exist apart from and will survive the loss of the material form.*

Astral Projection *details experiences Michael had even in childhood, where he assumed incorrectly that everyone was astrally conversant. He discusses the life force psychic mechanism which operates the sleep-wake cycle of the physical form, and which budgets energy into the separated astral form which determines if the individual will have dream recall or no objective awareness during the projections. Astral travel happens on every occasion when the physical body sleeps. What is missing in awareness is the observer status while the astral body is separated.*

Masturbation Psychic Details *is a surprise presentation which relates what happens on the psychic plane during a masturbation event. This does not tackle moral issues or even addictions but shows the involvement of memory and the sure but hidden subconscious mind which operates many features of the psyche irrespective of the desire or approval of the self-conscious personality.*

Online Resources

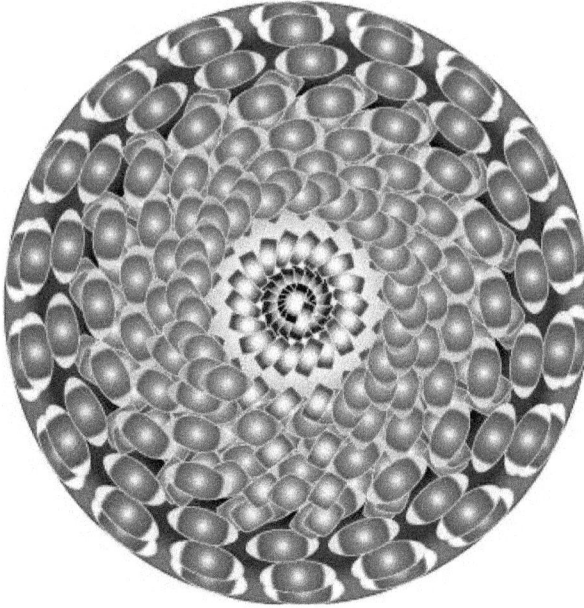

Email:	**michaelbelovedbooks@gmail.com**
	axisnexus@gmail.com
Website:	michaelbeloved.com
Forum:	inselfyoga.com
Posters:	zazzle.com/inself

www.ingramcontent.com/pod-product-compliance
Lightning Source LLC
Chambersburg PA
CBHW072342090426
42741CB00012B/2889